This book is to be ret...

The Encyclopaedia
of Cult Children's TV

RICHARD LEWIS

First published in Great Britain in 2001 by
Allison & Busby Limited
Suite 111, Bon Marche Centre
241-251 Ferndale Road
London SW9 8BJ
http://www.allisonandbusby.ltd.uk

A catalogue record for this book is available from the British Library

ISBN 0 7490 0576 9

Printed and bound in Spain by
Liberdúplex, s.l. Barcelona

RICHARD LEWIS has been a tone-deaf musician, a colourblind graphic designer and a not very well-read bookseller. He has worked in locations as diverse and exotic as France and Leamington Spa, but now works in London as a journalist. He lives close to the river Thames with a large collection of children's videos which is now for sale. This is his first book.

For Alice, Georgia, Ana and Milena

Prologue

Preface and acknowledgements

As a man whose first serious boyhood crush was Jana of the Jungle, I was at first unsure whether I should take on this project. After all, some skellies are best left in the closet. Or at least under the bed, where the less hormonally active Jamie kept his magic torch. But regression therapy has its uses. The dark, hairy foreboding that was Yoffy from *Fingerbobs*, the sepia-tinted safety that was *Bagpuss*, the hypnotic tartrazine trance that was *Roobarb*: these, and many more, are the shows that formed our collective perspectives, growing up.

Which accounts for a great deal. Who, for instance, can forget the tripped-out, staring eyes of Mary out of *Mary Mungo and Midge*? Or the perpetual psychedelic tea party of *Chorlton and the Wheelies*? Remember Kiki, the voyeuristic frog who spied on Hector and Zaza in their garden? Clearly a forerunner to *Big Brother*. Thanks a lot, Kiki! How about *Ludwig*, that strapped-in submissive, forever attached to some fetishistic tweaking device? That is not to mention the legendary Seaman Staines and Master Bates.

Our infant viewing schedule has (probably) turned us into a generation of drug crazed, deviant peeping toms, disaffected by the realisation that the employment marketplace is not actually based on mutual cooperation and respect, like *Trumpton*. Where oh where are Brian Cant and Floella Benjamin, and why won't they save us?

Whatever our own personal shortcomings in adult life, these shows have stuck in our minds and they will not go away. Why else would it be that we find ourselves at three in the morning, altered by substance intake and too much mindless tribal dancing, arguing over the lyrics to "Time Flies By", or the name of Paddington's nasty neighbour? These things, at certain times, matter. Someone had to set it all straight. Finally

I agreed to regress when I figured it might be a way to blame some of my failings on Cheggers. I urge you to do the same.

So weep for your lost innocence, oh commuting office-politicians. Forget your missed deadlines, your caffeine'n'VDU migraines and your maxed-out credit cards. Come with me instead, on a journey back to *Chigley*, to Moominvalley, to Wheelie World, high above the streets and houses, where it was all so honest and simple. Where it was perfectly ordinary for a camp man in dungarees, a big woolly bear, a fey pink hippo and a bitchy zipped-up gimp to get in bed with each other and sing a song.

What is a cult?

Almost as soon as I began to research the book, it became clear that there were as many cult followings as there were TV shows. This made it a much bigger project than was first envisaged. Your unfavourite cartoon from the '70s is probably the subject of passionate debate on some web group or other. So, after the doctor finally agreed to double my valium, I widened my search. Then, after several days submerged in various tomes and catalogues at the BFI, I realised I could not cover every show. A line had to be drawn. Naturally, I chose an arbitrary line, starting somewhere around 1960 and ending roughly around 1988. Shows outside that period tend to have been left off. *Noddy*, for instance, didn't make it. Nor did *Rupert the Bear*. *The Woodentops*, *Bill & Ben*, *Andy Pandy* and *Muffin the Mule*—all very old shows—have been vigorously and very well covered by the media. There seemed little point in going over old ground. *Larry the Lamb* only just made it by the skin of his sheep teeth. Similarly, at the other end of the scale, *Ren and Stimpy* and *The Simpsons* didn't get a look in. They were all too recent and too easily remembered.

The purpose of this book, I decided, would be to fill in the gaps of memory; to answer the questions vaguely forming at the back of people's minds, about the shows they only half forget. In many cases the shows are entirely lost. No tapes or archives exist for a great number of cult favourites. It was disturbing to discover just how much sterling work was simply thrown away. This book should, then, provide a single reference for those seeking simply to remember. I have veered away from transmission (tx) times and exact dates, although they are available, should you care to look. That just seemed like the Dark Side, and my anorak is in the wash (see **Lizzy Dripping**). The dates given refer to the year in which the show was first broadcast. Finally, I decided the book should ask the questions other encyclopaedias dared not ask. Were Tony Bastable's sideburns really alive? Was the Snork Maiden really "doing" Moominpappa? Because I know that's what has been on your minds.

Programmes that were obviously the work of Satan, such as the *Keith Harris and Orville Show* have been given a wide berth, simply for reasons of good taste. Also, I had to drop the family shows—such as *The A-Team*, *Knight Rider*—and sitcoms such as *The Fresh Prince of Bel Air*. They weren't really kids' shows. Schools programmes, too, have been omitted. They could easily be the subject of a whole book. So, with a heavy heart and some regret, I jettisoned *Look And Read*, *You & Me*, *My World*, *Words & Pictures* and so on.

I have taken pains to be as accurate as possible in my factual research, but the opinions expressed are just that: opinions. Not that they belong to me, particularly. I have merely tried to reflect what I gather is the general feeling about a show. This kind of information has come from trawling the chat rooms and fan websites on the internet, and by asking everybody who came within a few yards of me what they thought. People of all generations were canvassed, often down the pub, in states of woozy nostalgia and embarrassing candour, and I am confident that I am representing a general view. Please feel free to differ, although preferably not in writing as there are only three people at my publisher's office. Hate mail may be sent via my website at http://freespace.virgin.net/goods.in.

Use of bad words

At many and various points in the encyclopaedia I plan to use the words idiot, catamite, midget, doofus, loon, fatso and blimp, for comic effect. The reader might be forgiven for believing that these words carry a pejorative meaning. But these are purely descriptive and not mocking. The reader should take note that I, myself, am both an idiot and a midget, who is well on the way to becoming a blimp. If I seem to employ the words with especial zeal, it is simply that I am identifying enthusiastically with my fellow miniaturised idiot fatsos. In any case, I have been obliged to adopt a bantering tone as part of my publishing agreement, and a man has to make a living. I have not yet—as this book is published—been a catamite; but had I been, I should be proud of my economic prowess.

Thank you

The information came from many sources, without which the book could not have been written. The chief resources for this book were the shows themselves. Thanks to everyone who lent me tapes. Secondary to that were the memories of a lot of people, mercilessly hounded for their nostalgia. You know who you are. The BFI and its catalogue, library and helpful staff were all invaluable.

I am indebted to Rosa Collinge, whose patience and additional research is hard to repay. I would like to thank Louis Barfe for sustained informative contributions and tapes; also Jane and Andrew Lewis, Raj Yagnik, Josic Cadoret, Heidi Ziemer, plus Phil Norman, the Bullet List participants and the tv.cream team for extra help at the eleventh hour. Special thanks go to Jeffrey O'Kelly, Nigel Plaskitt, Oliver Postgate, Geoffrey Hayes, Jane Tucker, Fred Harris, Mike Hayes, and the Grange Hill production office. I am grateful to David Shelley at Allison & Busby, who commissioned and edited the book, and provided a great deal of humour, energy and encouragement. Debbie Hatfield— who long ago spotted a *Hong Kong Phooey* video in my flat and dobbed me in to David—Fiona Hague, Alan Jessop and the Compass team are all worthy of medals for their hard work. Jane Gregory is due recognition for brokering the deal so honourably. My gratitude also goes to Danuta Kean, Jenny Bell and Nicholas Clee—my editors—for putting up with a tired, book-crazed laggard in the office for more months than was strictly necessary.

Parents, don't make the mistake of thinking your kid only learns between 9.00 a.m. and 3.00 p.m.

George Bush

Muttley, get me out of this cream puff!

Dick Dastardly

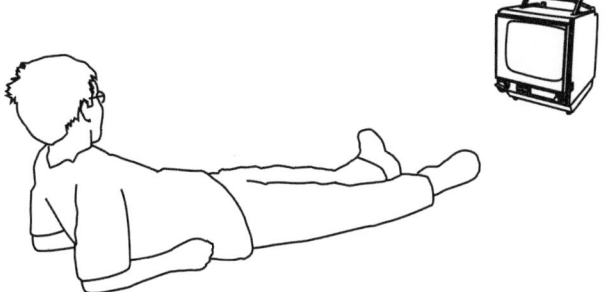

Adventure Game, The

BBC TV. Produced by Patrick Dowling. A BBC production. UK, 1980–86

Did you ever push kids into the artificial pond at school and boom "You are now in The **Vortex**, bu-wa-ha-ha-ha"? Did you ever try to pay for your school dinner with **Drogna** currency you had made yourself out of atomic particles from the chemistry store cupboard? And did you ever stand behind the school library spider plant and wobble it as you talked, pretending to be **Aspidistra** the Rangdo on his plinth?

Celebrity idiots—and brainiacs like former Goody and doctor Graeme Garden (see **Bananaman**), and *Tomorrow's World* proto-Vorderman Judith Hann—were abducted by Moira Stewart in a dragon costume and forced to take the Piccadilly Line to a mysterious location. There they were walked about a badly-designed studio set, which everyone pretended was the planet Arg, and they were obliged to make imbeciles of themselves, blowing through straws and speaking backwards, for the entertainment of a plant (the aspidistra). Do you remember them grinning like buffoons, filmed for posterity using a BBC computer? Never mind, then. You missed little.

The aspidistra was subsequently given a moving role—meaning that it moved about—and was played by Kenny "R2-D2" Baker. He was later replaced by a teapot. The vortex occupied random spaces on a game board, on the floor, on which contestants hopped. They hoped not to hop onto the same segment as the vortex. If they did, they lost, and that was somehow bad. If there was entertainment in this contrived format, then it was in watching celebrities on the spot making idiots of themselves. But since that is what they were paid for and you were thirteen with spots, the joke was on you. Although it was not a children's show *per se*, children were the only people who watched it. *The Adventure Game* was brought to you by Patrick Dowling, the man who also gave us **Why Don't You**, **Take Hart** and

Vision On. While *The Adventure Game* was harmless enough, this encyclopaedia's feeling is that it was the show which begat *The Crystal Maze*, and for that Mr Dowling owes us big.

Alan
See Josie and the Pussycats

Actually Freddy from **Scooby Doo**—same face, same clothes, same voice by Frank Welker—Alan was the impossibly-chested boyfriend of Josie, the strawberry blonde who fronted her own girl "band". He was coveted by the badger-haired Alexandra, who contrived to fall into his arms and generally be alone with him at every turn. What did he think about all this? Who knows? He had no personality of his own.

Alberto Frog and his Amazing Animal Band
See Bod

He had trouble choosing his milkshakes. He had a band. They were animals. They were not amazing. For some, he interrupted **Bod** and broke the spell. For others he was the bit they were waiting for. Many people loved Alberto, and his non-appearance on many *Bod* videos has turned him into a cult hero in his own amphibian right. Mine's a strawberry, though.

Algernon Winston Spencer Castleray Razzmatazz
See Razzmatazz, Algernon Winston Spencer Castleray

DCM-eating rastafarian loon also known as Dudley comic L. Henry in too-hot-for-tots weekend non-**Swap Shop** hot slot.

Animal Kwackers

ITV. A Yorkshire Television production. UK, 1975

Quick, get out the biscuit tins and knitting needles and drum along. Rum entertainment show featuring a so-called pop trio (see **Josie & the Pussycats**), Rory, Twang (see **Rainbow**) and Boots—three actors in animal costumes playing musical instruments. Not at all a lame copy of the already lame, but freakily entertaining **Banana Splits**, then. A total of 39 20-minute episodes were made by Yorkshire and aired to unfortunate children between 1975 and 1978. Inspired the author of this encyclopaedia to nag for his first (and only) drum kit: a two-foot high, all-tin affair from Chad Valley. Banging.

Animal Magic

BBC TV. A BBC production. Directed by Robin Hellier. UK, 1962-83

Johnny Morris OBE—who died in 1999 aged 82—will be remembered by at least two generations of children as the voice of Salty the Seal. More than that, Johnny *was* animals. All of them—including Wendy the Elephant. Aside from presenting an informal and informative show about nature and its creatures—with Dotty the ring-tailed lemur crawling over his shoulder—Morris pioneered a mode of presentation which had him dubbing his voice characterizations over footage of animals doing their thing. Cut to squirrel, scampering. Cue breathy voice: "Hello? What's this? Ooh, I'll just have this nut." That sort of thing. What stopped this from being a mere charade was the sensitivity he showed to the characters of the animals. He, er, brought them to life.

Morris was aided and abetted in the studio by Terry Nutkins—addressed affectionately by Morris as "Nutkins"— whose demonstration of how to record insect noises will be hard to forget. "I'm using a parabolic reflector," he explained, "and that's not a dirty word." Heaven forbid. Not at BBC Bristol.

The show typified an era of Bristol-produced BBC programmes (**Why Don't You**, **Take Hart**, **Vision On**) in its stoic professionalism on a budget. It had a slight done-in-the-shed feel which did not detract from its quality. A tapir might take a dive, Morris would follow and interview its keeper from the floor as the latter lay holding on for dear life. Fantastic. Of course, pretending to be an animal could not last forever. Different modes of presentation prevailed. Morris's approach was considered unscientific by new BBC cheeses, so *Animal Magic* finally bit the dust in 1983, after 21 years of continuous broadcast and 400 episodes. It made way for formats like the equally good, but different, *Really Wild Show*.

———

Ant Hill Mob

*See **Wacky Races** and **Penelope Pitstop***

Band of miniaturized hoodlums in bespoke tailoring who drove the **Bullet-Proof Bomb** and spent too much time trying to protect **Penelope Pitstop**. They came into their own in a spin-off show, **The Perils of Penelope Pitstop**, in which they were constantly on hand to "save" the flighty pink-clad beauty from the evil clutches of the **Hooded Claw**. They were led by **Clyde**—not Clyde Barrow of Bonnie Parker fame, but a gruff-voiced mafioso in a pork pie hat.

———

Arabian Knights, The

A Hanna-Barbera production. USA, 1968

Historically inaccurate political drama based in the Middle East. Also a cartoon. The evil **Bakaar** (voiced by Paul Frees) had usurped the throne of **Prince Turhan** (Jay North). His Arabian Knights were duly dispatched to seize it right back. Using only a few magic carpets, unlikely transmogrifications and words not really in the Arabic vocabulary, such as Shazan, they rose to the challenge. Standard cyclops and Medusa battles ensued. **Princess** "Siiiiiize of an earwig" **Nida** (Shari Lewis) was mistress of many disguises. By use of the cunning "size of . . ." invocation she could transmute (see **Battle of the Planets**) into any living beast. It had a limited use. Someone might have been coming at her with a sabre; she would give it "size of a seagull" and swoop up into the air away from danger. Once in the air, as a bird, you are pretty much committed to a retreat, unless you can succesfully take out a marauding Mongol with sheer guano-power. Nevertheless, the scripts required that she prevail, so prevail she did. Enemies obediently stood still and waited for their lame doom (see also **Hong Kong Phooey**). Fariik (John Stephenson) was the plausible-sounding magician while Raseem (Frank Gerstle) was the he-man figure.

A total of 19 episodes were made and shown on **The Banana Splits Adventure Hour**. Relive them now, title by title. The Ransom/The Joining of the Knights/A Trap for Turhan/The Great Gold Robbery/Isle of Treachery/The Wizard of Ramnizar/Sky Raiders of the Desert/The Sultan's Plot/The Reluctant Empress/The Challenge/The Great Brass Beast/The Coronation of Bakaar/The Desert Pirates/The Royal Visitor/The Spy/The Fabulous Fair/The Jewels of Joowar/The Prisoner.

———

Arkansas Chuggabug
*See **Wacky Races***

Hillbilly-themed vehicle, more like a motorized front porch than a car. It had a red cast-iron stove and was driven by the non-proactive **Lazy Luke** and his pet, **Blubber Bear**, an enormous mammal in a tiny crash helmet. The bear sat on the rocking chair and Luke sat on the bear—perhaps a comment on Arkansas habits, or perhaps not.

Army Surplus Special
*See **Wacky Races***

Militaristic vehicle entered in those crazy wild wacky races. It was driven by a Tom Clancy type: **Sergeant Blast** and his scrawny-necked inferior **Private Meekly**.

Arnold, Kevin
*See **Wonder Years, The***

Kevin Arnold was the 12-year-old lead character in ***The Wonder Years***, played by Fred Savage. He had an IQ-free older brother called Wayne, who beat on him, and an older sister, Karen, who was going through a hippy-influenced adolescence and getting involved with boys. Aside from siblings, Kevin had two main things. Thing one: a thing for Winnie Cooper, his next door neighbour, who played hot and cold with him in her Alice band over the course of several years. Thing two: a klutzy best friend called Paul Pfeiffer, who may or may not have been based on Morocco Mole (see **Secret Squirrel**). Arnold was cute for a few years and then adolescence struck. Cue the axe.

Around the World with Willy Fogg
A BRB International production. Spain, 1983

From the people who brought you **Dogtanian**. That, in a way, says it all—although the encyclopaedia fears a fuller explanation is called for. Not much fuller though.

Rather loosely based on the Jules Verne novel, *Around The World in Eighty Days*, this slow-moving animation replaced the characters with animals, dressed in the buttoned-up fashions of England in the early 1900s: a chilling image, if ever there was one. Fog—a fox—was chewing the fat with several other bellicose old bastards with port and gravy stains down their fronts at London's Reform Club when the possibility of going around the world in 80 days was mooted. Don't ask why, it's not important. Lord Guinness—one of many churlish old goats to mutter their way through supper at the club, except that Guinness actually *was* an old goat—was up for it, but sadly wheelchair-bound. Fog volunteered out of bravado. A £10,000 bet was made—a lot of money in those days—and 26 episodes of animal fun ensued.

Fog the fox takes a hamster with him, has capers with a cad by the name of Transfer, who has been hired to fox the fox and—to cut a long story short—he picks up a foxy feline called Romy and gets back home in time to win the bet. *Willy Fog* had not the charm of *Dogtanian*—which sounds like a compliment for *Dogtanian*, but isn't.

Aspidistra the Rangdo
See The Adventure Game

Referred to as Uncle. Nominally the ruler of Arg, actually a plastic plant. It was replaced in later episodes with a teapot.

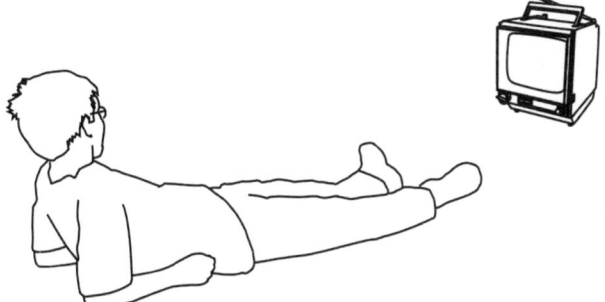

Baggy Pants and the Nitwits

NBC. A De Patie-Freleng Enterprises production. USA, 1977

Playground Conversations You Never Hear, No. 32: "Wow, did you see *Baggy Pants and the Nitwits* last night?" This gloomy cartoon double-bill, from US producers De Patie-Freleng (see **Bailey's Comets**, **Pink Panther** and **Doctor Snuggles**), was first aired in 1977 and ran for just one 13-episode season in the US before leaking into the UK like acid out of old batteries. Baggy Pants was a cat-faced Charlie Chaplin pastiche. He dressed and waddled like that comedian of yesteryear, in a variety of unthrilling escapades. The lack of dialogue and canned laughter did little to boost the appeal to children of this slow-moving nostalgia piece, inked from a dreary palette of browns and greys.

The Nitwits, by subtle contrast, were two clapped out superheroes: Gladys, enormous frump with wrinkled stockings, and **Tyrone**, tiny old fool with droopy white moustache. The dismal duo had been called out of retirement to help fight crime, with the aid of Tyrone's flying walking stick, **Elmo**. Tyrone, in the advanced stages of senile dementia, bungled everything and Gladys was generally the brains behind any success (see **Hong Kong Phooey**, **Captain Pugwash** etc).

Voiced by Arte Johnson for Tyrone and Ruth Buzzi for Gladys, *The Nitwits* was an adaptation of a well-known sketch on Rowan and Martin's *Laugh-In*. That is to say, it was well-known to American pensioners. Tyrone's fumbling attempts to solicit amorous activity from the matronly Gladys added a slightly unsavoury element to the piece. Add in the fact that the word "pants" generally has a different meaning in the UK to the States and you have an offering which was, all in all, enough to make the average under-ten crawl off somewhere dark to do its homework.

Bagpuss

BBC TV. A Smallfilms production. Created by Peter Firmin and Oliver Postgate. Written by Oliver Postgate. Directed by Peter Firmin. Music by John Faulkner and Sandra Kerr. Narrated by Oliver Postgate. UK, 1974

"We will stick it with glue, glue, glue." So sang the mice on the mouse organ, providing in their rodent way a neat commentary on the way animators Oliver Postgate and Peter Firmin had gone about creating the magical world of *Bagpuss*. Much has been made of the fact that the duo—as the prolific, acclaimed Smallfilms—produced *Bagpuss*, **The Clangers**, **Pogle's Wood**, **Ivor the Engine**, and **Noggin the Nogg** in a tiny pig sty on Peter Firmin's farm. But the fact is hardly outstanding on its own; after all, it is not as if the pigs were still in it. More impressive is the enduring quality of their creation, and the affection with which it is remembered.

The premise of this engaging make-believe show was that a little girl called Emily had a bunch of stuff. She had found, collected and kept not only Bagpuss, "the most magical saggy old cloth cat in the whole wide world," but a host of other dolls and assorted bits of sentimental junk, in the way people do. With Emily, though, it was something like a compulsive habit. Each episode she would collect another poor, abandoned, broken toy and bring it back to her shop, where—via Bagpuss and his friends—she would festoon it with love, until she got bored, moved onto something else and the programme ended. The shop itself was not of the type which actually did business. The toys were not for sale. Ostensibly left for their owners to collect, they were really Emily's. Unusual? Not really. Did you never set up shop at home and invite your parents to "buy" your most treasured Star Wars key rings and Munch Bunch pencil tops, with the strict proviso that they didn't actually keep them?

They were all alive, the toys: all it took was the sound of Emily's voice and they would all wake up. They were at her beck and call, a population of malleable puppets who would do her bidding and talk to her and never ever leave her because they were trapped. Each one owed her its life.

Perhaps. Or perhaps it was a simple parallel of that special box of special things all children keep somewhere special.

"Bagpuss, dear Bagpuss, old fat, furry cat puss, wake up and look at this thing that we bring," ordered Emily. The cat would yawn, stretch and wake, in lurching stop-motion. And when Bagpuss woke up, all the other people in the "shop" woke up too. The picture would change from sepia to colour and the whole magical fantasy playground would come alive (in Emily's mind). **Madeleine** the maternal doll, sitting up in her chair with those scary wide eyes and mad stripy dress; **Professor Yaffle**, the cantankerous old woodpecker, who was actually a bookend; **Gabriel** the singing, banjo-playing amphibian (not to be confused with **Alberto Frog and his Amazing Animal Band**), who did a kind of Maurice Chevalier impression; and the mice on the **mouse organ**, a team of rodent charlatans who squeaked and sang and pretended to fix things "we will fix it, we will fix it" but generally did a cowboy job on it, incurring the lethargic disapproval of the tubby kitty.

Wait a minute. "Bagpuss is not to be called a 'tubby kitty'," says Oliver Postgate, his creator. What's more "he did not comment on the mousework." Mr Postgate can't be wrong. Perhaps, then, there was just something in the fatty catty's expression which made him seem so superior to the rodents.

Anyway, they all had a good look at Emily's new item, tried to nurse it back to health and work out what it was. But their experience was limited by the fact that they were not even real. A story would be read, a song would be sung, but in the end they were pretty much resigned to life as a series of fleeting moments in Emily's fertile imagination and would eventually lapse back into a kind of gloomy torpor. Today was just like yesterday and tomorrow would be the same. It was predictable and homely. There is a kind of reassurance in that. As if in comment, the world—as seen through the Smallfilms camera—would respond to Bagpuss's renewed slumber by turning back to sepia stills and becoming (in this encyclopaedia's imagination at least) infused with the faint smell of mothballs, dust and old shortbread (see also **Ffestiniog**).

Wait a minute. "The imagination boggles wondering," says Mr Postgate, "where the author dreamed up the dismal ending! No mothballs." He goes on to point out that, in fact, "Emily has NO part to play in the series except to bring things she finds." So don't go getting all creative. Fondly remember *Bagpuss* the way its producer intended or not at all ...

Link: www.martinday.co.uk/bagpuss.htm.
Readers who are sceptical about Mr Postgate's assertion that Emily had no part to play, might find the above site interesting reading. Not for the faint-hearted, though. Or for the sane.

Bailey's Comets
CBS. A DePatie-Freleng Enterprises production. Created by Joe Ruby and Ken Spears. USA, 1973

"Skateroo to the next clue!" *Bailey's Comets* followed the all-American efforts of a six-strong roller skate treasure hunt team—headed by pubescent man of action Barnaby Bailey—to win a $1m prize. In a similar scenario to **Wacky Races**, the Comets were hampered and plotted against by 16 other teams: the Black Hats, the Cosmic Rays, the Broomer Girls, the Duster Busters, the Gusta Pastas, the Gargantuan Giants, the **Hairy Madden Red Eyes**, the **Mystery Mob**, the **Rock 'n' Rollers**, the Ramblin' Rivets, the Roller Bears, the Roller Coasters, the **Yo Ho Hos**, the Stone Rollers, the Texas Flycats and the **Dr. Jekyll/Hydes** (whose uncontrollable ability to switch madly between good and evil added a random comic element to the proceedings).

Just like in real life, the teams' members all possessed one obvious and overdrawn character trait which informed every action they took (the Yo Ho Hos were all pirates, the Rock 'n' Rollers were, well, guess). Usually this involved villainy. But the Comets were far too scrupulously honest to ape the double-dealing of their competitors: a predictable moral stance, which usually meant they triumphed. Just like in real life.

Giving the fatuous running commentary from a helicopter was a character called Gabby, voiced by stalwart voice artist

Don "**Scooby Doo**" Messick. Also in the cockpit was pilot Dooter Roo, voiced by the versatile Daws Butler (see **Snagglepuss**, **Hair Bear**, **Wally Gator**). The climax of each episode came when the next clue was found and, pausing only for a quick team-briefing, the Comets would skateroo away, clean around the world.

It is possible that creators Joe Ruby and Ken Spears (who also created *Scooby Doo* for Hanna-Barbera) were unaware that within this frivolous animation was actually a workable (if frivolous) live-action format. In retrospect, it seems plausible—if bizarre—that *Baileys Comets* was the inspiration for Channel 4's 1982 *Treasure Hunt* format, created by Anne Meo and personified in the UK by Anneka Rice. *Bailey's Comets* was doubled at one point in the UK with the excellent **Grape Ape** by some inspired programmer.

Bakaar
See Arabian Knights, The

Cod Arabic impaler-type loon, obsessed with rule. Seized the throne of **Prince Turhan,** then sat on it. The character was voiced by Paul Frees.

Ball, Benny The
See Top Cat

Small blue tubby kitty. Wore a white jacket. Blissfully unaware of everything. Based on Private Doberman from *Sergeant Bilko*, he was voiced by the same actor, Maurice Gosfield.

Bananaman

101 Productions. Produced by Trevor Bond. Directed by Terry Ward. Written by Bernie Kay. UK, 1983

At 29 Acacia Road lived a cretin called Eric Twinge, possibly the best-named character in this encyclopaedia. Sadly he came not from the best show. This schoolboy nerd lived an amazing double life, according to the opening titles. For when Eric ate a banana, an amazing transformation occured. Eric *was* Bananaman—ever alert for the call to idiocy. Voiced by the Goodies (Bill Oddie, Graeme Garden and Tim Brooke-Taylor), *Bananaman* survived the transition from the short-lived *Nutty* comic to badly-drawn animation by employing a healthy dose of irony. Quite funny, largely due to the quality of the voice artists, it nevertheless came a poor second to **Danger Mouse**, to which it was a sort of rival. Eric's fantasies about Fiona the newsreader played second fiddle to head-on encounters with nemesis Genberal Blight, Dr Gloom and a band of aliens called Nerks. He had a friend, Appleman, and a crow. Seen worse (see **Superted**).

Banana Splits (The Banana Splits Adventure Hour)

A Hanna-Barbera production. USA, 1968

One banana, two banana, three banana, four. Four bananas made a bunch and so did many more. Over hill and highway the banana buggies went. But just who were those crazy animal quackers, flipping like a pancake, popping like a cork? They were Fleegle, Bingo, Drooper and Snork. They looked like what you might see if you watched Hanna-Barbera cartoons after eating chemicals—the living, breathing embodiment of Cartoon Hell in all its oversized, luminous, grinning glory.

More precisely, the Splits acted as musical comperes for a raft of second rate Hanna-Barbera entertainment shows and pop videos. Firstly, **Danger Island**: a stunningly wooden live action drama of the "how-are-we-ever-going-to-get-off-this-place-without-being-scalped-and-eaten?" kind, shot in spectacular colour of the postcard touch-up kind. Then came **The**

Three Musketeers, a cartoon reading of the Dumas novel of the same name (not to be confused with **Dogtanian and the Three Muskehounds**). It was tame, compared to **The Arabian Knights**, an Ali Baba cartoon spectacular, complete with metamorphosis action. "Siiiiize . . . of an eagle." **The Adventures of Gulliver** was a Lilliput-related cartoon caper, featuring a cunning dearth of laughs. The crowning glory was **The New Adventures Of Huck Finn**. Tearaway Tom Sawyer starred in this unconscionable time-travel charade. *Microventure* was a lame dose of miniaturised mad scientist mayhem in cartoon form. Lastly, and leastly, **Hillbilly Bears**, a country cousin cartoon carry-on in which the best thing was the names of the characters.

Those Banana Splits in full, then. **Fleegle** played the guitar and sometimes read the "news". He had long ears, for he was a beagle. Fleegle the beagle, you see. It rhymed. Jeffrey Winkless had the thankless job of wearing the suit. The man with his voice was Paul "**Bubi Bear**"Winchell (see also **Dick Dastardly**). **Bingo** was a grinning orange gorilla, and Mickey Dolenz looka-like voiced by Daws "**Snagglepuss**" Butler (see also **Wally Gator** and **Wacky Races**). The man inside Bingo was Terence Winkless (relation). **Drooper** was the name of the lion gui-tarist. He had his own your-letters segment, "Dear Drooper". The man who wore that suit for money was Daniel Winkless (relation). He was voiced by Allan Melvin. **Snorky** was the spot-eared elephant "at" the organ. They were all out of Winklesses by this time, so Robert Towers wore the suit. Snorky never spoke. The Winklesses employed "stage" surnames—such as the hunky, all-American-sounding Brock and Owen—but this encyclopaedia is not buying that. They were called Winkless. Not everyone can boast a name like that—if you've got it, flaunt it.

Banana Splits, then: the **Multi-Coloured Swap Shop** of the US (see also **Animal Kwackers**). Mute brothers in animal suits are judged by this encyclopaedia to have been a distinct improvement on Noel Edmunds. Bit like *The Monkees*, though.

Barbapapa

BBC TV. A Polyscope production. Created, illustrated and written by Annette Tison and Talus Taylor. France, 1974

And now—unusually for an encyclopaedia—a French linguisti-cal gag. *Barbe à papa* (pause for laughs). Literally "daddy's beard", *barbe à papa* is the French phrase for candyfloss. Barbapapa the children's character, however, was a luminous blob who could change shape at will and had spawned a whole family of similarly mutating blobs of uselessness, which you couldn't even eat. Describing this motley midden as can-dyfloss would seem to be taking poetic license a little too far. But this was Paris in 1974. Baudelaire and Rimbaud were dead—someone had to pick up the baton.

That someone was Annette Tison, a French architecture

graduate, along with Talus Taylor, a Californian expatriate teacher. Legend has it that the couple met in a café and instantly formed a writing partnership, of which *Barbapapa* was the happy fruit. The sheer romanticism of profitably exploiting a marketing package across the world may not have been what drove them to marry shortly thereafter.

Barbapapa, the patriarch, was an unhappy cross between *Wicked Willy* (see also **Roobarb**) and the **New Schmoo**. His spouse was aptly named Barbamama, and was black with big Su Pollard glasses. Barbabravo, an offspring of this happy union, was a Sherlock Holmes type, complete with magnifying glass, while Barbabright was blue and clever. Barbazoo was chiefly known for doing things with animals. Barbabeau was the hairy artist, while Barbabelle was obsessed with her own appearance (see **Penelope Pitstop**). Barbalala was the house musician and, lastly, Barbalib was an orange female, with a *penchant* for books.

The animated television shows were produced by Polyscope, a now-defunct offshoot of Polygram (see **Doctor Snuggles** for an account of Polyscope's demise), and the storyboards for the shows were expanded into a series of popular books. And Barbapapa *was* popular in his time. Perhaps it was the polymorphous angle which caught the imagination. He and his family certainly had many practical uses. My favourite use for Barbapapa is random insertion of his name in meaningless, jargon-drenched business memoranda (see also **Snagglepuss**)—a time-buying tactic which proved useful to me when delaying delivery to my publishers of this manuscript:

Dear Allison & Busby

Thank you for the advance. **Further to** our conversation **re** KIDS TV 'Project Value'; as you know I have **facilitated** a **fast-track** schedule for a **value-added, content-rich, single-channel publisher-facing solution, ETA** mid-Jan 2003. Can I suggest your KTV **team flag up** a **dedicated barbapapa** as a contingency. I shall be in NY **going forward** but, in my absence, please **liaise with** Barbara at my office **in the first instance**.

Thanking you in advance …

Links: Visitors to the creators' web site at **wwwusers.imaginet.fr/~mhp/** are assailed with possibly the most amusing copyright notice ever posted by people who draw outlines and colour them in:

> BARBAPAPA COPYRIGHT TRADEMARK
> INTELLECTUAL PROPERTY RIGHTS
> ...If you use the materials of BARBAPAPA without permission you cause damage to the creators of BARBAPAPA by confusing persons genuinely seeking information. You interfere with the freedom of persons who try to get proper information from the only sources who can advice [sic] them correcly, the editors of the BARBAPAPA books, and the creators themselves. You do not help the creators in any way, you only cause them damage, and you cause damage to everyone who is delayed in their search to try to obtain up-to-date information about BARBAPAPA ...

It hardly needs saying that, as a person genuinely seeking information, I was unable to find any on this site. The up-to-date Barbapapa information—so titillatingly dangled—was not available, nor was any information about the creators or the books and television shows. There is, however, a useful and informative site at: **www.naughtykitty.org/barbapapa.html**. Or, if your heart can stand the fun, there is the Barbapapa webring at **www.naughtykitty.org/barbapapa/barbaring.html**.

Barnaby the Bear

Barnaby (Aka Barnaby the Bear)

Created by Olga Pouchine. Narrated (UK) by Colin Jeavons. France, 1973

Barnaby the Bear was his name. "Never call me Jack or James" was his warning, delivered in the insistent title theme. Just what he might do if you did was never revealed, but let's be honest: one does not fool around with bears unless one is already of that predisposition (see **Rainbow**). Despite the pugnacious warning, however, Barnaby was, like all bullies, a wimp on a scooter.

Now, Barnaby lived and worked in a circus, owned and managed by the difficultly-named **Mr Pimoulu** (pronounced: *pimoulu*): a slightly demonic figure sporting a top hat (see also **Moominpappa**) and a moustache greased into two dangerous spikes (see also **Zebedee** and **Dick Dastardly**). Observing the first rule of business, Pimoulu forced most of his acts to multitask in administrative or supporting roles. A typical contract probably read: "Position: monkey, plus any other duties." He obliged his wife—a svelte blonde in a yellow twinset—to sell the tickets from a tiny wood kiosk before jumping onto the high wire, in the same twinset, and alarming the audience. **Sara the Seal** had to double up on drums or risk the dole queue. **Ricky and Dicky**, two cheeky primates, played all the instruments in the band and then did a trapeze act. Leading by example, Pimoulu—nominally ringmaster—condescended to do his own magic act, in which he humiliated a lion and then turned it into a domestic kitty.

Amid these death-defying dares, it is hard to imagine why Barnaby should have gotten to be the star of the show, when all he did was ride about on a scooter and sing his little song. No one claps when *I* do that. Nevertheless, the audience loved this fluffy cretin with an identity complex and forgave him his neurosis.

Barnaby's act and whole *raison d'être* hinged on his golden singing voice. Given this, one of the most endearing features of the show was narrator Colin Jeavons' complete inability to carry a tune in a bucket. "Birds taught me to sing," he would grate—alternately sharp and flat—in the theme song, adding: "If you want to sing this way ..." and offering instructions. But music was not the only attraction *chez* Pimoulu. Also available, according to the theme song, was the appetising combination of "treacle pudding, fish and chips, fizzy drinks and liquorice". Mmm.

Baron Silas Greenback
See Danger Mouse

Sworn enemy of **Danger Mouse**. Greenback—created by Mike Harding and based on a farmer he had taken against—was a giant, rasping toad and enemy of democracy, whose plans to rule the world—or throw it into chaos and confusion by stealing every important signpost—were hampered by the existence of DM. Recalling the famous James Bond nemesis, he stroked a fluffy white caterpillar called Nero. He was voiced, or rasped, by Edward Kelsey.

Basil Brush Show, The
BBC TV. A BBC production. Character created by Peter Firmin. Puppeteer: Ivan Owen. UK, 1968

Boom boom. The **Hartley Hare** of the canine world, Basil—a cross between a gravy stained old git in a tweedy cape, and your little brother—was created by Peter Firmin (see **Clangers, Pogles** etc) for a children's show called *The Three Scampys*. He arrived in 1963 and didn't leave until 1982. The Jelly Baby-eating fox—based on Terry Thomas's various screen cads—was considerably more memorable than his host show and in 1967 he was offered a segment on *The Nixon Line*, a vehicle for magician David Nixon. His success was so great that in 1968 he was given his own show, which ran for four series. Operated and voiced by the late, great Ivan Owen, Basil got through a host of straightmen during his run. He barked out that infectious laugh, banging his head repeatedly against the desk as the rights flew this way and that across 14 different countries. Ka-ching.

Rodney Bewes chaperoned the fox between 1968 and 1969, before becoming a Likely Lad. Derek Fowlds took over the reins from 1969 to 1973, before giving way to Roy North who suffered stoically for four further years from 1973 to 1977. The others were Howard Williams (1977-79) and Billy Boyle (1979-80), who was last seen heading towards Disney. The puppet also had a short recording career. A couple of LPs (remember them?) on EMI should be worth a bob or two (remember them?) by now.

He was axed by the BBC for unknown reasons, but we may not have seen the last of the naughty fox. Entertainment Rights—the global multimedia children's and family entertainment group which had been holding the Brush rights—struck a deal in May 2001 with Children's BBC to jointly develop a new comedy series to feature Basil. Expect much Hasbro merchandise to follow.

Batman

ABC. A Greenaway production for Twentieth Century Fox. Executive producer: William Dozier. Produced by Howie Horowitz. Directed by various including Robert Butler. Created by Bob Kane. UK tx ITV 1966. USA, 1966

"Holy catamites, Batman, what exactly *is* our relationship?" Millionaire playboy Bruce Wayne (Adam West) and his young "ward" Dick Grayson (Burt Ward) were shacked up together, amusing each other in opulent luxury while crime and chaos stalked the streets of Gotham City. Albeit in camp costumes. Whenever things got too much for police commissioner Gordon and chief O'Hara (ie always) they would reach for the batphone. When that happened, Wayne and Grayson knew what to do: put their pants on outside their tights and go out to fight. The batpoles were behind the book case, the batmobile was in the batcave and eveything else was in their bat utility belts. Then out they would go, the Caped Crusader and the Boy Wonder, into who knew what.

Would it be the wonky-legged Penguin (Burgess Meredith) in his purple suit? Or would it be that cold-blooded quizmaster the Riddler (John Astin)? What about the Joker (Cesar Romero), his mouth mutated by a chemical accident into a fearsome clown's grin? Would it be the dominatrix Catwoman (Eartha Kitt), purring mortally in her skin-tight leather? One of them, probably. And whoever it was, and whatever they were doing, you knew it would end in a stiltedly choreographed punch-up, punctuated with all the KA-POW, CRAK, POP, WHIZZZ of the 1939 comic strips by Bob Kane. A mere 120 episodes were produced, before ratings slumps forced the show off the air. Perhaps it was West's less-than-muscle-bound physique which didn't cut the mustard. *Batman*, of course, hit the mainstream eventually with high-budget feature films, (*Batman* by Leslie Martinson, 1989; *Batman Returns* by Tim Burton, 1992; and *Batman Forever* by Joel Schumacher, 1995) but the superlative '60s series by William Dozier remains a cult item. Who could ever forget that theme, by Neal Hefti: Dinner dinner dinner dinner, dinner dinner dinner dinner …

Battle of the Planets

BBC TV. A Gallerie International Films production in association with Sandy Frank Film Syndication Inc., in association with Tasunoko Production Co. Ltd. Written by Jameson Brewer and others. Japan/USA, 1978

One was called Keyop. "Brrrrrrrrrrrrrrrrr-root-toot-toot-toot!" That was his catchphrase. They were young, they had eerily big eyes, they wore baseball shirts and flares, they had shoulder-length hair; they were a Japanese sub-manga *anime* cartoon with dubbed American voices (see **Marine Boy, Moomin** etc). But more than that, they were a team. G-Force was its name, and its mission was to save the planet from the warmongering planet **Spectra**, an alien body whose mission it was to destroy Earth. Like firefighters, the members of G-Force hung about, indulging in recreational pursuits, waiting for the call. Unlike firefighters, when the call came they all dressed as birds and got in a spaceship called the Phoenix.

What distinguished these kids from others their age was the unique "cerabonic superpowers" they possessed. Basically these powers enabled them to "transmute" into their bird alteregos (see also **Arabian Knights, The**). Their vehicles also transmuted. There was something else special about the kids in G-Force. The commentary over the show's introduction sequence described them as "fearless orphans", although the encyclopaedia prefers to interpret this as "exploitable loners with nothing to lose".

There was Mark; he was the commander, and hero. He was firm but fair, full of pathos and compassion: standard traits in the average 17 year-old. Then there was Jason. He was a bit lairy and given to brooding. One was fat. His name was Tiny. One was a girl. Her name was Princess. Just to make sure we all knew she was a valued and capable member of the top intergalactic peace-keeping force, the animators had her wear a very short pink dress and perform continual somersaults, causing hormonal distress to ten-year-old boys the country over.

Watching over them from Centre Neptune (a submarine building with school glockenspiels on the walls) was their computerized co-ordinator, 7-Zark-7—the John Inman of the robot world. Forever fussing, he would occasionally flit across the floor, his gold cape trilling behind him:"I don't know why I worry so much about G-Force," he would fidget. Zark may have been camp, but he was not gay. He had an ongoing relationship with Susan, a breathy, female-voiced computer, who used to give his electrodes goosebumps. He was voiced by Alan Young, very much in the C3PO vein.

Centre Neptune was the nerve centre for Universal Defence and Security, which was in turn presided over by the hairy and foreboding presence (see **Fingerbobs**) of Security Chief Anderson. Anderson was—one must presume—taking time out from his usual job as a porn star, if his bushy moustache and action sideburns are anything by which to judge. He certainly was not the most reassuring chief of security a universe could have hoped for, as you will see for yourself in this gripping dialogue from "Ghost Ship of Planet Mir":

MARK: Chief, there's a fog machine we want to knock out, but it could be one of Mir's defences.

CHIEF: We don't have any information on that, but go ahead. Chance it.

That's the spirit. It's only a drawing. What could it hurt? Anderson reported to President Kane of the Intergalactic Federation, who presided not just over Earth, but over all its colonies and allied planets in other galaxies, even those "galaxies beyond space", wherever that is (see **Ffestiniog**). The balance of power was ably demonstrated by the symbolic sequence in the episode above where Anderson lights Kane's fat cigar. Perhaps that's how such an incompetent got promoted so high ...

Then there was Keyop. He was genetically modified and, as a result, he dressed as a duck and said "proot". Allowances were made and everyone patronised him gently. When Princess said: "It's *my* turn to go with Mark," Keyop's useful comment was: "Proop. Lovey dovey Marky Warky." Keyop's tweeting antics would sometimes push the mercurial Jason just too far and the temperamental one would round on the duck-faced one. Poor Keyop. He would foot and twoot and fweep and the fat one—who dressed as an owl—would come to his rescue. It's a wonder they ever got any universe-saving done, but they did, and always in the nick of time, via use of the Fiery Phoenix function. It was never explained and, looking back, this encyclopaedia finds it's good not to know.

The score—a mixture of *Star Wars* pastiche and muzak—was provided by the imitable Hoyt Curtin (who did a better job with **Scooby Doo**). The rousing *Star Wars* stuff formed the backdrop to battles and action sequences, but the muzak had a special use. For deep within the tough, fearless exterior of G-Force there beat a human heart. A heart that knew the pain of losing a family. A heart that knew loneliness. A heart that learned its lessons the hard way. Yes, there was always a softer, human-interest, sub-plot which allowed Mark to show his compassionate side. This side of his character was usually made manifest in close-ups of his face in static emotion-shots (i.e. gritted teeth). Cut to sunset; mix up muzak; introduce small child; bucket optional.

Battle of the Planets was a version of the brilliantly-named Japanese series *Science Ninja Team Gatchaman. Gatchaman* clocked up a violent and bloody 205 episodes. The American cartoon—a much-watered-down brew—was compiled from 85 *Gatchaman* episodes. The twee 7-Zark-7 was added by American animators Gallerie International, to bridge the gaps where bloodshed and death had been edited out.

Belle and Sebastian

RTLF, A Gaumont France production. Executive Producer: Ettienne Laroche. Produced by Helene Gagarine. Directed by Jean Guillame. Written by Cecile Aubrey. Music by David White. France, 1967

Aaah. Lovely doggie (see **Littlest Hobo**). This it's-grim-down-south-of-France drama series followed the mountain-based adventures of a young boy and his enormous white dog in a small Pyreneean village. Grumpy Grandpa was much in evidence, as were various big, beardy rough, tough men, who didn't like dogs or small, sensitive boys. Pierre Mehdi played the hapless Sebastian, forever calling "Bell-uh Bell-uh" as various undesirables plotted, for some deeply suspect reason, against him and the dog.

Based on the books by Cecile Aubrey, 13 25-minute episodes were shot in glorious black and white and unleashed on an unsuspecting world over three series: *Belle et Sebastien*, *Sebastien et la Mary Morgane* and *Sebastien parmi les Hommes* (Sebastian among the men . . .). Not without a certain imported **Danger on the Danube Delta**-style allure, *Belle and Sebastian* usually caught viewers unawares during the summer holidays in between **Why Don't You** and *Laff Olympics* (see **Hanna-Barbera**).

(A Japanese *anime* version—made by MK Company, Visual 80 Productions and Toho Co—was shown on cable station Nikelodeon in the US relentlessly over six seasons from 1984 to 1990. Has been sighted in the UK.)

Benny the Ball
See Top Cat

Small blue, straight-man to TC's funny man. The unwitty kitty was voiced by Maurice Gosfield.

Benn, Mr
See Mr Benn

Bert
See Sesame Street

Long of head, whiny of voice, single tuft of hair. He wore the kind of polyester top which was simultaneously a v-neck and a polo-neck. He lived with **Ernie**, with whom he shared a bedroom, but not a bed and whom he ordered about relentlessly, to no real effect. He was voiced by Frank Oz.

Bertha
BBC. A BBC production. Produced by Ivor Wood. Written by Eric Charles. Directed by Derek Mogford. Music by Brian Daly. UK, 1985

Bertha was a big green machine, with buttons to push and levers to pull. She lived in the Spottiswood factory, managed by the vocationally-named Mr Willmake and his sound-effect

secretary Miss McClackerty. Bertha spat objects out out her great toothy mouth on a conveyor belt tongue (see also **Chock-A-Block**). She clicked and whirred. There was a little robot fiddling with her, which might have accounted for the clicking and whirring. That was T.O.M. (Talk Operated Machine), the brainchild of chief designer Mr Sprott's assistant Tracy. He took the **Cli Cli** role. Ted Turner fixed her when she went wrong, Mrs Tupp brought the tea and Roy Willing—Turner's brainless apprentice—took the **Shaggy** role of humorous bungler. Gentle panacea for littl'uns, from the Ivor Wood stable (see **Wombles, The**), narrated by the late Roy Kinnear.

Bessie
See Chigley

Old steam train. It was the pride and hobby of aristocratic layabout **Lord Belborough** who, like all landed gentry, performed a useful role in the community, in this case by bringing out the rolling stock to carry bags of biscuits from the Chigley Biscuit factory before standing the tired workforce a much needed waltz (surely pint?) on his barrel organ. Time flew by when he was the driver of his train, and he rode on the footplate, there and back again, according to the lyrics of his song. Bessie was also the name of a stuck-together lump of margarine containers, toilet rolls, cotton wool and about half a pound of Sellotape (see **Doctor Snuggles**) you pretended was a train, chuffing it around the carpet, kitchen floor, parents' dressing table and finally the bath, where it melted into a lump of sog and you ran away. Admit it.

Big Gruesome
See Wacky Races

One half of the **Gruesome Twosome**. Behind the wheel of the **Creepy Coup**, he endeavoured to win that wacky race. He was

49

some kind of monster in the Frankenstein vein, but with a fringe. He was voiced by Daws Butler and his partner was **Little**, a mauve Dracula.

Black Beauty, The Adventures of

ITV. A Talbot TV/LWT production. Executive producer: Paul Knight. Produced by Sidney Cole. Directed by John Reardon. Script by Ted Willis UK, 1972.

Could easily have been called The All-New Black Beauty Show, such was the disparity between these stories of strapping black stallion action (see **Champion, The Adventures of**) and the Anna Sewell novels on which they were supposedly based. The only part that had any lasting impression on almost the entire online community was its theme. But what was it called? ITV reports it was the stirring "Galloping Home", written by Dennis King.

Black Pig, The
*See **Captain Pugwash***

August vessel of the tubby cap'n and his band of unproblematically-named pirates.

Bleep and Booster
*BBC. A BBC production. UK, 1964. See **Blue Peter***

Earth boy Booster and his robot Bleep in space-related hiccups. Shown on **Blue Peter** and transferred to the Annuals for a while. Narrated over black and white stills. Gripping, for 1964.

Blockbusters

ITV. A Central Television production. UK, 1983-93

"Put yourself on the hot spot." Televised daily humiliation for sixth-formers, in the days before *Home and Away*. Gonks and teddy bear mascots were a must as one loner versus two idiots competed in a connect-4 (or 5, depending on which team you were in) style board game, where each question correctly answered gained you a space on the board. Each hexagonal space had a letter with which began the answer. "What T, everybody," teacherly presenter Bob Holness might have begun, "is a state of apathetic inertia induced by watching this show day after day while eating your tea?" Bzzzzd. Is it torpor, Bob? "Correct, and that's Blockbusters. So good luck as I ask you to... put yourself on the hot spot." Best of three games gave you a shot at the Gold Run: a multiple-letter hot spot challenge. RIP, ATV; they were all there, waiting to be deciphered.

You could accumulate cash at £5 for every correct answer. Rapacious contestants who clocked up needless extra points and cash, having first blocked their opponents, were given short shrift by Bob. Prizes included horrible action breaks with white water rafting and abseiling, and the occasional weekend for two in Venice (Who will you take? I don't know). High points included cliffhanger tension—"and we'll find out if he makes that connection ...on the next edition of Blockbusters". Low points were the "chat" bits where Bob asked shambling, cocky adolescents about their vain aspirations—*Why do you want to be a child psychologist?*—or questioned them on their idiosyncrasies: *So, Nigel, why is your nickname Nomates? ... Tell me about your gonk ...* Riveting. Humour elements included the ritual asking of "Can I have a P please, Bob" and sporadic hand-jiving over the credits. Grooh. Michael Aspel presented a more recent BBC2 version using adults, but the show lacked even the mild charm of the Holness version. Sky One was showing a version with Liza Tarbuck in 2001. Unsurprisingly, the format originated in the US.

Blue Peter

BBC TV. A BBC production. Created by John Hunter Blair. UK, 1958–ongoing

If only you could have bought "double-sided sticky tape" in your local WH Smith, life would have been different. *Blue Peter*, then: Totaliser and military band fun from the BBC. Make a Christingle and candelabra out of tinsel and clothes hangers (here's one we set fire to earlier). Paint your tortoise with non-leaded paint. Seek out and attempt to use something called sticky-backed plastic (possibly Sellotape, see **Doctor Snuggles**). Raise money for charity appeals by staging your own *Blue Peter* bring-and-buy sale. Send old coins and shoes. Whoops, here's some elephant poo, a steel band and a documentary about an old ship. Look out, Percy Thrower's cursing vandals in the *Blue Peter* sunken garden, Joey Deacon's fallen asleep and Peter Duncan is making a hibernation pit for hedgehogs out of a cardboard box. Help!—multi-instrumentalist Mike Oldfield is re-recording the theme tune using something called a multi-track tape recorder. He's wearing his *Blue Peter* badge, which means he could get a reduced price ticket to the Bath & West show, should he choose to go. Special assignments from Cambodia. Party on.

What can be said about this show that has not already been said? Hardly a cult, it is a national institution, but an encyclopaedia (even this one) would be incomplete without it. Like faded jigsaws and old shortbread in a village shop window (see **Ffestiniog, Bagpuss** and **Sally & Jake**), the beauty of *Blue Peter* is that it has remained utterly untouched for 43 years. It has a timeless quality insofar as it has always seemed slightly out of date. Having lost some of its power in many people's eyes with the end of the Leslie Judd, Peter Purves and John Noakes presenting triumvirate, trouble was clearly afoot when ageing DJ Simon Groom took over the Noakes slot with his own Shep (Goldie). He played "Funky Town" on his "decks" and advertised the latest annual by saying the inside cover showed "pictures of me and Tina (see **Lizzy Dripping**) in 28 different positions". The production team should have known better than to let the innuendo king loose on live TV with a documentary about knockers. Further highlights included a two-year bout of pre-chocolate photo Anthea Turner and a Peruvian marching powder cock-up with Richard Bacon. Early shows and Annuals included excellent space-age (non-animated) cartoon strip called **Bleep and Booster**, when space was cool.

In anyone's book 43 years is a long time. Presenters come and go so—lest we forget—here is a round up. You might want to get a grown-up to help you with this bit. Christopher Trace (1958-67): died in 1992. Leila Williams (1958-62). Anita West (1962-62). Valerie Singleton OBE (1962-72): arrived in conjunction with twice-weekly billing; had two dogs called Petra. John Noakes (1965-78): action man with own catchphrase: "down, Shep"; left to present *Go With Noakes*. Peter Purves (1967-78): avuncular. Lesley Judd (1972-79): became a prisoner on **The Adventure Game**. Simon Groom (1978-86): not another film about his parents' farm! Christopher Wenner (1978-80): who? Tina Heath (1979-80): really **Lizzy Dripping**; had *Blue Peter* pregnancy. Sarah Greene (1980-83): good prospects, but ended up with Mike Smith. Peter Duncan (1980-84, then 1985-86): apeared in *Flash Gordon*, **The Flockton Flyer** and a nasty suit designed by a *Blue Peter* competition winner; went on to "star" in the not-quite-convincing *Duncan Dares*. Janet Ellis (1983-87): former **Jigsaw** presenter who left under a cloud of pregnancy. Michael Sundin (1984-85): died tragically at a young age. Mark Curry (1986-89): barrel bottom? Caron Keating (1986-90): bit racy and famously Gloria Hunniford's daughter; had funny hair—for a bit. Yvette Fielding (1987-92). John Leslie (1989-94); heartthrob; famously dumped Catherine Zeta Jones, allegedly so she wouldn't hamper his career. Diane-Louise Jordan (1990-96): short but sweet. Anthea Turner (1992-94): before all the silliness. Tim Vincent (1993-97): bit dull. Stuart Miles (1994-99): left to pursue "new challenges". Katy Hill (1995-2000): promoted from within, she had been a BBC administrator. Romana D'Annunzio (1996-98): went into theatre, whence she came. Konnie Huq (1997-): she came from Channel 5; still at it. Richard Bacon (1997-98); bit sniffy (see **Noseybonk**); went on to join *Big Breakfast*, which knows no shame (see

Cheggers). Simon Thomas (1999–). Matt Baker (1999–). Liz Barker (2000–).

Blue Peter, then: amazing really. Actually a kind of flag.

Bod

BBC. A Bodfilms production. Produced by David Yates. Written and designed by Joanne and Michael Cole. Music by Derek Griffiths. UK, 1975–76

What exactly was Bod? Was it some form of child? It had no hair, slit eyes, wore a yellow dress with leggings and looked like the space alien out of *Close Encounters*. We didn't know what it was, we just knew it was coming. "Here comes Bod." The suave tones of narrator John le Mesurier (of *Dad's Army* fame) did nothing to reassure Bod's more easily alarmed pre-school viewers, who hung onto their seats through Farmer Barleymow, PC Copper and Aunt Flo until the show metamorphosed into the milkshake-happy **Alberto Frog and his Amazing Animal Band**. You knew where you were with talking animals, or, at least, there was a precedent for them in children's TV. But there was no precedent for *Bod*, which is probably why it has become one of the best remembered pre-school shows of the '70s era. That consumers are now offered a 'Gold Edition' video speaks volumes about the kitsch adult appeal of this kids' favourite.

Part of that appeal was the funky music, supplied by **Play School** veteran Derek Griffths. Another contributing factor was undoubtedly the setting. Bod was in space. That is to say, not actual outer space, but it might have been—no one would have known. The backgrounds were non-figurative colour washes, giving them the hip, minimalist look of early **Pink Panther** or **Roobarb**. In addition, surreal things happened. People might fall down a hole into a giant cake, and that would be perfectly all right. No need to comment, just concentrate on getting out. Philosophical concepts were thrown out and left to hang. Most importantly, when you add all this together, it did not patronise children and bore them to stupefaction with tired formats (see **Button Moon**), creepy puppets (see **Hartley Hare**), reworkings of old stories and hammy presenters wildly twitching with bogus joviality (see **Rainbow**, etc) and mired with innuendo. Kids are not stupid: they know the few genuinely happy adults in life are either mad or on medication. *Bod* was dry, ironic even. It understood that you cannot always explain everything, that not every scenario has a winner, loser, a goody, a baddy and a moral. Sometimes things happen for no reason at all. More than that, it was cool. Just look at the way the characters' legs moved— pure class. The show was written and designed by Joanne and Michael Cole, who also brought you the understated **Fingerbobs**.

Book Tower, The
ITV. UK, 1979-89

More of a rival to **Jackanory** than **Magpie** was to **Blue Peter**, *The Book Tower* not only read stories to children but discussed books and the act—or hobby—of reading. It ran for 10 years over 11 series with distinguished author and actor presenters such as Tom Baker (see **Doctor Who**), Stephen More, Neil Innes (see **Puddle Lane**), Dick King Smith, K M Peyton, Quentin Blake, Nicholas Fisk and Roger McGough—a move which lent the show considerable authority and impact. Sadly, the producers, following the old if-it-ain't-broke-fix-it-and-fix-it-bad rule of broadcasting saw fit to replace such presenters during series 10 with the likes of Mark Miwurdz (possibly not his real name), Timmy Mallet (actual name), and Wincey Willis. And that was pretty much the end of a good show. Top marks. *The Book Tower* broadcast a dramatisation of Gene Kemp's *The Turbulent Term of Tyke Tyler*, which is often hazily confused with **Educating Marmalade**.

Bouldermobile
*See **Wacky Races***

One of the cars competing in those zany, wacky races. It was driven by the Slag Brothers: Rock Slag, voiced by Daws Butler (see **Wally Gator**, **Snagglepuss**, etc) and Gravel Slag, voiced by Don Messick (see **Bailey's Comets**). Guess what it was made of.

Botch
*See **Hair Bear Bunch, Help! It's The***

"Ooh. Ooh. Mr Peevly!" Brain-free ample-bellied assistant to **Mr Peevly**, zoo keeper of the **Wonderland Zoo**, who in turn reported in obsequious fashion to the superintendant. Botch was obsessed with promotion, the promise of which was often dangled as a carrot to "get those bears," but never granted by his boss, who was ill with ego and duplicitous self-aggrandisement and bitter with his own failure. Peevly spent most of his time undermining Botch in front of the bears and berating his skill and competency, whilst denying him the opportunity for training or development. Little did Peevly realise that the joke was on him, since he hired the so-called ninny in the first place. The interplay between the two provided—unusually for Hanna Barbera—a useful glimpse of life as a grown-up. Face it, you're either one or the other. The unhappy underling was voiced by Joe E Ross, who also did a fine job as **Sergeant** "Ooh. Ooh." **Flint** in **Hong Kong Phooey**.

Box of Delights, The
BBC1. A BBC/Lella Production. Produced by Paul Stone. Animation by Ian Emes. Directed by Renny Rye. Written by Alan Seymour. Music by Roger Limb. UK, 1986

Six-part Pandora's box serial mayhem from BBC veteran producer Paul Stone (see also **Tom's Midnight Garden**, **Lizzy**

Dripping). A small manchild is transported from the olden days into nightmare scenario after nightmare scenario, after repeatedly fiddling with his box. A sobering lesson for all small boys. Notable actors were Patrick Troughton as Cole Hawlings and Nick "Heartbeat" Berry as Pirate Rat. Beautifully shot and everything, kept a good few thousand kids up at night, although possibly not fiddling with their boxes if they knew what was good for them.

Bracket, Mr
See Chigley

Lord Belborough's butler. When visitors came to call at **Wingstead Hall**, he strode with the perfect balance of pomp and deference up the corridor to find his laird, who was usually amusing himself in his tweeds.

Braveheart
See Inch High, Private-Eye

Not an awful film featuring men in skirts, but something equally useless. It was the cowardly dog belonging to the idiot boyfriend of the incapable niece of a midget detective.

Brain
See Top Cat

TC's cohort in a blue t-shirt. The name was ironic. He was voiced by Leo DeLyon (see **Spook**)

Brains
*See **Thunderbirds***

Goggle eyed, lab coated inventor and IT support boffin on **Tracy Island**.

Bubi Bear
*See **Hair Bear Bunch, Help! It's The***

"That's exactly what I-sa troyda rasin say da troyda say." Midget bear with unique speech impediment, voiced by Paul "**Dick Dastardly**"Winchell. No one understood what the hell he was saying, least of all the self-obsessed zoo keeper **Mr Peevly**. He was best used by wannabe wideboy Hair to cloud the issue. When the bears mounted their invisible and pretend motorcycle, Bubi (pronounced "booby") sat on the pretend handlebars.

Buford Files
NBC. A Hanna-Barbera production. USA, 1978

Orginally a segment on *Buford and the Galloping Ghost* in the US, *The Buford Files*, whose name was a limp take on NBC's live-action private detective hit *The Rockford Files*, was aired in its own right on BBC 1 for a short while in the early '80s. Never much more than an also-ran in the UK—partly because we were still getting good vintage **Scooby Doo Where Are You?**—this slightly tired format (see also **Goober and the Ghost Chasers**) had the usual group of teens solving mysteries, this time with an ageing and badly drooped bloodhound called Buford. The episodes were set in the bayous of the American deep south, necessitaing the constant use of those little boats with flat bottoms and fans at the back, which some viewers (possibly only the author) tried lamely to duplicate with lego on the carpet. The dog was voiced by Frank Welker, which was a sad comedown for the voice behind *Scooby Doo*'s macho **Freddy**.

Bullet-Proof Bomb
*See **Wacky Races***

Sometimes wheel-less limousine "driven" by a midget band of doofus hoods, the **Ant Hill Mob**. They dressed like Bugsy Malone—Italian suits and trilby hats—and had grey circles around their mouths to indicate that they had not shaved, and so were obviously of dubious provenance and character. As villains they were a flop, since they all loved **Penelope Pitstop** and considered it their gangster duty to rescue her from the evil doings of **Dick Dastardly** and Sylvester Sneekly (see **Penelope Pitstop**). Their little legs came out of the bottom of their car.

Bully Bundy the Show Business Rabbit
*See **Jamie and the Magic Torch***

High flown thespian and giant bunny. His feet were enormous. Was given to quoting from Shakespeare: "Is this a lettuce I see before me".

Bungle
*See **Rainbow***

Was in need of a slapping. Instead he did the slapping (allegedly) when suit-wearing actor Stanley Bates was reportedly involved in a "road rage" incident.

Button Moon

ITV. A Thames production. Executive producer: Charles Warren. Produced and directed by Stan Woodward. Written by Ian Allen. Puppets by Ian Allen and Alistair Fullerton. UK, 1980

Fun with kitchen utensils. Or, kitchen utensils at least. "We're off to Button Moon, follow Mr Spoon." Mr Spoon, of course, was only part spoon (his arms). They were wooden spoons. The kind your mum let you mix cake with. He had a daughter, Tina Teaspoon, and a Spouse, Mrs Spoon. They would fly off to the moon, through Blanket Sky, in their rocket ship made from an old Heinz baked bean can and a funnel. The man in black holding the rocket was just visible against the black background. There they would glimpse the overacted antics of the plastic bottle army, or other loons, through the telescope. Often on at lunchtimes when you were bunking off school, *Button Moon* gave you an unhappy glimpse into the kind of ropey old nonsense they were serving up for pre-school tots in those days. Hardly in the same league as Thames long-runner **Rainbow**, the show was characterized by really quite poor production values, witless scripts and horrible voices. Nevertheless, seven series were made by Thames and aired between 1980 and 1988. The show was narrated by Robin Parkinson. Peter "**Doctor Who**" Davison, sang the sugary-sweet theme song with his spouse Sandra Dickinson.

Buzz Wagon
*See **Wacky Races***

Contender in those way out wacky races. It had a log-cutting theme and was driven by **Rufus Ruffcut**, a grinning maniac lumberjack in the requisite shirt, and Sawtooth, a beaver with buck teeth.

Bygones, The
See Cloppa Castle

The Bygones were feudal puppets ruled by Queen Ethelbruda, and her husband King Woebegone, a man in the advanced stages of melancholia. The feckless Prince Idelbone and the able-bodied Princess Tizzibel were their caricaturised progeny. Partial to fossil fuels.

Button Moon: © Pearson TV

61

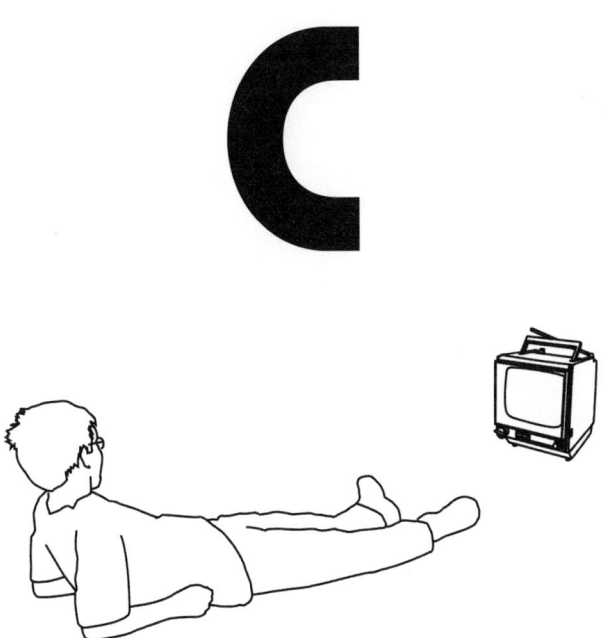

Camberwick Green (See also Chigley, Trumpton)

BBC TV. A Gordon Murray Puppets production. Created, written and produced by Gordon Murray. Animated by Bob Bura and John Hardwick. Narrated and sung by Brian Cant. Music by Freddie Philips. UK, 1966

"Here is a box, a musical box. Wound up and ready to play." So intoned the voiceover during the opening sequence of Gordon Murray's classic stop-motion animation. And out of the box rose spinning people. If that was a bit freaky, then what followed soon soothed any jitters the pre-school viewer might have had. Camberwick Green was a utopian little village, where everyone co-operated with everyone else; where every job related to every other job, and the people related to each other. It was a small village so it's probably fair to say they *were* related to each other (see **Sally & Jake**).

Each episode would bring up a different character from the music box, and the camera would follow their day's machinations. Narrator Brian Cant would engage in a dialogue with them. "Are you going on your rounds, **Doctor Mopp**? You are? Can we come too?" And the mitten-handed characters would nod. You wouldn't know from the soundtrack that the former **Play School** presenter was crouched in a cupboard at the time, speaking into a tape recorder, since his voice carried the assured—and ever so slightly bossy—tone of an infant school teacher.

Mrs **Honeyman** was the village busybody. She wore a dress with a skirt down to the floor and appeared to float over the ground. The village was kept in line by PC McGarry (number 452), a "big, friendly policeman". **Windy Miller** made the flour that made the bread. Actually, Micky Murphy made the bread, with Windy's flour. Fish were mongered by Mr Carraway, while milk was delivered by Tommy Tripp. For the most part, this little eco-system was self-sufficient, and maladies could always be solved by Dr Mopp. But introduce one minor hiccup to the smooth self-sufficiency and it was time to call in the troops. The "soldier boys", such as they were, lived at **Pippin Fort** (not to be confused with **Pippin** and **Tog**), where they were constantly being inspected by **Captain Snort. Sergeant Major Grout** called them into line with a three-note ditty on the melodica. Then they got into their army truck and sang a little song about it. "Riding along in an army truck / In a humpity bumpity army truck." Delivered in a vocal sense by Cant with all the necessary pomp, the songs were created and executed by Freddie Philips, who played a mean acoustic guitar. But what could the trouble be? What catastrophe had occasioned this bout of martial intervention. It was usually no more problematic than a shortage of breeze *chez* Windy, and the troop would all whistle for the wind to get the mill sails rotating again.

Charming to the last, the show cannot really be said to have delivered more than a cursory bout of learning. If you believed all you had to do for food was whistle, you were certainly setting yourself up for a fall, and possibly a slap in the face. Camberwick Green was the first of three stop-frame classics from the house of Murray, the excellent spin-offs being **Trumpton** and **Chigley**.

Captain Caveman and the Teen Angels
NBC. A Hanna-Barbera production. USA, 1980/86

"Zowie, Cavey," said the curvy "teen" with the blonde afro hair and the flared hipster slacks. The hirsute midget would beat his chest, brandish his lumpy club and holler his name into the wind. Delving deep into his body hair, he would usually produce something to solve the dilemma of the moment. Explosions and collisions often ended with his body hair being ripped from him, revealing a skinny nerk (see **Bananaman**) in polka-dot boxer shorts. What was going on? While the show's concept would seem at first to be the warped product of a mind on medication, the real answer is more mundane.

In 1980, Hanna-Barbera were casting about for something to fill out *The Flintstones Comedy Show*. A rather contrived *Superman* pastiche segment was duly produced wherein

Wilma Flintstone and Betty Rubble both had jobs at the Daily Granite newspaper (or news slate, more accurately). For some reason they got into terrible scrapes and had to be continually rescued by the neanderthal superhero Captain Caveman, who was, unpredictably, a geeky office clerk from the Daily Granite in disguise. A likeness of the character had previously appeared driving the **Bouldermobile** in the guise of both Slag brothers in **Wacky Races**. Captain Caveman also appeared on *Scooby's All-star Laff Olympics* in 1977.

Captain Caveman and the Teen Angels was a development, if not an advance. The hairy dwarf was teamed up with Dee Dee, Brenda and Taffy, a *Charlie's Angels*-style trio of alarmingly-busted young women who hung on his every word. They did quite a lot of hanging on, since the majority of his vocal output went "oog". The purpose of the set-up was never made clear. What were we to make—as nine-year-olds—of this dubious *ménage à quatre*? Where had they come from and what were they doing? The answer is: nowhere special and nothing much, respectively. Nevertheless it made undemanding viewing for those of us, goggle-eyed with passive entertainment, who cared to sit transfixed in front of it after school, knee deep in Lego, our pockets sticky with half-masticated Bazooka Joes. The team insisted on solving mysteries and fighting crime, which always seemed to be a waste of all that sexual energy to some, as they sat gazing vacantly at the coloured dots, wishing it was **Battle of the Planets** instead and waiting to go to swimming club.

The idea that Hanna-Barbera did not quite know what to do with this character appears to have been given weight by the range of formats they shoved him in. In 1986 they tried something else: *Captain Caveman and Son*. It appeared as a show-within-a-show (or spin-off within a spin-off) on *The Flintstones Kids*. The kids watched it on the old stone telly as the Simpson kids watched *Itchy and Scratchy*. As far as this encyclopaedia can establish, this derivation was never shown on UK television, but you didn't miss much. It was the Cavey equivalent of *Scrappy Doo*.

Cavey was voiced by old master Mel "*Bugs Bunny*" Blanc—slumming it a bit, one presumes (see also **Ant Hill Mob**). Dee Dee was voiced by the croaky Vernee Watson; Marilyn

Schreffler supplied the voice of Brenda, and Taffy's voice was created by Laurel Page.

Captain Pugwash

BBC 1. Written, illustrated and produced by John Ryan. Voices by Peter Hawkins. Music by Johnny Pearson. UK, 1959

"Kipper me capstans!" Captain Pugwash—the Flat Stanley of teatime telly—was artist, writer and producer John Ryan's pirate-centric animated kids series. Animated, that is, in the sense that two people got either side of a cardboard set and wobbled it as Peter Hawkins voiced the characters and Johnny Pearson, the composer, played the accordion. Later there was a John Carey-produced cell animation which, although slicker, never quite carried the same charm as its stuck-together-with-glue-and-cost-a-tenner predecessor. That said, the animation technique devised by Ryan was actually a highly sophisticated (if labour-intensive) system of articulated arms which moved key elements (like eyes and tongue) on a static plateau. The system became known in the industry as Pugwashing and contributed an instantly recognisable quality of eeriness to the show (see **Mary Mungo & Midge**) as characters remained motionless, save for their eyes which followed you, or their tongues, which might wag.

For the thinking sort of child, Pugwash was an interesting lesson in social division. He was a thief, a bully and a pompous, portly bungling buffoon, whose irritatingly clean cabin boy did all the clever stuff, for no credit. But viewers were invited to side with the fat fool when he went to battle with sworn enemy **Cut-throat Jake**, pirate captain of the **Flying Dustman** ("Creeping catfish!"). For not only was Jake obviously evil, but also bearded and hairy (see **Fingerbobs**). You could tell he was evil because his band of ruffians were unshaven and generally swarthy-looking and Jake had a deep voice and a dagger in his teeth. Pugwash and his chums, by contrast, were a much better class of thief and given to shaving properly on those high seas. Both crews fought unceasingly over treasure, buried, sunken and other. Comfortingly, there was never any shortage of treasure.

Which is fine, but I suspect that is not why you are reading this entry. You want to know about Seaman Staines, Master Bates and Roger the cabin boy. Various newspapers were obliged to print apologies after it was suggested that the BBC pulled off the programme because it found out the names were rude.

Fact: Pugwash, skipper of the **Black Pig**, had a crew of three—Barnabas, Pirate Willy, Master Mate and Tom the cabin boy. Four men and a boy, innocently whiling away the time in an enclosed space. The adult-oriented characters never existed. John Ryan did not write them. There was no Seaman Staines; there was no Master Bates. The urban myth, whilst funny in a Finbarr Saunders sort of way, becomes much less so when you understand that Ryan's livelihood depended in part upon his many visits to schools, where he gave talks and workshops. According to sources close to Ryan, schools no longer asked him to call when the "story" broke.

But sources close to Pugwash suggest that the Captain's diction in the hands of Peter Hawkins was not always as it could have been, and that the words "Master Mate", delivered with Hawkins' unique combination of nasal and glottal characterics, could possibly have been misconstrued. It depends on the maturity of your outlook. This encyclopaedia takes the view that Ryan's tubby skipper has been foolishly interfered with.

————

Captain Snort
See Camberwick Green

Called the shots at **Pippin Fort**.

Catweazle

ITV. A London Weekend Television production. Created by Richard Carpenter. Produced by Quentin Lawrence and Carl Mannin. Directed by Quentin Lawrence, David Reed and David Lane. Written by Richard Carpenter. UK, 1970–71

Tramp action from novelist and screenwriter Richard Carpenter. Although he looked like a tramp, Catweazle (Geoffrey Blaydon) was in fact (for fact read fiction) a wizard from Norman times who had bungled a spell and gotten himself trapped in the 20th century—with "hilarious" results, such as not understanding electrickery. A youthful farmer's son called Carrot Bennett befriended him—and his "fam-il-i-ar," Touchwood the toad—and tried very hard to send the old fool back whence he came. When he succeeded, the writer had Catweazle louse up again for a second series of century mismatch misdemeanours. Doh (see **Crackerjack**)!

Champion, The Adventures of

UK tx BBC 1 1956. A Flying A Production. Created by Gene Autry. Produced by Gene Autry, Eric Jenson and Louis Gray. Directed by George Archainbaud. USA, 1955

Champ-iuuun . . . thu *won*-der-*horse*, sang Frankie Laine, possibly into the wind. When that happened you knew it was time for stallion shenanigans, dredged up from the bowels of black and white TV history and served up for the millionth time as a Saturday morning filler/school holiday filler/Sunday morning ironic post-clubbing slot filler. The show was in fact conceived—perhaps in error—by singing cowboy Gene Autry, who put his money where his mouth was and actually made the show, to the tune of 26 episodes. He owned the actual horse, you see. Champion was best chums with a small boy called Ricky (Barry Curtis) who lived with his Uncle Sandy and attracted rough men and trouble the way some boys can't help but do (see **Belle and Sebastian**). Champion always saved the day, rearing up quite a lot to scare off foes and villains, leaving

Ricky to slope off and fool around with **Rebel** the dog. Nostalgic—even back in the '70s.

Charlie Rat
*See **Doctor Snuggles***

Brain-free rodent crony of **Willy The Terrible Fox**.

Cheggers Plays Pop
BBC TV. A BBC Manchester production. Produced by Peter Scott Ridsdale. Directed by Johnie Stewart. Designed by Peter Mavius. UK, 1978

What do the following top tunesmiths have in common: Suzi Quatro, Showaddywaddy, Darts, Shakin' "Shakey" Stevens, Dollar, Bucks Fizz, Rocky Sharpe and the Replays, B.A. "Bang Bang the Mighty Fall" Robertson, Jona "Stop the Cavalry" Lewie, Bananarama, Toyah, The Thompson Twins, Haircut 100 and Bad Manners? That's right, they're all crap. But more than that, they all appeared on *Cheggers Plays Pop*, the inflatable-heavy quiz show with the dishearteningly easy pop music questions. Look out, here he comes, running then doing a little skip. Weyhey! The Hot Box Quick Quiz put pop pickers in the hot seat as they were grilled on tedious teenybop trivia. "Name two members of Godley & Creme." Limahl? "Triffic! Weyhey!"

"Alls you godda do," Keith "Cheggers" Chegwin would begin, before sending teams of hapless tweens capering over a giant bouncy castle to pick up foam balls in their mouths and spit them through a hoop into a bucket without falling from a slippery stool into a paddling pool full of water. It was a mild improvement on *It's A Knockout* in the sense that Cheggers is and was a mild improvement on Stuart Hall. The show was a product of BBC Manchester and pioneered the two-teams-of-kids-in-different-coloured-t-shirts-thrown-in-foam format, and as such can claim to have been the progenitor of *Funhouse* and

71

all other gunge-based team game shows with hyperactive presenters. Remember, for example, *On Safari* with Christopher Biggins and a pre-layby Gillian Taylforth in leopardprint loincloth? Although Biggins could never be said to have been hyperactive.

Chegwin Checks it Out, a behind-the-scenes sort of show, came in 1987 and went in 1988, after which Chegwin checked out himself (see **Chock-A-Block**) for a nice drink, and a good sit down that would last until his *Big Breakfast*-lead resurgence, public nudity and live web-casts from his bedroom.

Chigley See also **Camberwick Green, Trumpton**

BBC TV. Stop-motion animation. A Gordon Murray Puppets production. Created, written and produced by Gordon Murray. Animated by Bob Bura and John Hardwick. Narrated and sung by Brian Cant. Music by Freddie Philips. UK, 1969

Nothing was better than "being at large, in charge of a gay inland waterway barge". Exciting though this sounds, the reality was more mundane than the reader's imagination has, no doubt, suggested. But that sums up *Chigley* quite well. The third—and most satisfying—of Gordon Murray's animated **Camberwick Green** trilogy, *Chigley* concerned itself with the minutiae of quotidian life in an upwardly mobile hamlet close to **Trumpton**.

In days of yore *Chigley* had been the domain of landed lazybones **Lord Belborough**, a confirmed bachelor who was generally to be seen pottering aimlessly about in his tweeds looking for a tome in his ancient library or dimly supervising the topiary in the ornamental gardens of his stately home, **Wingstead Hall**. But times had changed. Money was tight and Belborough had been obliged to let the public in, for money, and give them rides in his restored steam engine, **Bessie**.

Meanwhile, escalating rents in Trumpton had (probably) forced Mr Cresswell's Chigley Biscuit factory onto a cheap greenfield site close to the canal and Treadle's Wharf. Planning permission was probably not hard to come by, since Trumpton's council amounted to little more than its egotistical Mayor, who enjoyed putting his signature on things. "All done by efficiency," the factory boasted an automated production line and a giant workforce of dungareed journeymen who worked with all the robotic precision of the Trumpton clock. Chigley was also home to a commercial pottery—run by Harry Farthing and his tomboy daughter Winnie—which dispatched regular orders to the outside world. Sometimes, however, delays in the supply chain caused a panic. In these cases, Bessie was called upon to help out and supplicators knocked on the doors of Wingstead Hall. Mr **Bracket**, the butler, strode up the corridor, past the ancestral paintings and Ming vases, with the perfect balance of pomp and deference, to find his master. Belborough, of course, unfailingly obliged, giddy with the hokey joys of social purpose. "Time flies by when I'm the driver of a train," he would chirrup, ostensibly to himself, "and I stand on the footplate there and back again."

Time had indeed flown by since Belborough's type had any place in the scheme of things. Chigley people made their money through trade, and were proud of it. Evidence of an outdated feudal system and capitalist market forces working in harmony would, however, seem to be compromised by the closing scene of each episode. At 6 o'clock sharp the factory whistle blew and the biscuit workers were marched out in lurching stop-motion into the car park, where they were obliged to waltz in formation with girls in peasant smocks and headscarves as Belborough wound the handle on his restored Dutch barrel organ. He might have been on the verge of bankruptcy and humoured by the local tradesmen, who grew wealthy while he foundered in his tweeds and dithered like an overgrown child on his toy train, but—in the end—he had found a way to ensure those filthy proles danced to his tune.

That tune was provided by Freddie Philips. Former **Play School** presenter Brian Cant (see also **Play Away**) delivered the dry commentary.

Chippy Minton

See ***Trumpton***

Chippy was, as his name suggests, **Trumpton**'s carpenter. He owned his own private plane (geddit?).

————————

Chock-A-Block

BBC TV. A BBC production. Executive producer: Cynthia Felgate. Produced by Michael Cole. Directed by Nick Wilson. Music by Peter Gosling. UK, 1981

Chock-a-bloke checking in. Chock-A-Block was a toothy machine with a gaping mouth and a conveyor belt (see **Bertha**). Out of it came items which formed raw material for the day's fun and play. The Chock-a-bloke—at least initially—was former **Play School** presenter Fred Harris in a boilersuit, while the Chock-a-girl was former *Play School* presenter Carol Leader, in another boilersuit. The executive producer was former *Play School* producer Cynthia Felgate, possibly in a boilersuit, although who would have known? It is possible—and this is just an idea—that this pre-school show was an attempt to recapture the magic of the defunct *Play School*. Despite the worthy credentials, fine presenters—and a good healthy dose of kid-attracting whirring cogs and gurgling noises—*Chock-A-Block* had neither the charm nor the staying power of its predecessor. Perhaps it was the boilersuit angle. Perhaps it was changing agendas at the BBC. Whatever the reason, *Chock-A-Block* has now checked out, to be remembered fondly if hazily.

Chocky

ITV. Supernatural drama. A Thames Television production.
Produced and directed by Vic Hughes. Executive producer:
Pamela Lonsdale. UK, 1984

Based on the creepy novel by John Wyndham, this equally
creepy supernatural spooktacular featured a boy beset by a
strange green glowing figure in the corner of his room who
spoke to him deep inside his head. Space aliens? So they were
saying. Early signs of paranoid psychosis? Maybe ... Enough to
give you nightmares as a concept, the special effects and music
combination sent you properly "into one" and rooted you to
your seat, where you broke out in a cold sweat. You quickly had
to read *Mrs Pepperpot* afterwards to wash your brain of the
weirdness and spook. You watched it with petrified fascination
and ghoulish compulsion.

Alternatively: based on the superlative and engaging novel
by John Wyndham, this charming adaptation told the story of a
lovely little boy and his special friend. You watched it with your
mum. Whatever your angle, the show was well made, quality
drama, and spawned the spin-off *Chocky's Children*. (Still
creepy though, I'm saying)

Choo Choo

*See **Top Cat***

One of TC's cronies. He was the sensible one, voiced by Marvin
Kaplan.

Chorlton and the Wheelies

ITV. A Thames Television/Cosgrove Hall Production. Written
by Brian Trueman. UK, 1976–79

The Wheelies were an affable bunch of big-nosed Kinder Egg
toy lookalikes—inexplicably on wheels. They trundled around

in something called Wheelie World, where they were endlessly tortured by the green faced and evil **Fenella,** the Kettle Witch. She lived at Spout Hall, between Wheelie World and the Sad Lands with her servants the **Spikers** and the **Toadies** and wore an elongated Fez hat.

It was Fenella's vocation to be miserable—she was only happy when she was miserable—and to achieve true misery it was necessary to subjugate the Wheelies and generally throw them into unrelenting doom. But the Wheelies acquired a secret weapon in the clumsy, lumbering shape of Chorlton, a Happiness Dragon, who hatched one day from an egg and had—to judge from his dialect—evidently come from Halifax. Chorlton was good at one thing: spreading happiness, which he did without knowing it, or indeed without knowing anything. "Eh-up little old lady," he was wont to cry cheerily at Fenella, sending her into spasms of rage. Chorlton was blissfully unaware of Fenella's evil, because he was stupid. But that was exactly the way to confound her, which is why the Wheelies—especially the blonde, freckle-faced **Jenny**—loved him.

The extent of Fenella's evil should not be underestimated. This encyclopaedia considers it significant that the first ever word she uttered in the first ever episode was **Ffestiniog** (see also **Ivor the Engine**). In fact, the show was rich with comedy accents, all supplied by narrator Joe Lynch. Chorlton's humourous, "ecky-thump"Yorkshirisms aside, Fenella was clearly Welsh, a characterisation which, unfairly perhaps, encouraged the viewer to equate Wales with extreme doom. **Reilly,** Fenella's bungling, one-eyed telescope, was "bejaysus" Oirish. Claptrap von Spillderbeans, the book of evil spells, was distinctly Germanic; and the Toadies, Fenella's band of fungus sneaks, inflected like a cross between Spike Milligan (as Eccles in The Goons) and Chairman Mao. That the obvious goodies—the Wheelies—were all English in vocal tone, from the cheeky cockerney **Zoomer**, to the ditzily upper-crust Queen, might be cause for disapproving tuts from right-on liberal readers, were it not for the fact that they were all basically useless. Except for Jenny. Lovely pair of wheels, that girl.

Chris Rabbit
*See **Henry's Cat***

Rodent chum of Henry's cat. Good name, so worth a mention.

————————

The Clangers
*BBC1. A Smallfilms production. Created, written and pro-
duced by Oliver Postgate. Music by Vernon Elliot. Set design
and puppets by Peter Firmin. UK, 1969-74*

Life isn't easy when you're made of knitting. Especially when
there's little or no gravity. Sometimes it's all you can do to get the
dustbin lid closed against the cold of the planet surface and boil
up some blue string pudding. The Clangers had neighbours. There
was the Soup Dragon, a benevolent, scaly, volcano-dwelling relative of **Idris**, who ladelled out supper in return for a trinket or
two bunged into the hole. Oliver Postgate, creator and producer
of *The Clangers*, claims the Soup Dragon never took payment for
soup, in trinkets or otherwise, but it occurred at least once. The
Froglets were orange, scrapy-voiced, bug-eyed jumping beasts.

Major Clanger, Mother Clanger, Small Clanger and Tiny
Clanger were small, pink pig-like creatures who communicated via a swanee whistle activated off-camera. The swanee
whistle is not usually an instrument noted for its expressive
qualities, but in this case, it gave the Clangers not only voices,
but speech. Family-orientated, the Clangers were given to
demonstrative behaviour and were permanently comforting
each other and indulging in group hugs. Again, Mr Postgate
takes issue with this assertion (see also **Noggin the Nog**, **Ivor
the Engine**, **Pogles Wood** and **Bagpuss**) and the author finds
himself in the strange position of disagreeing with the show's
genius creator. They did indeed hug one other. Mr Postgate,
perhaps, has confused the expression "group hug" with "group
sex", which they certainly never indulged in on camera. When
they were upset they put their ears over their eyes.

The stop-frame animation series was made by Postgate and
Peter Firmin—as Smallfilms—in Firmin's barn. The series began

in 1969, a matter of months after NASA's moon landing. In one episode, an astronaut leaves behind an American flag. Mother Clanger had it for a tablecloth.

What sets *The Clangers* apart from so many other children's animation shows is the care and attention Firmin and Postgate put into its production. From Vernon Eliot's gentle flute and xylophone score to Postgate's avuncular narration, this series of short films was imbued with a gentleness and a subtlety lacking in so much that came after it. This is probably why Smallfilms' output, more than that of any other production house, is remembered so vividly and fondly. *The Clangers*, like *Bagpuss*, is one of the all-time classics.

––––––––––

Claptrap von Spillderbeans
See Chorlton and the Wheelies

Dusty, Teutonic and often reluctant book of spells belonging to **Fenella** the Kettle Witch. Voiced by Joe Lynch.

––––––––––

Cli Cli
See Marine Boy

Cli Cli was little more than a dramatic device. He was an errant small child whose narrative job it was to louse up Marine Boy's efforts to keep sea-peace with well-intentioned bungling.

––––––––––

Clifton House Mystery
HTV. An HTV production. Produced by Leonard White. Directed by David Hugh. Written by Harry Moore with Daniel Farson. UK, 1978

Clifton is a posh part of Bristol. HTV was an independent West Country-based television station under the ITV umbrella. This six-part supernatural chiller had a local theme, which added extra spook value for those resident in the HTV catchment area—and utter obscurity for those who weren't.

A family moved into a house in Clifton, but could not work out the architecture. From the outside there appeared to be an extra room, which was not apparent from the inside. They wished they had not bothered looking when they discovered the hidden room, full of ghosts and fear and desperation and doom. Eek. Possibly a plot by Bristol's middle classes to keep the riff raff out of Clifton. Terrifying, if you saw it.

Cloppa Castle

ITV. An ATV production. Produced by John Read and Mary Turner. Directed by Mary Turner. UK, 1977

Chunky-nosed feudal fantasy fun and political satire brought to you by former Gerry Anderson Supermarionation puppeteers John Turner and Mary Read (see **Thunderbirds**, **Stingray** etc). The **Bygones** were a forward-looking bunch of primitive people ruled by the authoritarian Queen Ethelbruda—a hawk-nosed vision in plaits—and her ennui-riddled husband King Woebegone. Their offspring—the foppish Prince Idelbone and the comely Princess Tizzibel—brought about as much joy as Jest-a-minit the jester, or Mudlin the hapless magician. Happily, Cue-ee-dee the inventor had discovered a rich supply of crude oil (it starts to go a bit dark here) under the castle and was permanently engaged in exploiting this commodity for everyone's gain, with a series of chunky inventions.

But the Bygones' dreamy fossil fuel idyll was not to last. Sadly, a rival clan— Beoswayne and the Hasbeens—had designs on the oil and so began the bloody and unending territorial battle. Elbow, the bruising head of the Queen's bodyguards, and Osmosis, his semi-permeable inferior, had the job of keeping the Hasbeens the right side of the castle walls. An impressive 52 11-minute animations were stumped-up for by Lew Grade's spendthrift ATV (see **Pipkins** and **Tiswas**) and aired in 1977. Unsighted since, *Cloppa Castle* has become one of the (great?) lost (classic?) children's shows. An odd one for sure.

Clunk
See Dastardly and Muttley in Their Flying Machines

An excellent forerunner to Keyop (see **Battle of the Planets**), Clunk had an impressive range of vocal tics and the habit of hiding his head inside his coat. He made the aeroplanes.

Clyde
See Ant Hill Mob, Wacky Races and Penelope Pitstop

Diminutive doyen of grey-chinned, go-getting gangster group.

Cockleshell Bay
ITV. A Thames Television/Cosgrove Hall production. Directed by Jackie Cockle. Written by Roy Davis. Narrated by Brian Trueman. Music by Stuart J Wolstenholme. UK, 1980

Cheese and chutney chirpiness from Cosgrove Hall. This twee animation related the exploits of two seaside-dwelling children—Robin and Rosie—who liked to have a bit of fun with Old Mr Ship, the gnarled and hoary fisherman. The only thing better than fooling around with an old man was getting fed by an old woman. Gran always called them away to munch on lunch: cheese and chutney sandwiches. Just smell that salty air. Their adventures were written by Roy Davies and narrated by Cosgrove Hall favourite Brian Trueman (see **Danger Mouse, Chorlton and the Wheelies, Jamie & the Magic Torch, Screen Test** etc).

Colonel K
*See **Danger Mouse***

Boss of the secret service and of **Danger Mouse**, Colonel K
was a country gent-style beaver with a bushy white moustache.
He appeared on-screen to DM in the mouse's subterranean
den, and delivered his orders.

Compact Pussycat
*See **Wacky Races***

Steered by the classy, cosmetics-driven **Penelope Pitstop**, the
Compact Pussycat had various in-built automations, like
extendable mirrors and prosthetic lipstick. As it was a woman's
car, it was pink, as was Penelope.

Compost Corner
*See **Tiswas***

Heap of mire, presided over by David "Lenny Henry" Bellamy. It
was where Tarrant put you for random misdemeanours on his
anarchic Saturday morning show, **Tiswas**.

Convert-a-Car
*See **Wacky Races***

Driven by **Professor Pat Pending**, the Convert-a-Car was a
(supposedly) high-tech vehicle capable of changing specifica-
tion (ie turns into helicopter/boat, etc) at the touch of a button.
Very useful for cheating.

Coot Boot
*See **Doctor Snuggles***

Oddly-beaked messenger bird.

Cosmic Cat
*See **Doctor Snuggles***

Pointy-eared, wide grinned Cheshire-type feline and friend of **Granny Toots**.

Count, The
*See **Sesame Street***

One! One peanut butter sandwich! Ah—ah—ah. Two! Two peanut butter sandwiches! Ah—ah—ah. Three! Three peanut ... etc.

Crackerjack
BBC TV. A BBC production. Produced by Johnny Downes, Brian Whitehouse. Directed by Brian Penders. Music by the Bert Hayes Orchestra. UK, 1955-84

It was Friday, it was five to five ... The list of *Crackerjack* presenters reads like the cast of *Mother Goose & The Beanstalk* showing at a run-down pier near you. Eamonn Andrews, Leslie Cowther, Ronnie Corbett, Peter Glaze, Michael Aspel, Don MacLean, Bernie Clifton, Ed Stewart, Stu Francis, The Krankies. The encyclopaedia would list more but a sudden migraine has gripped the author.

This variety game show for kids, with special guests such as the lastest pop pin-up and The Great Soprendo—a format relevant in 1955, but poisonous in 1981—occupied that microscopic area on the scale of dreadfulness between being stuck in a Boy Scout Gang Show and being stuck in a hospice with tertiary syphillis. Lucky children were humiliated in front of their school chums, and openly exposed to the sort of humour which can rot a young brain in seconds, for the dubious privilege of winning a set of *Crackerjack* pencils. How is it, you may ask, that the show lasted so long? There is no obvious answer. Conceived and first broadcast in 1955, *Crackerjack* ran for an almost incomprehensible 29 years. Along the way, a dazzling array of durable "TV personalities" were dressed up as pirates in cardboard sets and forced to deliver excruciating lines for money. It was precisely the kind of light entertainment that Morecambe and Wise mocked so well.

Readers who survived the 1976–81 vintage will remember presenter Ed Stewart. Younger readers will remember Stu "Stu-Pot" Francis, known by his humorous catchphrases. He could crush a grape. He could also jump off a doll's house. If pushed, he could wrestle an action man (see also **Jana of the Jungle**). Credentials indeed. The show's heavy duty reliance on Scotland's most dismal product (and the world's scariest husband and wife team)—The Krankies—may well have been the cause of its timely death in 1984. A transmission listing for episode one of series 26 in 1983 reads, beguilingly: "Basil Brush, Gary Numan".

Sadly, the defunct *Crackerjack* begat an evil offspring before it died: *Crush A Grape*. This vacuous vehicle for Stu-Pot's catchphrase began its first and only series with The Krankies and ended 16 weeks later—perhaps tellingly—with Paul Shane. In between, the usual suspects were all wheeled out to perform their tired old variety "acts": Keith Harris and Orville, Bernie Clifton, The Grumbleweeds, The Great Soprendo, Basil Brush, Jim Bowen and more Krankies. When *Crush A Grape* died, seaside towns enjoyed an entertainment boom. It has been mooted that Peter Glaze's constant cries of "Doh!" were an influence on Matt Groening, creator of Homer Simpson. But that seems about as likely as a *Crackerjack* revival.

Crazylegs Crane
*See **The Pink Panther Show***

This down-at-heel, wrinkly and knock-kneed geriatric bird had his own mid-show segment on *The All-New Pink Panther Show*. The triple-bill was probably an attempt by producers De Patie-Freleng to appeal to a kids-only audience, having originally launched the Pink Panther as a cartoon character for adults. In any case, *All New* was a shadow of the former **Pink Panther Show**, which featured Inspector Clouseau and Sergeant Deaux-Deaux in the middle segment. Friz Freleng created the Panther and Inspector characters for the titles of Blake Edwards' *Pink Panther* feature films, made famous by lead actor and former Goon Peter Sellers (see also **Potty Time**).

––––––––––

Creepy Coupé
*See **Wacky Races***

Pronounced "coup". A runner in the wacky races, this auto with a gothic theme was steered by the **Gruesome Twosome**: **Big** and **Li'l**. They did spooky stuff in the style of the Addams Family.

––––––––––

Crimson Haybailer
*See **Wacky Races***

It *wasn't* a haybailer but it *was* crimson. More a kind of Fokker monoplane than an agricultural tool, it was driven by the Teutonic **Red Max**. Not the most memorable of the Wacky Races vehicle/character combinations.

Crystal Blob
*See **Chorlton and the Wheelies***

The Crystal Blob was the function of a certain spell—the Doomsday Special—cast by **Fenella** the Kettle Witch in "Chorlton & The Ice World", a 1976 30-minute Christmas episode of the animated short. Initially, **Claptrap von Spillderbeans** is reluctant to unleash the rubric to Fenella, as she has not passed her Witches' diploma. But in the end he gives in. Fenella recites the spell, and the Crystal Blob does its evil deed, turning Wheelie World to ice and activating an army of sinister snowmen. The Crystal Blob is mostly remarkable for the number of times narrator Joe Lynch is obliged to say "crystal blob" in various comedy voices in the course of the script. Chorlton, true to form, has not the faintest inkling that the Blob might be less than friendly. He considers it akin to Blackpool illuminations, and mentions this to a Latin-American dancing duck. The episode was written—as was the series—by Brian Trueman (see **Jamie and the Magic Torch**, **Danger Mouse**, **Screen Test**).

Crystal Tipps and Alistair
BBC TV. Animation. A BBC-Q3 London co-production. Created by Hilary Hayton. Designed and written by Graham McCallum and Hilary Hayton. Music by Paul Reade. Directed by Richard Taylor. Produced by Michael Grafton Robinson. UK, 1972

Look out, it's the girl with the unfeasibly frizzy hair. Was she a girl, or was she a woman? Impossible to tell, such was her ambiguous lifestyle. She lived alone in the kind of twee, ornamental cottage previously only seen as line drawings on packets of doilies and shortbread tins, where she was constantly having tea and cakes with Alistair the dog, who sat at table with a napkin at his collar. What was she doing there and how was she supporting herself? Was the crazy-limbed doggy bringing home the bacon? No—he was bringing home an egg. They hatched it on the table in a tea cosy and it turned out to be a fantastic trippy bird of paradise which flew around the house in a mad way. Mind the tea cups! Don't stain the doilies! Even the wallpaper was enough to bring on a migraine.

They went to the park, they did their exercises, they went home, they found a psychedelic butterfly, they went to an art gallery. And wherever they went, they went with a dazzling flurry of busy colour and kaleidoscopic pattern. Luminous flowers, tangible rainbows. What was in that tea? Perhaps Crystal's curiously dilated pupils hold the answer.

Originally aired in 1972, *Crystal Tipps and Alistair*—dubbed by some as "Crystal trips with Alistair"—was a series of interludes in the dopamine-heavy life of a big-haired girl and her sausage-eared dog. It managed without narration, it managed without dialogue. So transfixed were you by the bodily contortions afforded by Hilary Hayton's animation style; by the brightly hued creatures, manifold plants and surprisingly communicative score (by Paul Reade) that the last thing you wanted was to start hearing voices. Fifty 5-minute episodes were made in all, including: "Cave Cricket", "Topiary", "Pussy" and "Bump In The Night". The show was resurrected for Children's ITV in the '80s before coming home to roost more recently at the BBC. Excellent, odd and, despite having endured, distinctly of its time—in the sense that people do not paint pictures like that anymore, outside of Rampton. Flower power, in a very literal sense.

———

Cut-throat Jake
See Captain Pugwash

Hairy, beardy bad man (see also **Belle & Sebastian**, **Danger on the Danube Delta** and **Champion, The Adventures of**). Arch nemesis of clean-shaven **Captain Pugwash** and his bogus brigands. Carried a knife in his teeth. Actually quite frightening in the original John Ryan animation, due to the static face/moving eyes technique. Less so in subsequent cell animations.

DCM

*See **Razzmatazz, Algernon Winston Spencer Castleray**
and **Tiswas***

Stood for "De Condensed Milk", delivered in comedy Jamaican accent by Lenny Henry as **Tiswas** denizen Algernon Razzmatazz. With bread, it was his fetish food. Mildly more appetising than the foam fare offered by the **Phantom Flan Flinger**.

Dai Station

*See **Ivor the Engine***

Moustachioed and be-capped Welsh stationmaster and lover of timetables, rules and "regoolations". Looked after the Merioneth and Llantisily railway.

Danger Island

A Hanna-Barbera production. Directed by Richard Donner. USA, 1968

Help-here-come-the-natives live action deadwood by Hanna-Barbera, who really could have done better, and indeed did (see **Top Cat**). A bunch of all-American dweebs got stuck on an island peopled by naughty savages who, quite rightly, felt inclined to scalp the intruders at every possible opportunity.

The All-American team included Professor Irwin Hayden (Frank Aletter) and his spouse, Leslie Hayden (Ronnie Troup). Link Simmons was played by Jan Michael Vincent, while Morgan was played by Rockne Tarkington. Naughty natives included the generically-named Chongo (Kahana), Mu-Tan (Victor Eberg) and Chu (Roderigo Arrendondo). The latter is not to be confused with **Choo Choo**. A total of 36 episodes of this cliffhanger nonsense were directed by

Richard Donner—whose later and less embarrassing credits include *The Omen* and *Superman*—and aired as part of **The Banana Splits Adventure Hour**.

Danger Mouse

ITV. A Cosgrove Hall/Thames TV production. Executive producer: John Hambley. Produced by Brian Cosgrove, Mark Hall. Directed by Brian Cosgrove & Chris Randall. Written by Brian Trueman & Mike Harding. Music by Mike Harding. UK, 1981-91

"Cripes, DM!" *Danger Mouse*—the title being a take on Patrick McGooghan's *Danger Man*—was a witty, skillfully executed cartoon series from Manchester-based animator Cosgrove Hall. The show followed the adventures of the eponymous mouse, a curt, serious-voiced secret service agent with an eye patch, and his corking sidekick **Penfold,** a speccy mole in an ill-fitting suit. The duo lived under a London postbox in a luxury pad with sunken furniture and a huge TV screen. Orders came in from HQ via the screen from **Colonel K**, a tweedy old beaver with a handlebar moustache and an undoubted extramural interest in huntin' shootin' and fishin'. Trouble usually meant one thing: the rasping **Baron Silas Greenback**, a giant toad and enemy of democracy (voiced by Edward Kelsey) whose plans to rule the world—or throw it into chaos and confusion by stealing every important signpost—were hampered by the existence of DM, the "misbegotten mouse and his asinine assistant Penfold".

Greenback—created by musician Mike Harding and based on a farmer he had taken a dislike to—hatched his megalomaniac plans with the aid of **Nero**, a kind of fluffy white caterpillar, and his Sicilian henchman **Stiletto**, whose cries of "Si, Barone," did not necessarily mean he had understood. If Stiletto bungled it, there was always the International Conference of Evil-Doers to be called upon.

Cosgrove Hall had come up with the idea of a rodent secret agent with a mole sidekick (see **Secret Squirrel**) but didn't

Danger Mouse: © Pearson TV

know where to go from there. Harding was called upon to solve the problem. He took the premise, expanded it and created a couple of draft episodes, before handing over writing duties to Cosgrove Hall favourite and sometime **Screen Test** presenter Brian Trueman. What Harding and Trueman created between them rewrote the rules of children's animation and delivered a highly sophisticated series—full of irony, subtle puns, and allusions to TV and literature—making it a teatime favourite with adults too. The animation style recalled the early work of Monty Python animator Terry Gilliam, with its colourised photographs, while the scripting and delivery was reminiscent of *The Goons* in its oblique jumps and self-referential gags: "He'll never last another episode".

But the masterstroke was the inspired casting. DM was voiced by *Only Fools and Horses* star David Jason, whose Del-Boy character had echoes in DM's boorish bossiness. Penfold was voiced by the inimitable comic actor Terry "& June" Scott, whose *Carry On* voice lent the hapless mole an appropriate Boys-Own innocence (see **Famous Five, The**). "Cripes, DM! What are we going to do now?" "Penfold . . ." "Yes, Chief?" "Shush." The duo's well-honed sense of comic timing gave the series a professional edge missing from much of children's television, helping to guarantee that ratings-boosting adult following. The whole package was topped off with Harding's score—a compelling blend of Romanian gypsy band chic and the exaggerated drama of radio classic *Dick Barton, Special Agent*. Rival animators 101 Productions attempted to challenge DM's supremacy with their own **Bananaman** in 1983, casting the Goodies in voice roles. But if 101 could compete on actors, their animation could not come close to replicating the quality and energy of the Cosgrove Hall series. So, *Danger Mouse*, then: classic comedy, really. Surely due for a revival.

NB. A character from one DM storyline, Count **Duckula**, was spun off by Cosgrove Hall into his own show in 1988, but sadly its storylines wandered and the series failed to deliver the same quality, despite being popular.

Danger on the Danube Delta

Original title: Négyen Az Árban. A Hunnia Játekfilmstudio production. Directed by György Révész. Music by András Bágya. Hungary, 1961

Tense moustache and dubbing action as a group of Hungarian kids attempted to escape a band of convincingly violent hoods by means of flimsy boat in this many-parted serial import in the **Belle and Sebastian** vein. Shallow water shenanigans ensued as the vessel went its reedy way to the delta. Which way? Which way? Whoa, look out for the rapids. Tune in next week. Hungarian dialogue audible low in mix (see also **Singing Ringing Tree, The**). Classy. Transmission details were not available. It is possible the guilty programmers have tried to erase it from their memories. As Tears For Fears sang: "memories fade, but the scars still linger …"

Daphne

See **Scooby Doo**

"Yikes, my hairdo!" Curvy redhead in purple dress and green scarf. Did not add masses to the Scooby dynamic, since **Velma** did all the work and **Shaggy** did all the goofing. Was she "doing" the impressively-chested **Freddy**?

Dastardly and Muttley in their Flying Machines

NBC. A Hanna-Barbera production. USA, 1969

Those magnificient men—well, one rather inadequate man and his mediocre pooch—took to the air in this World War One spy comedy cartoon caper. Orders come down the telephone line in the unintelligable voice of the Colonel. **Clunk**—very much in the Keyop role (see **Battle of the Planets**)—invented the Heath Robinson-esque winged machines, before disappearing into his coat and experimenting with his range of vocal tics. The idea was to stop the tenacious carrier pigeon delivering its message. Failure abounded and Muttley was usually urged to "do something" about it. A spin-off from the earlier, better **Wacky Races**, *Dastardly and Muttley* was nontheless an amusing vehicle for the man and mutt double act.

Degrassi Junior High
*See **Kids From Degrassi Street, The***

Adolescent spin-off from the elementary school soap.

Dennis the Badger
*See **Doctor Snuggles***

Hardworking assistant to midget messiah and inventor **Dr Snuggles**.

DeNuccio, Jennifer
*See **Square Pegs**; **Slash, Johnny** and **Fennifer***

She was hot, she was cold. She was snooty and rich. She was "popular". All the girls in **Square Pegs** wanted to be like her, or at least be liked by her (nothing doing if you were not of the right stock or if you were fat, not beautiful or wore glasses or mouth braces)—all the boys simply wanted her. Actually an abysmal character. She epitomised high school snobbery in this off-beat teenage sitcom.

Deputy Dawg

NBC. A Terrytoons production. USA, 1960

"Why **Musky**, dag nabit, you cotton pickin' pesky varmint!" When he wasn't asleep (see **Dylan**), Mississippi's laziest lawman Deputy Dawg spent a good deal of time getting upset about the minor felonies of Musky the Muskrat and Vince van Gopher (see also **Officer Dibble**). Since he was—predictably—a bungler, he generally ended up getting bawled out by his human boss, the Sheriff. The latter owned an ice factory and had better things to do. Vince, meanwhile enjoyed clinging onto Musky's tail. In the superlative episode "National Lazy Day" Musky and Vince planned to steal a quantity of watermelons and pies in order to force the canine cop to chase them and, in so doing, lose the prize. The Dawg ended up winning jointly with Musky, who decided he was too lazy to collect the award. The syndicated cartoon was such a hit with '60s audiences that producers Terrytoons had to hire more staff to keep the episodes churning out. The voices were provided by Dayton Allen and Lionel Wilson, who would often satirise celebrities via the show.

Devo plastic hair

*See **Slash, Johnny***

It was a kind of wig, but you had to be there.

Deaux-Deaux, Sergeant

*See **The Pink Panther Show***

Supposedly dimwit sidekick of cartoon Inspector Clouseau, on the original **Pink Panther Show**. He was a uniformed French police officer, with requisite hat which covered his eyes, giving him the look of a buffoon. But the real buffoon was, of course, the artless inspector C. Just like in the movies, where Clouseau was played by former Goon (see **Potty Time**) Peter Sellers,

Clouseau just could not get it right and was the cause of mental instability to his commissioner. The segment provided talky-style relief from the dialogue-free Pink Panther shorts which sandwiched it in the original triple-bill show.

Dick Dastardly
*See **Wacky Races***

Crazy hat, crazy guy. Mr Dastardly was the evil driver of the **Mean Machine**, along with his neanderthal-jawed dog, **Muttley**. His goal was to win the Wacky Race by hook and crook. He tried any amount of mean-spirited tricks to foil his competitors, but he was, of course, bungling, so the evil never paid. He maltreated his dog too, so when it all went wrong for Dick, Muttley would snicker his trademark laugh. Dastardly and Muttley were such a successful pairing that Hanna-Barbera span off a separate show as a vehicle for them: **Dastardly and Muttley in their Flying Machines**, in which the duo competed against various airborne freaks to eliminate a bird. Mr Dastardly was voiced by Paul Winchell (see also **Bubi Bear**).

Diff'rent Strokes
NBC. A Columbia Tri-star Television Production. USA, 1978

"Wodju talkin' about, Willis?" Inter-racial fun in the Park Avenue appartment of Philip Drummond, rich, white president of

multi-national conglomerate Trans-Allied, who had "taken on" two poor black kids—Willis and Arnold—from Harlem. The show was built on the premise that the benevolent white man could teach America a lesson about brotherhood and generosity by helping these black unfortunates. But why were they so poor and underprivileged in the first place? Willis and Arnold were actually the sons of none other than Drummond's own housekeeper who, having worked herself into the ground trying to raise her sons on the pittance she received from one of America's wealthiest men, persuaded Drummond in her dying breath to adopt them. They were poor because he made them so, but still he picked up the credit for their deliverance. He condescended to teach the rambunctious brothers important moral lessons about being nice and living right, neatly forgetting that one does not usually get to be the wealthy president of a multinational conglomerate by being nice, but more normally by being ruthless, self-seeking, politically adept and by exploiting naïve emerging markets in developing African countries.

Even more sorry than the idea were the episodes themselves. In particular, the one when Arnold and Willis made an effort to discover their African roots, but eventually realised how un-American they were being and apologised, stands out. Adding an additional unpleasant ingredient to the mix was Drummond's prim, preppy, goody-two-shoes daughter Kimberley, who appeared in a succesion of turtleneck sweaters, A-line skirts and the hair of Trisha Yates (see **Grange Hill**). Star of the show, however, was the miniaturised Gary Coleman as Arnold. He popped his eyes, stuck out his lower lip and delivered his comic line "wodju talkin' about" with all the precocious confidence of an actor much older than he looked. He was, of course, but he couldn't help that. He had a (much publicised) kidney condition, leading to a transplant at age five which had stunted his growth to such an extent that the only other TV role he got was as a similar carnival sideshow character on the ratings-grabbing *Buck Rogers In The 21st Century*. Such exposure can warp even an averagely-sized person's outlook. After his alleged assault of an autograph hunter, Mr Coleman took to working as a security guard—an unusual career move for a tiny person—and warned reporters not to talk to him about his career on *Diff'rent Strokes*. It's hard to blame him. It is also hard to imagine that the US group currently campaigning in the media with the subtle tagline "Leave Gary Coleman Alone" is providing him with much comfort.

But the now thirtysomething Mr Coleman—who reportedly divides his time between model railways, DVDs and the odd film role—is but a minor casualty of *Diff'rent Strokes* celebrity when compared to his co-stars. Todd Bridges, who played Willis, suffered a sustained bout of media drubbing in the US, as he went from courthouse to courthouse on minor felony charges. He was convicted of drugs and weapon offenses, much to the prurient delight of lesser US newspapers. But the Associated Press reports that, despite his transgressions, Mr Bridges was community-spirited enough to save the life of 50 year-old paraplegic Stella Kline. The woman had apparently been fishing in her electric wheelchair when, in a freak twine/chair controls accident, she plummeted to certain drowning in three feet of water at Balboa Park Lake in San Fernando Valley, Los Angeles. Mr Bridges "dived in" to save her. According to the AP's report, he believed God had put him there at the right time. Meanwhile, Dana "Kimberley" Plato was arrested for attempted armed robbery before bowing out for good in 1999—at the age of 34—in what many regarded as a suicide.

It is, perhaps, unusual for such a high proportion of lead actors in a successful children's TV sitcom to go on to lead such unhappy lives, hounded by the lesser journals, treated like freaks and pariahs, derided and mocked for their changing fortunes. US journalist Joal Ryan claims they were and are the blameless victims of a cultural "curse" in her book *Former Child Stars* (ECW Press, ISBN 155022428X). Despite Ms Ryan's seemingly good intentions, one can't help but feel she is not helping by putting a picture of the 10 year-old Gary Coleman on the front cover, framed by the book's subtitle: "The Story of America's Least Wanted". There is unsubtle and then there is downright cruel. But what, in the first place, prompts vulnerable children to bid for fame in America's so-called celebrity-or-bust culture? Takes all sorts, I suppose.

Diff'rent Strokes was first aired on NBC in 1978 and ran until 1985. The show moved to ABC for two further seasons before it (probably) withered under its own hypocrisy and died in 1986, having packed the all-grown-up Kimberley off to Paris. A total of 189 episodes were made, featuring guest appearances by such screen legends as David Hasselhoff, Janet Jackson, Molly Ringwald and, er, Nancy Reagan.

_____

Doctor Jekyll/Hydes
*See **Bailey's Comets***

Team from the De Patie-Freleng roller skate derby cartoon, itself an answer to **Wacky Races**. The Dr. Jekyll/Hydes were sinister limeys whose helfulness turned to evil in an uncontrollable puff of smoke.

_____

Doctor Mopp
*See **Camberwick Green***

Medical man and top hatted driver of old-fashioned car. Didn't speak much.

_____

Doctor Snuggles
A Jeffery O'Kelly/Topcraft/De Patie-Freleng/Polyscope production. UK tx: ITV 1980. Created by Jeffrey O'Kelly. Holland, 1979

He was a friend of the animal world. Inventions came out of his briefcase. He hopped around on a duck-headed talking pogo-stick umbrella called **Jefferson** and knew of **lavendar sheep** and camels who lived in the sky. No, do not adjust your dopamine levels, it was only *Dr. Snuggles*, cult hit for 10 year-olds. In 1980.

But what had so caught that childish fancy? The Doctor himself was a strangely-trousered, benevolent midget fatso with a slightly messianic air, whose sole aim was to make the world a better and happier place. He was a friend to the animals and made fantastic inventions in his shed **Rickety Rick** which, like all sheds, was alive and capable of ennui. Then he would take off in his home-made rocket, **Dreamy Boom Boom,** with his robot factotum **Mathilda Junkbottom** and his hardworking assistant **Dennis the Badger**. His mission: to spread good cheer to the world. That world was a colourful cornucopia of trippy fantasy, rich in its imagination and almost limitless in its scope for storytelling. Don't just take my word for it—here's *Dr Snuggles'* equally benificent and expansive award-winning creator Jeffrey O'Kelly, a self-confessed "cosmic Paddy" who was "very friendly with **The Smurfs**":

"I went to Chelsea art school and was a painter. Then I was an actor and a film maker. As a film maker I won lots of prizes. Then I tried to eat the prizes which is when I came up with Doctor Snuggles . . . I summoned **Michael Bentine** from the desert and asked him where was the magic place to live and he said Morocco. Then I asked where the goose were more prevalent and that's when I ended up in France . . . I lived on an island in the Seine and the [co-] creator of **Barbapapa** [Talus Taylor] used to walk around with a dog the size of a small cow and wear his cap at a jaunty angle and attract all the women . . . My ex-wife tore up the *Snuggles* manuscript in Gibraltar, into little pieces. So there was I running around the streets of Gibraltar trying to put it back together." Luckily Mr O'Kelly was with a mysterious man who had "just invented Sellotape so he taped it all up for me. I sold my Volkswagen to have it typed up."

That, believe it or not, was only the beginning. Disney liked *Snuggles* but, according to Mr O'Kelly, the media giant would only buy the format outright, giving its creator no further interest in it. So Disney was sent packing. A disastrous alliance with a Dutch exploiter ended in a settlement out of court, giving Mr O'Kelly a free hand to sell the format to Polygram's then daughter company Polyscope. "I signed a 54 page contract thinking that one day I would be more intelligent and drive a truck through it." Miffed that Polyscope sat on the format for three

years, preferring the less content-rich *Barbapapa*, he did. A team of lawyers was engaged, Polyscope went into receivership somewhere along the line and Mr O'Kelly regained his rights in 1985. Six episodes were eventually made by the Japanese animator Topcraft. The quality was good, but the US broadcasters did not, apparently, dig Japanese work. So Warner breakaway De Patie-Freleng Enterprises (see also **Pink Panther**, **Bailey's Comets** and **Baggy Pants and the Nitwits**) was engaged. Since its creation *Dr Snuggles* has been broadcast in 73 different countries. Airing in Canada and in Germany until 2004, its last showing in the UK was on Channel 4 in 1999. A further 26 new episodes are now ready to go into production and funds are being sought. There are also plans to use the internet to beam "edutainment" packages to the world.

Not surprisingly, given the legal tussles, at one point in the *Snuggles* saga Mr O'Kelly became ill. "It was like a negative acid trip. I was in the oldest French hospital and I had to sell my bed to afford the medicine so I could keep alive". As **Freddy** from **Scooby Doo** might say: somewhere in there is a clue.

Mr O'Kelly claims that if there is one message that he wanted *Dr Snuggles* to put across it was to be creative, be imaginative and follow your dream. "My one dream and desire in life was to get *Snuggles* out there," he says. "I don't know why ... But it's kept me all these years and sent my kids to school. Even now, all the money is *Snuggles* money". He appears to have baulked at companies who wanted exploit the format's commercial potential at the expense of its creative value. He also appears to have had very exacting standards when outsourcing that creative work. Two writers who did not make the grade were the late Douglas Adams (bestselling author of *The Hitch Hiker's Guide to the Galaxy*) and the similarly fêted John Lloyd (writer and producer of many fames and, with Douglas Adams, author of the hilarious *Meaning of Liff*). Mr O'Kelly rewrote their scripts.

Taking on multinationals is not a recommended path for those who like to live the quiet life. But in Mr O'Kelly's case it seems to have been worth it. Since launching his website at www.doctor-snuggles.com, Mr O'Kelly has received reams of e-mail messages from people, now all grown up, who say *Dr*

Snuggles influenced them to be creative. So what's the moral? Behind every seemingly frivolous kid's cartoon is an embattled creative genius leaving juggernaut conglomerates withering in his wake? Perhaps. Or is it that we should love and embrace our fellow men? "Auld bastards!" says Mr O'Kelly. He could be right. My thanks to him for his charming and illuminating conversation and for allowing me to use his illustrations. Big up, Jeffrey.

Link: **www.doctor-snuggles.com**—Mr O'Kelly apologises for the spelling mistakes:"The bloke who did the website for me is dyslexic. I've tried to threaten him, but he's from Bournemouth."

Link: a photograph of France's Mr Barbapapa, Talus Taylor (pictured with jaunty cap and oversized dog) is available at **www.naughtykitty.org/barbapapa.html**

Doctor Who

BBC. A BBC production. Created by Sydney Newman. Produced by Verity Lambert, Innes Lloyd et al. Directed by Waris Hussein, Douglas Camfield et al. Written by Terry Nation, Anthony Coburn, Dennis Spooner et al. Music by Ron Grainer and the BBC Radiophonic Workshop. UK, 1963–92

Very much the Moonies of television cults, *Doctor Who* is second only to *Star Trek* in its ability to attract sociopaths, hobbyists, theorists, collectors, role-playing gamers, fanatics and, frankly, experts. There is little this encyclopaedia can put forward which has not already been the subject of a keynote address at some high-priced, stale-smelling conference in Leicester, called something like SADCON or TOTALCON. However, in keeping with the general spirit of producing a reference book (even of the type that ends up in your toilet), the author feels it relevant to offer a few facts for the moderate or novice enthusiast.

The format was the 1963 creation of Sydney Newman, then head of BBC drama. His intention, reportedly, was to provide an educational show for children about science and history. This was born out by the presence, in the show's first incarnation, of assistant Susan's teachers. The educational idea was soon dropped by producer Verity Lambert in fine style, and Daleks—invented by writer Terry Nation—appeared forthwith.

The Doctor himself was a rogue Time Lord from the planet Gallifrey. A mere 720 years old, he had reached this veritable age by "regeneration", a device which enabled actors to run off and become *Worzel Gummidge* if they wanted. He travelled through space and time in a machine called a TARDIS, an acronym for Time And Relative Dimension In Space. His model was faulty, though, and dumped him in random locations, such as disused quarries and Wookey Hole. It should have been able to change its outer appearance in the manner of a chameleon, but was stuck in Police Box mode. He got it working at one stage, when special effects became cheaper, but that wasn't nearly so much fun.

That rise and fall in full, then. William Hartnell (1963–66) was the hoary old grandpa to young Susan (Carol Ann Ford). Assisting ably were Peter Purves (see **Blue Peter**) as Steven and Maureen O'Brien as Vicki. The first regeneration brought a new character. Patrick Troughton (1966–69) was a scruffy individual, obsessed with his recorder. His assitants were Polly (Anneke Wills), Ben (Michael Craze), Jamie (Frazer Hines and Zoe (Wendy Padbury).

John Pertwee's white-haired dandy, keen on frills, (1969–74) got involved with some earthbound unit called UNIT, led by Brigadier Lethbridge-Stewart (Nicholas Courtney). The Brigadier was generally trying to stem the alien tide of a luminous amoebic liquid with nothing but a small handgun. He was bally useless at it too, don't you know. Luckily the Doctor had his sonic screwdriver. Also helping out was Liz Shaw (Caroline John). Pertwee ran off to "be" *Worzel Gummidge*.

Tom Baker's interpretation (1974–81) had the Doctor as a big-haired, big-scarved, long coated intellectual. Baker's commanding physical presence and other-worldly voice had much to do with this regeneration's status as the definitive Doctor Who, although its long run (seven years) helped. His assistants were Sarah Jane Smith (Elizabeth Sladen), Harry Sullivan (Ian

Marter), the loinclothtastic Leela (Louise Jameson) (see also **Jana of the Jungle**), Romana (Mary Tamm and Lalla Ward), and the idiot robot canine K9 (voiced by John Leeson [see **Jigsaw**]). Baker's sense of drama held viewers and distracted them from the very low budget.

Then it all went wrong. Peter Davison, though a very fine actor (and singer: see **Button Moon**), had a hard act to follow. He failed to capture the nation's imagination as the smart, slightly effete Doctor in his 1982-84 run, despite a damn good effort. Helped by Tegan (Janet Fielding), Nyssa (Sarah Sutton), the despicable Adric (Matthew Waterhouse) and Turlough (Mark Strickson), ratings began to fall. Colin Baker (1984-86) played an irritable Doctor and ratings slid further still, helped by Peri (Nicola Bryant) and—a strange choice for a show in need of a ratings boost—Bonnie Langford (see **Just William**) as Melanie Bush. The last ditch stand—and indeed last straw— was dear old Sylvester McCoy (1987-92) (see also **Tiswas**, **Vision On**, **Jigsaw**) with Sophie Aldred as the tomboyish Ace. McCoy, after a shaky start, found his feet and acquitted himself nobly as the Doctor, but the nation was simply not up for it. It seemed that the show had descended into farce and ratings slumped to an all-time low.

Various monsters and adversaries came and went. The most popular, of course, were the Daleks, genuinely terrifying armoured beings on wheels with hideously modulated voices, screeching "ex-terminate". The fact that they couldn't get up and down stairs did not stop them. The Cybermen, whose expressionless robot heads with slit eyes had their own handles, were equally terrifying. The Sea Devils, who came lumbering, all scales and gills, out of the water had a good go as did the Robots of Death. But budgets were budgets. Monsters were all very well, but sometimes you had to use a sinister liquid or, indeed, a few grisly cats. Failing that, there was always the Master. The Doctor's arch nemesis usually turned up when the Monster budget had been spent. He was a fellow Time Lord, but with none of our Doctor's haplessness. He had two things: a mean streak plus a TARDIS that worked.

A stunning 679 30-minute episodes were made over 29 years. There are even people who can tell you what happened in all of them. The *Dr Who* Bible is generally accepted to be the 1998 tome *Doctor Who: TV Companion* by David J. Howe and Stephen James Walker, ISBN: 0563405880. There, the reader will find all the gory details this encyclopaedia cannot possibly (be bothered to) include. If that does not satisfy, Howe *et al* have amassed a veritable arsenal of *Dr Who* reference works, including a whole book about the Sylvester McCoy years ...

Dogtanian (and the Three Muskehounds)

A BRB International production. UK transmission: 1985 BBC1. Executive producer: Claudio Biern Boyd. Director: Tom Wierner, Robert Barron, Byrd Ehlman. Writer: Claudio Biern Boyd. Music: Guido and Maurision de Angelis. Spain, 1981

"Huh? I'll get you rascaaaals!"

Cartoon pooch version of the popular classic. Diminutive Dogtanian—a puppy—befriended the canine Athos, Porthos and Aramis and flitted from Gascogne to gay Paree to fight for the king. On the way he fell in dewey-eyed love with the demure Juliette (a dog), over a rumbling backdrop of general Huguenot persecution. What would Dumas have made of this doggy adaptation of his *Three Musketeers*? Not a lot, perhaps. The rest of the world, however, thought it a hoot. The hilarious cartoon series was produced by BRB international in Spain, where people talk a lot faster. This created an interesting challenge for the American voiceover artists, when it came to dubbing, and gave the show a breakneck pace, unique among children's shows (even BRB's own **Willy Fog** was slow-moving by comparison). By far the most oblique, yet compelling, aspect was the theme song:

> Yapacan yapacan, they cross their swords and pray.
> Yapacan yapacan, they're never far away.
> Yapacan yapacan, they're always ready to fight or to sing.

That's right, one or the other. Could go either way. Highly entertaining stuff really, heartily missed.

Double Deckers, Here Come The
See Here Come The Double Deckers

Dougal
(See Magic Roundabout, The)

Loosely resembling an enlarged Shredded Wheat, Dougal was **The Magic Roundabout**'s uncouth and egotistical mutt. His passion for sugar was overshadowed only by his passion for himself. His character was largely invented by English scriptwriter Eric Thompson, who discarded Serge Danot's original Pollux character along with the rest of the French scripts when he reworked them for UK transmission. Dougal would have perhaps found a soul-mate in **Parsley the Lion**, whose opinion of himself in The **Herbs** was exemplary. Gave **Dylan** a hard time over the latter's lax attitude to his rabbitorial duties.

Dreamy Boom Boom
See Doctor Snuggles

Home made rocket ship of the portly inventor.

Drogna
See Adventure Game, The

Fake currency with denominations that foxed even professional brainiacs like Heinz Wolff and Judith Hann. Exercised celebrity minds in **Why Don't You** producer Patrick Dowling's **Adventure Game**: the *Krypton Factor* for couch potatoes.

Duckula
*See **Danger Mouse***

Danger Mouse spin-off featuring the vegetarian, blood-avoiding vampire Count Duckula. The show followed the attempts of his more bloodthirsty relations to wean him off the broccoli set him on the right bloodsucking path. A fairly good premise was let down in many people's eyes by rambling scripting and lazier-looking animation.

Dusty
*See **Hickory House***

Mop haired puppet sidekick of **Humphrey Cushion** on the 1973 Granada pre-school show *Hickory House*. The mop hair was, undoubtedly, a function of the fact that Dusty was, indeed, a mop. His features—no eyes but little red nose sticking out of the mop hair—gave Dusty the look of the various puppets on **Potty Time**, Michael Bentine's surreal children's offering.

Dylan
*See **Magic Roundabout***

Blissed out bunny. For the most part asleep, the languourous rodent was occasionally seen strumming an orange guitar in an advanced state of tranquilised torpor, before the effort became too much for him. When he first arrived in the garden, **Zebedee** and **Dougal** were shocked at his un-rabbit like demeanour. They thought he should have been hopping about. "Weren't you told?" Zebedee asked. "I was told," Dylan replied. "But I didn't dig ..."

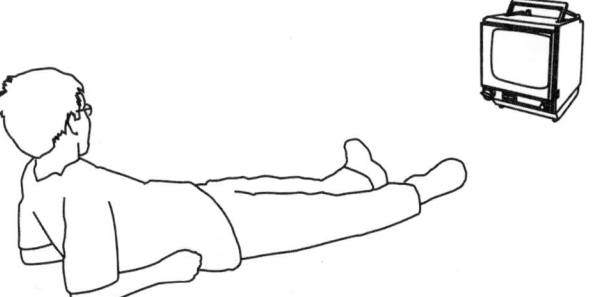

Educating Marmalade

ITV. A Thames production. Executive producer: Pamela Lonsdale. Produced by Sue Bertwhistle. Directed by John Stroud. Created by Andrew Davies. Theme music by Bad Manners. Incedental music by Andy Roberts. UK, 1981–83

Marmalade Atkins (played by Charlotte Coleman) was a very naughty girl indeed. That was pretty much it. She had been expelled by 10 schools, the only place that would take her was a convent school and the series began as she sewed Sister Conception to the altarcloth. Tanks were called in to get rid of her. The quality of Andrew Davies' scripting and Coleman's acting carried what could have been an exceptionally rum deal. Directorially of the **Rentaghost** school—all slap and no stick—the show begat spin-offs *Danger—Marmalade At Work* in 1984 and *Marmalade Atkins In Space*. Then the plot was lost somewhat and the show dissolved into zero-gravity nonsense with T-Bag, the intergalactic Grotbags (see **Emu's World**).

Elmo

*See **Baggy Pants and the Nitwits***

Walking-stick belonging to super hero **Tyrone**. Something approaching humour was derived from Elmo's erratic power of flight on this otherwise downbeat segment in the 1977 De Patie Freleng double-bill.

Emu's Broadcasting Corporation

BBC1. A BBC production. UK, 1975-80

Emu's first airing in his own show, which lasted for five series. And a fine show it was, by most accounts. EBC1 was a spoof television channel, run by the late Rod Hull in partnership with his unsavoury-looking and aggressive glove puppet, Emu, with support from Billy Dainty and Barnara New. Segments included spoof shows, such as Emu Trek and Open Emuversity. The show had a merciful sense of irony and Hull and his antipodean ward were at the height of their comic powers. A fixture on the variety and chat-show circuit, where he would attack amiable hosts at random while Hull feigned innocence, Emu was something of an institution. So it seems fitting that Hull, on the edge of mania at all times, may have had a home-made imitation Emu with which he attacked visiting vicars, uncles and family friends.

Emu's World/Emus's All Live Pink Windmill Show/Emu's Pink Windmill Show/Emu's Wide World/Emu's World

ITV. A Central production. UK, 1982-84/1984-85/1986/-1987/1988

Emu's World

"Ah yes," recalls journalist and sometime contributor to tv.cream.org Louis Barfe, "Emu's World . . . one lanky puppeteer in search of a format." In truth, Hull's dignity (never quite overflowing) and Emu's humour (ditto) did not fully survive their move from the BBC to the commercial Central Television, formerly the excellent ATV (see Tiswas, Pipkins).

Basically, there was "somebody at the door". That door was the only thing that separated Hull and his unpleasant glove puppet, Emu shacked up in a pink windmill with a lot of children from Grotbags the witch and her crocodile. She wanted the children. Hull wasn't letting go. Creepy.

Emu's World went through several incarnations, all vile (although not unpopular), from *Emu's All-Live Pink Windmill Show* in 1984 right through to *Emu's World* again in 1988. The viewer might have been forgiven for thinking Central never quite knew how to package this, by now, deeply anachronistic variety act. There was something forced and unsatisfying about all Emu's Central appearances and Hull finally bowed out of TV in 1988, only to be resurrected for systematic ridicule by Richard Herring, Stewart Lee and the actor Kevin Eldon in the second series of BBC2's adult comedy show *Fist Of Fun*, in 1996.

The previously quoted Mr Barfe also remembers being enlisted from the audience to "help out" Mr Hull on stage at the Britannia Pier in Great Yarmouth in 1979: "He smelled funny, and Emu's beak hurt my face." Nasty.

Link: Nastier still, the phrase "Emu's World", when keyed into a certain search engine, delivers the website of a Japanese sado-masochistic transvestite escort agency. Whole subject best left and forgotten, really.

Ermintrude
See Magic Roundabout

Pink cow with a flower in her mouth.

Ernie
See Sesame Street

Bert's chum with the stripy shirt. Played Dopey to Bert's Grumpy. Was known to need a glass of water in the middle of the night ... He was voiced by the late Jim Henson (see also **Muppet Show, The** and **Fraggle Rock**).

Evans the Song
See Ivor the Engine

Besuited choirmaster of the Grumbly and District Choral
Society.

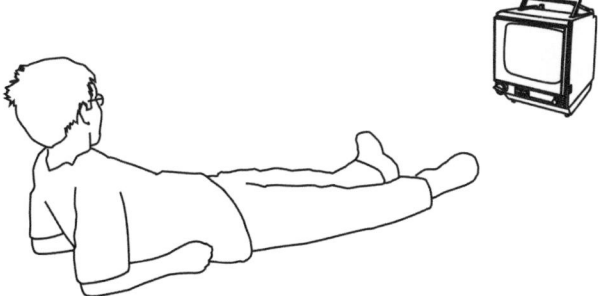

Famous Five, The

ITV. A Southern Television production. Directed by Peter Duffell. Novels by Enid Blyton. UK

Upper-class twit, tomboy and Timmy the dog crime-solving action drama series based on the ripping yarns of Enid Blyton. The show faithfully brought the novels to life in all their period glory and gloom. It was tanktops and plus-fours ahoy as this group of delightfully-spoken and insipidly polite stage-school children looned about on rocky islands, in secret passages and generally defeated naughty grown-ups in their wicked ways. The children's jolly-hockey-sticks-radiogram-ginger-beer-and-bread 'n' dripping crime victories rang a little hollow for some viewers who were, perhaps, not brought up during the war. Quintessentially English—where England equalled china cups and doilies (see also **Ffestiniog**), indifferent, monied parents and men who stood at the fireplace in tweeds, wracked with erudite ennui and nostalgia for the Raj—the series was ably parodied by French, Saunders, Mayall, Edmundson, and the rest of the Comic Strip crew in *Five Go Mad in Dorset*. Verdict: perfectly harmless Sunday afternoon teatime show, deemed better than *Songs of Praise* by many. Went well with cucumber.

Fancy Fancy
See Top Cat

Fancy was the white scarf-wearing, brown coated romeo of that New Yoik alley on the 13th precinct, where TC busted his chops to make a nickel. Fancy was generally offering some blushing kitty a bouquet of second-hand flowers when he got the call to action from TC: a prolonged bashing of the trash can lids.

Fenella the Kettle Witch
See Chorlton and the Wheelies

Hook-nosed, green, Welsh evil-doer and tormenter of the Wheelies. She had slaves: the **Spikers** and the **Toadies**. She had a book of spells called **Claptrap von Spillderbeans** and a one-eyed telescope called **Reilly**, who she stole from the end of a pier. She lived in **Spout Hall** (basically a black kettle), suffered from spasms and hated happiness. She could also bounce through floors, a trick that Chorlton kept cheerily asking her to teach him, to her spasmodic bemusement. She was voiced by Joe Lynch.

Fennifer
See Square Pegs; Slash, Johnny and DeNuccio, Jennifer

Johnny Slash's pet-name for the high-handed Jennifer only served to confuse and irritate the object of his unrequited affections. Offering her a turtle did not help.

Ffestiniog
A town in North Wales

Oliver Postgate's **Ivor the Engine** did much to perpetuate the notion that Ffestiniog is anywhere you would want to go. If ever you are in Porthmadog—and it could happen—you might see enticingly twee advertisements tempting you to take the Ffestiniog railway up through the mountains. Don't. It is not that the railway is bad—far from it. Rather, this charmingly cramped train deposits the unwary tourist in the drizzle-ridden, rubble-strewn, slate-grey mountain hell that is the charming and authentic trap of Ffestiniog, and doesn't come back for ages, forcing you and your cagoule out into the mist to shop for souvenirs. Choose between the one shop, with its yellowed and detumescing jigsaw, petrified Bounty bar (complete with white bloom) and 1,000 ceramic Welsh old women in lace doilies and **Fenella** hats. Once you are in, do not be offended if the local people stare darkly at you and talk behind their hands. Tip: do not eat the shortbread.

––––––––

Fingerbobs

BBC TV. Live action animation. A Q3 London production. Story and design by Joanne and Michael Cole. Music by Michael Jessett. Directed by Michael Grafton-Robinson. UK, 1971

"I wonder what Yoffy wants with all these stones . . ."

Lunchtime pre-school show delivers dose of extreme mellow. Yoffy lifts a finger . . . and a mouse is there. Not really a mouse of course, just a bit of paper, but close enough. They were easy to make out of a cone of paper and half-moons for ears, especially if you had a *Fingerbobs Annual* to show you how. There was also Gulliver the seagull, done by putting your hands together and flapping them like wings. As brooding, bearded pesenter Yoffy (in polo-neck and neckerchief combination) nodded his head just perceptibly—as if to say hello—whimsical minimalistic music on flute, xylophone and drum (see also **The Moomins**) told the viewer his or her television set was now being controlled by the Woodcraft Folk.

The show would open with Yoffy—the assumed name of former **Play School** presenter Rick Jones—fiddling with something or other on his desk. **Fingermouse** would pretend to arrive (he was really attached to Yoffy's hand) and pretend to ask him what he was doing. Yoffy would then pretend to send the pretend mouse off to collect a good deal of things: stones, feathers, bits of bark, beans. Various characters assisted: **Scampi** the shrimp and a tortoise called **Flash** were regulars. Then they would bring them all back to Yoffy who would introduce the story, which was illustrated, sometimes in lurching stop-frame animation, with all the bits and bobs the toys had collected. Charming, mellow and very folksy, **Fingerbobs**—the original 1972 artefact—is not to be confused with *Fingermouse*, a spin-off show which delivered 13 new episodes in 1985. *Fingerbobs* was written and designed by Joanne and Michael Cole, who went onto to more surreal things, with **Bod**.

Fingermouse
*See **Fingerbobs**, above*

Finkerton Organization
*See **Inch High, Private-Eye***

Owned and run by Mr and Mrs Finkerton, the "Organisation" sent the midget sleuth Inch High and his useless companions off on crime fighting missions, in the **Huge Mobile**. The pair were voiced by John Stephenson for Mr Finkerton, and Jean Vander Pyl for his wife.

Flash The Tortoise
*See **Fingerbobs***

Groovy reptile, ironic name. He was really Yoffy's glove with a paper dome on top.

Flockton Flyer, The
ITV. A Southern Television production. Produced and directed by Colin Nutley. Written by Peter Whitbread. Music by Jugg Music. UK, 1977-78

Possibly not a cult offering, but this entry might pleasantly jog your memory. *The Flockton Flyer* was a stirring 14-part loco-motive-based period drama featuring a young Peter Duncan (as Jimmy), who was to go on to present **Blue Peter**, shortly before his voice broke. A family moved into a small village and attempted to take over the old railway, which was falling to bits. The locals hated them, but that did not put them off. We *will* provide a regular train service, they cried. A bit gloomy—in a Hovis advert sort of way—unless the infant viewer happened to have a crush on the blonde Jessica (Caitrin Strong), in which case it was required viewing, no questions asked.

Flumps, The

BBC TV. A BBC/David Yates production. Produced David Yates. Written by Julie Holder. Animated by David Kellaher. Music by Paul Reade. UK, 1977

Those Flump names in full, then, since it's promised on the jacket. In descending order of seniority: Grandfather Flump, Father Flump, Mother Flump, Perkin, Posie and Pootle. Six owl pellets, kitted out in the bobble hats and cloth caps left over from a **Blue Peter** bring and buy sale. One of the more fondly remembered children's shows, *The Flumps* was written by Julie Holder and brought to life by David Yates (see **Pigeon Street**) and the stop-frame animations of David Kellaher. Thirteen episodes were made and aired in 1977, after lunch on Mondays. Much like the **Pogles**, the Flumps had a strong sense of masculine rule, with Mother Flump usually consigned to the dishes and the cooking. In one episode she had a headache. It might have been Grandfather that did it for her. The old boy was known to parp out a tune on his flumpet (a pun on the word "trumpet") until baby Pootle stuffed a carrot into it. Other than that it was fairly standard story-telling: the kind of subjects delivered by countless other shows. What made *The Flumps* different was the owl pellet angle. They were cute.

In "Secrets", the first episode, everyone was telling poor Posie a secret and telling her to keep it under her hat. Trouble was she couldn't find her hat. Where is it, where is it? Twelve more hilarious episodes followed, featuring magnet and roller skate capers, adventures with rockets and balloons, not to mention the evergreen "forgotten" birthday/surprise party mix up.

The best episode was "Where's Grandfather?" That one had real promise, until they found him.

Links: **www.psychoflump.clara.net/flumps/**
Meet the evil mutant Flumps.

Flying Dustman, The
See Captain Pugwash

The name of the boat skippered by scary and bearded (see **Fingerbobs**) brigand **Black Jake**, and his crew of woeful wrong-doers.

Follyfoot
ITV. A Yorkshire Television production. Executive producer: Tony Essex. Produced by Audrey Southcott. Created by Monica Dickens. UK, 1971–73

Clip clop. Soft-focus equine-interest show with creepy but catchy "Lightning Tree" theme song by The Settlers (not an antacid tablet but a popular music group). The storylines—created by novelist Monica Dickens—centred around a group of adolescents who liked to help out on Follyfoot Farm, a kind of hospice for decaying horses run by someone called the Colonel (Desmond Llewellyn). *Follyfoot*—according to this encyclopaedia's research (conducted down the pub)—was popular with a young female audience, but evidence suggests a heavy reliance on horses, father-figures, military men and folk music may have made this show a bitter pill to swallow for many boys. A total of 39 half-hour doses contained active ingredients: Gillian Blake as Dora; Arthur English as "Slugger"; Christian Rodska as Ron Striker, Paul Guess as Lewis Hammond and Steve Hodson as, er, Steve. Earlier episodes may have contained traces of Robin Stewart as Paul. Do not exceed stated dose.

Fraggle Rock
ITV. A Jim Henson production. UK, 1983–87

"Let the music play ..." Living in all alone in a lighthouse can do things to a person (see **The Moomins**). In this case, the lighthouse keeper of Fraggle Rock (Fulton Mackay, then later John Gordon Sinclair) had only a dog for company and began to see Muppets (see also **Sesame Street**) popping out of every crevice. Or did he? The dog was wise to the Fraggles and their well-established community, but the lighthouse keeper refused to believe. Jim Henson's puppet creations—including the prosaically-named Wembley, plus Gobo, Boober and Red—gave it large on Fraggle Rock over 85 half-hour shows. A talking trash heap with Dame Edna specs dispensed wisdom when required by the Fraggles, who were in turn dwarfed by the Gorgs, a family of puppet giants. The plots were nothing much to write to the mainland about, but the Muppets, as ever, gave excellent entertainment. The show gave birth to the term "Fraggle" as used to descibe any kind of miniaturized cretin, student or wastrel. An animated version, which ran from 1987–88, missed the point somewhat. "The trash heap has spoken."

Freddy
See Scooby Doo

Large-chested natural leader. He wore an orange neckerchief. He always had a plan, and it always involved **Shaggy** and Scooby—the two least likely to get anything done—going one one way, and the rest going the other. Was there anything going on between him and **Daphne**? You hoped so, otherwise it would have been a shameful waste of all that sexual energy and silhouette figures of them side by side in the sunset, while Shaggy and the dog goofed off and **Velma** did all the brain work. Freddy was voiced by Frank Welker (see **Buford Files, The**), and the character reappeared In **Josie and the Pussycats** as **Alan**, Josie's coveted boyfriend.

Fun Factory

ITV [tx LWT]. A Granada production. Produced by Sandy Ross. Directed by Ian Hamilton. UK, 1982

If your definition of fun was Billy Barty and Jeremy Beadle in your living room instead of **Tiswas**, then this was the show for you. Really a minor footnote, save for the fact it once—probably unsuitably—featured flowerpot hat-wearing US pop nerds **Devo** singing "Girl U Want" (see also **Square Pegs**).

G

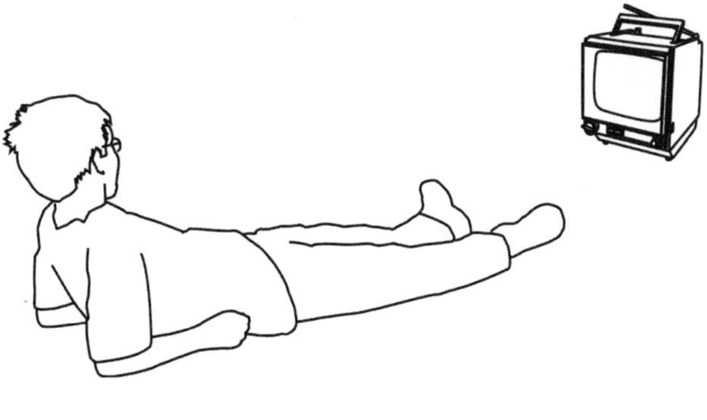

Gabriel
See Bagpuss

A toy toad in a straw boater with a banjo. Played songs. Then fell asleep.

Gator
See Inch High, Private-Eye

Idiot boyfriend of **Lori**, Inch High's niece.

Ghosts of Motley Hall
ITV. A Granada production. Directed by Quentin Lawrence. Written by Richard Carpenter. UK, 1976

The televised blatherings of a whole lot of ghosts (see **Rentaghost**), doomed to haunt their decaying ancestral Home, Motley Hall. Various generations of the hilariously-named Uproar family roamed the dusty carpets and halls as the undead. Bodkin was an Elizabethan jester (see **Rentaghost**), short on actual humour (see **Rentaghost**). Next was the 18th century dandy (see **Rentaghost**) Sir Francis Uproar, known as Fanny. General Sir George Uproar was an old British Army General. Making up the set were Matt, the stable boy and the enigmatic White Lady. The show was written by Richard "**Catweazle**" Carpenter.

Godzilla and Godzooky
NBC. A Hanna-Barbera production. USA, 1978

Scene: the ocean. Sci-fi trouble was never far away from Captain Carl Majors, Professor Quinn Darian, Brock, their young "assistant" (see also **Batman**) and Pete, their child. In their care—as is usual in these cases—was a baby radioactive dinosaur. Who could have guessed from its textbook doofus antics that the idiot reptile was none other than Godzooky, son of Godzilla. When the cyborg whale (or the stone creatures or the macro beasts) struck, Majors had only to sound his sonic alarm to summon the leviathan Godzilla from the deep. Naturally, the signal did not always work and Godzooky was called upon to squeek out to its progenitor. The waters rumbled, the air sparked with radium. The giant dinosaur surfaced to vanquish the evil that faced his human friends. Look out—lazer eyes. Pretty good stuff if ocean-based sub-manga sci-fi was your bag (see also **Marine Boy**).

These thirty-minute cartoons constitued Hanna-Barbera's attempt to get in on the Godzilla craze of the '70s. The series premiered on September 9, 1978 on NBC and the inevitable syndication brought him dripping to UK screens shortly thereafter. Godzilla himself was voiced by Ted Cassidy, while Godzooky voiceover duties fell to Don "**Scooby Doo**" Messick (See also **Muttley**). Captain Majors was voiced by Jeff David, Quinn by Brenda Thompson, Pete by Al Eisenman and Brock's voice was supplied by Hilly Hicks. As far as Hanna-Barbera cartoons go, *Godzilla* fell into the **Jana of the Jungle** and **Valley of the Dinosaurs** category, rather than the "wacky" gag-led sitcom strand of **Scooby Doo**, **The Hair Bear Bunch**, **Josie and the Pussycats** or **Wait Till Your Father Gets Home**. Godzilla, as a character, is one of those phenomena, like *Star Trek*, which attracts a huge cult following on its own terms. So if the reader is just getting started in Godzilla cataloguing, here is a handy shortcut.

Season one, which ran from 1978–79, brought us The Firebird / The Mega-Volt Monster / The Eartheater / Attack of the Stone Creatures / The Seaweed Monster / The Horror Of Forgotten Island / The Energy Beast / The Magnetic Horror / The Colossus Of Atlantis / Island Of The Lost Ships / The Breeder Beast / The Sub-Zero Terror / The Time Dragons. Season two, which ran from 1979–80, featured such legendary episodes as: The City In The Clouds / The Cyborg Whale / Microgodzilla / Pacific Peril / The Beast Of Storm Island /

Moonlode /The Golden Guardians / Calico Clones / Ghost Ship / The Macro Beasts /Valley of the Giants / Island Of Doom /The Deadly Asteroid.

Goober & the Ghost Chasers
A Hanna-Barbera production. USA, 1978

Invisible cartoon-dog ghost-chasing fun. By that I mean the dog was invisible, but on second thoughts, the fun was invisible too. Read it either way.

Grandad
BBC 1. A BBC Manchester production. Produced by Anna Home. Written by Bob Block. Created by Clive Dunn. UK, 1979-84

Permanently septegenarian actor Clive Dunn (of "Don't panic Mr Mannering" fame) came up with the idea for this awful show about an old curmudgeon doing anything he could to steal the limelight. It was written by Bob "**Rentaghost**" Block. What a team. Acted as a useful emetic if you had stuffed yourself to a toffee standstill with lemon bonbons. It was produced by BBC Manchester, the studio that brought you the equally good **Cheggers Plays Pop**.

Grange Hill
BBC1. A BBC production. Created by Phil Redmond. Executive producer: Anna Home. Produced by Colin Cant and others. Directed by Colin Cant and others. Written by Phil Redmond and others. UK, 1978-ongoing

It never occured to you to be afraid, starting Big School, that Gripper Stebson clones would sting you for your lunch money

131

or have their spineless goons duff you up. Neither did poor Zammo McGuire's 1986 descent into smack hell inspire you to shoot up once you were there. The fictional characters in Phil "Brookside" Redmond's high school soap went through these hoops so you didn't have to.

But that did not stop reactionary mothers and fathers the country over banning their poor progeny from watching the "scandalous" series. For *Grange Hill* was groundbreaking stuff in its time. As we sit watching *Beverley Hills 90210*, *Heartbreak High*, *Hollyoaks* (also by Redmond), *Neighbours*, *Home & Away* and their like, we forget that before *Grange Hill*, the format did not exist. A true soap, the show covered a broad raft of contemporary social issues: nicking stuff; getting up the duff; coming from a "broken home"; being fat; shooting up heroin in the school toilets and having one's first period (not necessarily at the same time); having a crush on someone you shouldn't (ie your teacher/pupil); bunking off; being picked on and; of course, forgetting your PE kit and having to do it in your pants on the day you have elected to wear your nylon Noddy y-fronts. (Actually, now that I come to think about it, the latter is one of my own memories.) Rather than seeking to shock, the show aimed to educate. A BBC press pack says the show aimed to deliver "realism and social relevance". Naturally, amid the gritty realism there was good hefty dollop of social stereotyping. Here is an example:

Poor old Roland Browning. The only person in the whole school who would give this high-voiced, speccy blimp with an advanced eating-disorder the time of day was a minute, skinny girl called Janet St Clair, who clearly adored the enormous sour-faced loner. "Ro-land," she would call. "I love you Ro-land." "Leave me alone!" he would squeak. And as he wobbled off in the opposite direction, his dingy grey shirt hanging grubbily out of his trousers, the ground trembled beneath him and squirrels on the playing field hid. Can this really be the moral: look beyond the blubber, the chip on the shoulder, the thick-framed NHS glasses and the permanent cheesy smell of Wotsits, girls, and there you will find a great man, worthy of your most tingling Judy Blume fantasy? Roland, of course, was bullied mercilessly by Stebson, causing him to play truant and end up on the (educational) psychologist's couch. He also walked out in front of a car. It wasn't really very funny and there was no easy solution. His short stint as the school usurer didn't last. Nor did his time as Stebson's evil henchman. Eventually he found solace in, er, cookery.

The other high-school axiom here is this: girls' hormonal action starts ahead of that of boys. In this climate of one-sided pubic change—which generally prompted six-foot girls in cheap deodorant and training bras to bend down and snog three-foot boys who were still wearing their football shorts and who smelled of Hubba Bubba—our Roly was more interested in his fish-paste roll than a bit of roly-poly. But it wasn't all AIDS and car crashes. The show also aimed to reflect the minor vissicitudes of school life, such as cheating and medical check ups. How refreshing it was to come home from school, having spent all your lunch money on cola cubes and then been sick over the bunsen burner, catching fire to your hair (haven't we all been there?), to have *Grange Hill* work through all of this, and more, for you.

The original, vintage, *Hill* featured Tucker Jenkins (played by Todd Carty, who went on to slap aftershave on his Johnson to ill effect in his own spin-off show **Tucker's Luck**); Pogo Patterson (Peter Moran), Trisha Yates (Michelle Herbert), whose catchphrase was "Don't be so shhtewpid", and Suzanne Ross (Susan Tully), who went on to further rock our worlds by having Dirty Den's lovechild in the first storyline of *EastEnders*. Erkan Mustafa, who played Roland, is currently doing a "bit of this and that"; Lee MacDonald (Zammo) is acting. Pogo Patterson (Peter Moran) runs a pub in Knightsbridge, London, while Jonathan Lambeth (who played the misunderstood and doomed artistic genius Danny Kendall) was working as a business news journalist for VNU Newswire, at the time of writing.

The characters changed, but two things remained: that slapstick theme tune, by Johnny Hawksworth, and that lone sausage, which flew, still attached to its fork, across the dining hall in the opening titles.

Granny Toots
*See **Doctor Snuggles***

She was old. She ran a hospice for cats.

—————

Grape Ape
ABC TV. A Hanna-Barbera production. USA, 1975

Here it comes: that same old talking beagle and giant gorilla combination. Grape Ape—a purple primate of few words, voiced by Bob Holt—would do anything for grapes. He had a friend called Beegle Beagle (Marty Ingels), whom the Ape addressed as Beegly Beagly. Beegly Beagly was a beagle. However, this Beegle Beagle beagle is not to confused with the other Fleegle Beagle beagle (see **Banana Splits**). That beagle drove a buggy but this beagle drove a van. The ape sat atop the van and scooted along with his foot. The show first appeared as a 10-minute segment on the *New Tom & Jerry/Grape Ape Show* (there's a snappy title). Beegle was a fairground hustler and the Grape Ape was his act. They got into "scrapes", but were rescued by grapes, as when the ape ate the grape, they'd usually escape. Sighted only rarely in the UK, *Grape Ape* was paired here with **Bailey's Comets** (a show from rival animator De Patie-Freleng). Good fun.

—————

Gruesome Twosome
*See **Wacky Races***

They drove the **Creepy Coup**. They tried to win the race. They were called **Big** and **Li'l**. They were ghouls.

Gulliver, The Adventures of
A Hanna-Barbera production. USA, 1968

This Hanna-Barbera cartoon serial—loosely based on the Jonathan Swift novel *Gulliver's Travels* and aired as part of the **Banana Splits**—concerned the father-hunting adventures of one Gary Gulliver (voiced by Jerry Dexter). That's right—Gary. Now, Gary is part of a little-known coterie of literary heroes and exponents including Wayne Whittington, Colin Copperfield, Barry Baudelaire and . . . oh, anyway, it's all about Lilliput. Following an unfortunate shipwreck, Gary and his dog Tag (Herb Vigran) were set upon by various mini people including the foxy Flirtacia (Ginny Tyler), the self-explanatory Eager and Glum (Don "**Scooby Doo**" Messick) and Bunko. There was missing treasure involved and stock evil imbecile Captain Leech was there to louse it all up via episodes such as The Valley of Time, Exit Leech and Tiny Island. Like everything else associated with *Banana Splits*, *The Adventures of Gulliver* was very rum indeed, but as such tends to be one of those that comes back to you in hideous snatches at three in the morning.

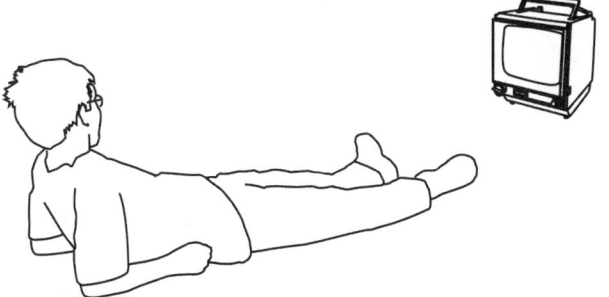

Hair Bear Bunch

See Help! It's The Hair Bear Bunch

Hairy Madden Red Eyes

See Bailey's Comets

Yet another team up against Barnaby Bailey. Were they beautiful? Guess.

Handful of Songs

ITV. A Granada Production. UK, 1973-82

Chirpy pre-school sing-song show with illustrations. "I saw a mouse." Where? "There on the stair . . ." Fronted by guitar-strumming Kathy Jones and Keith Field, who passed the baton to Keith and Maria Morgan in 1975, the show is mostly remembered for its hippy sentimentality and top title song: "We've got a handful of songs to sing you / new songs and blue songs and songs to bring you / happiness . . ." well, more or less. The formula worked well enough for 13 series, when it suddenly stopped working for some reason known best to the ITV programme controllers. Sweet.

Hanna-Barbera Cartoons

The most frequently remembered cartoons of the William Hanna and Joseph Barbera stable have been listed as separate entries in this encyclopaedia. However, given the sterling output of this animator over nearly fifty years, it seems fitting to quantify its achievement in as full a way as possible. There follows, then, a chronological list of the house's output in the 20th century, including the few live action shows.

The golden years, as you can see, were clearly the '60s and '70s. The rot had set in by 1980 with *The Frankenstones* and the '90s brought little of lasting merit, starting as that decade did with a Bill & Ted spin off and tailing off with the *Power Puff Girls*. The **Banana Splits** and the shows it showcased are grouped together in *italics*. But one of these shows is not like the others (see **Sesame Street**). Can you tell which it is (tip: it might be in **bold type**)?

1950s

Ruff & Reddy Show (1957); Huckleberry Hound (1958); Pixie & Dixie with Mr Jinx (1958); Augie Doggie & Doggie Daddy (1959); Quick Draw McGraw (1959); Snooper & Blabber (1959); Loopy De Loop (1959).

1960s

Yakky Doodle (1960); Yogi Bear (1960); Flintstones (1960); Hokey Wolf (1960); Snagglepuss (1960); Top Cat (1961); Lippy the Lion & Hardy Har Har (1962); Touché Turtle & Dum Dum (1962); Wally Gator (1962); Jetsons (1962); Magilla Gorilla (1963); Ricochet Rabbit & Droopalong (1963); Breezly & Sneezly (1963); Punkin' Puss & Mushmouse (1963); Peter Potamus & So So (1964); Yippee, Yappee, & Yahoeey (1964); Adventures of Jonny Quest (1964); Atom Ant (1965); Precious Pupp (1965); Hillbilly Bears (1965); Secret Squirrel (1965); Squiddly Diddly (1965); Winsome Witch (1965); Sinbad Jr (1965); Laurel & Hardy (1966); Space Kidettes (1966); Space Ghost (1966); Dino Boy (1966); Frankenstein Jr (1966); Impossibles (1966); Abbott & Costello (1967); Herculoids (1967); Young Samson & Goliath (1967); Fantastic Four (1967); Moby Dick (1967); Mighty Mightor (1967); Birdman (1967); Galaxy Trio (1967); Shazzan (1967); *Banana Splits (1968) included: Three Musketeers (1968); Arabian Knights (1968); Micro Ventures (1968); Danger Island (1968); Adventures Of Gulliver (1968); New Adventures of Huckleberry Finn (1968);* Wacky Races (1968); Perils of Penelope Pitstop (1969); Cattanooga Cats (1969); Motormouse & Autocat

(1969); Around the World in 79 Days (1969); It's The Wolf (1969); Scooby-Doo Where Are You (1969); Dastardly & Muttley and their Flying Machines (1969).

1970s

Where's Huddles? (1970); Harlem Globetrotters (1970); Josie & the Pussycats (1970); Pebbles & Bamm Bamm (1971); Help! It's the Hair Bear Bunch (1971); Funky Phantom (1971); Sealab 2020 (1972); Roman Holidays (1972); Amazing Chan & the Chan Clan (1972); Josie & the Pussycats in Outer Space (1972); Wait Till Your Father Gets Home (1972); Jeannie & Babu (1973); New Scooby Doo Movies (1973); Speed Buggy (1973); Yogi's Gang (1973); Addams Family (1973); Goober & the Ghost Chasers (1973); Inch High Private Eye (1973); Butch Cassidy & the Sun Dance Kids (1973); Superfriends (1973); Peter Puck (1973); Hong Kong Phooey (1974); These are the Days (1974); Devlin (1974); Valley of the Dinosaurs (1974); Wheelie & the Chopper Bunch (1974); Partridge Family: 2200 AD (1974); Grape Ape (1975); Dynomutt, Dog Wonder & Blue Falcon (1976); Jabberjaw (1976); Mumbly (1976); Clue Club (1976); C.B. Bears (1977); Shake, Rattle, & Roll (1977); Skatebirds (1977); Undercover Elephant (1977); Heyyyyy It's the King (1977); Posse Impossible (1977); Wonder Wheels (1977); Three Robotic Stooges (1977); Blast Off Buzzard (1977); Scooby's All Star Laff A Lympics (1977); Captain Caveman & the Teen Angels (1977); Yogi's Space Race (1978); Galaxy Goof-Ups (1978); Galloping Ghost (1978); Buford Files (1978); Godzilla (1978); Jana of the Jungle (1978); All New Popeye Hour (1978); Dinky Dog (1978); Scooby's All Stars (1978); New Shmoo (1979) Super Globetrotters (1979); Casper & the Angels (1979); Thing (1979); Scooby & Scrappy-Doo (1979)

1980s

Scooby's Laff A Lympics (1980); Bedrock Cops (1980); Dino and the Cavemouse (1980); Frankenstones (1980); Captain Caveman (1980); Drak Pak (1980); Fonz & the Happy Days Gang (1980); Richie Rich (1980); Space Stars (1981); Astro &

the Space Mutts (1981); Teen Force (1981); Kwicky Koala (1981); Dirty Dawg (1981); Crazy Claws (1981); Bungle Brothers (1981); Smurfs (1981); Laverne & Shirley (1981); Private Olive Oyl (1981); Trollkins (1981); Mork & Mindy (1982); Little Rascals (1982); Pac-Man (1982); Shirt Tales (1982); **Gary Coleman Show (1982)** [see **Diff'rent Strokes**]; Dukes (1983); Mochichis (1983); Biskitts (1983); Snorks (1984); Pink Panther & Sons (1984); Challenge of the GoBots (1984); Super Powers Team: Galatic Guardians (1985); Yogi's Treasure Hunt (1985); Galtar & the Golden Lance (1985); Paw Paws (1985); Thirteen Ghosts of Scooby Doo (1986); Pound Puppies (1986); Wildfire (1986); Foofur (1986); Flintstone Kids (1986); Captain Caveman & Son (1986); Sky Commanders (1987); A Pup Named Scooby Doo (1988); Popeye and Son (1987); New Yogi Bear Show (1988); Completely Mental Misadventures of Ed Grimley (1988); Fantastic Max (1988); Adventures of Don Coyote (1989)

1990s

Gravedale High (1990); Bill and Ted's Excellent Adventures (1990); Tom and Jerry Kids (1990); Pirates of Dark Water (1990); Fender Bender (1990); Monster Tails (1990); Young Robin Hood (1991); Yo, Yogi! (1991); Capital Critters (1992); Captain Planet (1992); Fish Police (1992); Droopy, Master Detective (1993); Screwball Squirrel (1993); SWAT KATS (1993); Two Stupid Dogs (1993); What a Cartoon (1993); Ted (1994); Real Adventures of Jonny Quest (1995); Space Ghost Coast to Coast (1997); Cartoon Planet (1997); Johnny Bravo (1997); Cow and Chicken (1997); Dexter's Laboratory (1997); PowerPuff Girls (1998); Ed, Edd, and Eddy (1999)

Hardy Har-Har
See Lippy the Lion

Gloomy, pessimistic hyena sidekick of **Lippy the Lion** in the 1962 Hanna-Barbera animation of the same name. Hardy revelled in doom: "Now we're for it, a-har, a-har-har-har."

Winning stuff. Voices by Daws "**Snagglepuss**" Butler. Earplugs recommended.

––––––––––

Hartley Hare
*See **Pipkins***

Species: rabbit. Type: manky.

––––––––––

Hattifatteners
*See **The Moomins***

Drifting, mute white creatures, loosely resembling unravelled condoms with hands. They travelled about in great numbers on boats and ate electricity, upon whose consumption they fluttered their hands and shimmered. They fascinated **Moominpappa**, briefly.

––––––––––

Heads And Tails
BBC 1. A BBC production. Presented by Derek Griffiths. UK

Former **Play School** presenter Derek Griffiths was the lithe-limbed, polo-necked musical phunkster behind this bird, beast and bug bonanza with episodes such as "Dog-a-long," "Ladybird ladybird" and "Skip to the Ewe". Griffiths also provided the legendary **Bod** theme.

––––––––––

Help! It's The Hair Bear Bunch
CBS. A Hanna-Barbera production. USA, 1971

"Quick, Square, ah, make like a motorcycle!"
"Ooh. Ooh. Mr Peevly! They're getting away!"

Three "groovy" bears lived in the **Wonderland Zoo**, where they were endlessly taunted and enslaved by mean, career-mad zookeeper **Mr Peevly**. He vowed to "get those bears one of these days" and send them back to the north woods, while they constantly contrived to stay in the zoo, in the lap of luxury.

There was Hair Bear, the ringleader: big of hair, **Top Cat** of voice (the mellifluous tones of this smooth talker were actually provided by Daws Butler, known for providing some of the more grating voices in animation [see **Wally Gator**, **Snagglepuss** etc]). He wore an orange waistcoat and a giant blonde afro. **Square Bear**, deep of voice, big of belly, wore a blue and green flowery sunhat over his eyes. **Bubi** (pronounced Booby), the little bear, had a unique speech impediment which caused him to add the unlikely phrase "atroyda raisin troydasay datray" into most of his sentencesasay datrays.

Their cave converted into a '70s bachelor pad at the flick of a rocky switch, with sliding doors and secret spaces reminiscent of **Tracey Island**. Their aim was to live a life of leisure and turn the tables on Peevly, whose aim was to secure promotion from the militaristic zoo superintendent and turn the tables on those troublesome bears. Hilarity ensued. You held your sides as Hair tried to raffle off the zoo and become the owner, or colonise Mars in a rocket and lead a miniaturized robot race. Sharp exits were ensured by the use of an imaginary motorcycle, made by simply assuming the position.

The characters were visually new, but personality-wise you had seen much of it before. Peevly, for example, was no more than **Officer Dibble** with a different uniform. His dimwit henchman Botch was a fatter **Sergeant Flint**, even voiced by the same actor, Joe E Ross. Hair Bear was a bigger, phatter, phunkier **Top Cat** and the other bears were run-of-the-mill sideshow foils. But the format was different enough to be diverting, familiar enough to keep those pre-teen eyes glued to the box. The shows stand up well to adult scrutiny as well, with humour working on several levels. "Ooh. Ooh. I'm on the choo-choo."

Hector's House

BBC TV. Created by Georges Croses. France, 1967

Hector—a pompous old dog with floppy ears—and Zaza—a petite, feminine kitty—lived in a house, but spent all their time in the garden. Their relationship was not obvious (a dog and cat surely should have been mortal enemies, or at least ironic critics of one another [see **Roobarb**]); but whether or not they were sleeping with each other, they clearly seemed to have found some common ground in their love of walking around with their arms straight out in front of them. It was as though they were not real at all but in fact basic glove puppets.

In the first two episodes, the couple's outdoor idyll was disturbed by a clearly disturbed frog called Kiki who, like all neighbours, had been spying on them for some time and interfering with their lives. There had been a bit of a palaver about a pink hat. Kiki had left it *chez* Hector during one of her spying visits and needed it back. But Hector caught her red-handed, whereupon they all become the best of friends. Perhaps the couple decided to let her into their circle when it became obvious that Kiki, too, was unable to bend her arms at the elbow. Such a condition can't have been that widespread—perhaps sufferers felt they should stick together, despite any sociopathic tendencies which might otherwise have divided them.

Whatever the reason, Kiki got her own gloryhole (is that the word?) in the fence, through which she could insert herself whenever she needed a bit of entertainment. Relatively ungripping adventures followed—this is 1967, remember—and whatever went wrong, Hector always took the blame in chivalrous

145

fashion. "I'm a great big jealous/curious/whatever-else-he-was old Hector", he would say, letting the gals off the hook. In "The Thistles", Hector made Kiki a necklace. Out of thistles. That went down well. In "Hector's Big Tidy", he tried to tidy the girls away. That's the spirit.

Created in France by Georges Croses and aired in that country as *Le Maison de Tou Tou* (for those of you who do not read French, Hector is undoubtedly the English word for *Tou Tou* [see **Barnaby**]). Despite being a bit tame, *Hector's House* held UK audiences by the simple device of being charming. Not as easy as it seems. The **Clangers** had it. **Button Moon** didn't. The first UK run came in the late '60s, but '70s reruns made the show popular.

Hemulens
*See **The Moomins***

The Hemulens represented everything that was tedious in humans. One might be a pedantic anorak with a butterfly collection, another might be a jobsworth park keeper. Yet another might be an incessant talker. Always patronising, and entirely without irony, the Hemulens were either bursting with insensitive bonhomie or bristling with high-handed authority. There was always one about in the Film Polski TV animation—as in life—and he or she unfailingly pissed everyone off. The rest are in the novels by Tove Jansson.

Henry's Cat
BBC TV. A Bob Godfrey Films production. Directed and narrated by Bob Godfrey. Produced by Mike Hayes and Bob Godfrey. UK, 1983

The man who brought you a wobbly green cartoon dog now brought you a wobbly yellow cartoon cat. Who was this man? It was Bob Godfrey, creator of **Roobarb** and **Noah and Nelly**

in **Skylark**, and pioneer of the wobbly cartoon style. Originally brought about by necessity—low budgets forced the use of paper instead of acetate cells and magic markers instead of costly inks—Godfrey returned to the boiling look for effect this time. Henry's Cat appeared with other talking animal friends: Douglas Dog, Denise Duck, Ted Tortoise, Sammy Snail, Pansy Pig and **Chris Rabbit**. The show, scored "mediocre" on this encyclopaedia's patented cult rating system (asking around in the pub) and so appears here chiefly as a nudge toward the mouldbreaking *Roobarb* and the excellent *Noah & Nelly*. Godfrey went on to make sex films, receive a lifetime achievement award and win an OSCAR (see **Roobarb**).

Herbs, The

BBC TV. A FilmFair production. Directed by Ivor Wood. Written by Michael Bond. Puppets by Ivor Wood. UK, 1968

Superlative seasoning-related animation written by Michael Bond—of **Paddington** fame—and produced by FilmFair, the

The Herbs: Parsley the Lion

Ivor Wood-led animation house which brought you The **Wombles** and The **Moomins**, **Simon in the Land of Chalk Drawings** and others.

The action centred around the stately garden of Sir Basil and Lady Rosemary. Sage the owl, though a bit leafy-looking for an owl, was an inhabitant. Constable Knapweed patrolled the grounds, dispensing a unique brand of law and order. Bayleaf the gardener kept the place tidy, as Mr Onion, the Chives (a group of naughty children), Tarragon, **Dill** the Dog and, of course, **Parsley the Lion** caused their mayhem. The pompous, cynical, weary-voiced old lion and the impetuous, egotistical panting dog, forever running around in giddy circles, established themselves over 40 15-minute episodes, as a double act to conjure with. Gordon Rollings provided the narration and the voices: the perfect interpretation of Woods' animation and Bond's deft scripting. If *The Herbs'* laconic tone, dry wit, surreal setting, and animation style all happily recalled the **Magic Roundabout** then it may well be because director Ivor Wood worked with Serge Danot on the earlier show and brought much of its magic to his new project. One of the all-time classics—as was the equally good spin off *Parsley the Lion—The Herbs* is remembered with enthusiasm by early viewers of both generations. The influence of Wood's animation and Bond's writing can clearly be seen in Cosgrove Hall's excellent **Chorlton and the Wheelies**.

Here Comes Mumfie

ITV. An ATV/ITC production. Produced and directed by Mary Turner and John Read. Created by Katherine Tozer. UK, 1975-78

Elephant fun for pre-schoolers. It's not how big it is, it's what you do with it that counts. Whether or not that statement contains the slightest germ of truth, it may have consoled poor Mumfie, who was distinctly under-endowed in the trunk department. It's not that it didn't have the length exactly, but it was thin like a twiglet and permanently erect in over-eagerness for adventure. Meanwhile, his Uncle Samuel E Phant's wizened old protuberance hung low and swayed with the weight and girth of a mature beast. Nasally challenged in such an obvious way, Mumfie over-compensated with his ears, which were enormous and pointy. Adding a further cruel twist of irony was Mumfie's best friend: a scarecrow with a substantial snout. With a hanky in one pocket and Panky the conveniently-named mouse in the other, the scarecrow's main pleasure lay in leading Mumfie astray. In awe of his ably-nosed chum, Mumfie was doomed to don his blue dungarees and rove in search of adventure, ever-watchful for the wicked witch whose mission it was to abduct him and drain his polite manners for her own use. This rather strange series of 10-minute puppet animations for the pre-school audience was based on the books published by Katherine Tozer in the 1930s, and clocked up a distinguished 52 episodes over four series, from 1975 to 1978. For the last year of its run it preceeded the similarly oblique **Cloppa Castle**. The production house with the fat wallet was Lew Grade's ATV which, memorably, brought us **Pipkins**.

Here Come The Double Deckers

ABC. UK tx BBC TV. Produced by Roy Simpson. Dirceted by Harry Booth. Created by Roy Simpson and Harry Booth. USA, 1970

Not an American show, but it was bought and aired by ABC after the British ITV turned it down. When ABC had a hit with it, the BBC bought it and aired it in the UK. What was all the fuss about, then? Not much, really. Melvyn Hayes (who went on to star in *It Aint Half Hot, Mum*) led—as Albert—the cast of precocious brats in this London bus related adventure series. More *Swish of the Curtain* than **Famous Five**, the *Double Deckers* never got too adventurous. No secret passages, smugglers coves or rough, moustachioed men (see **Belle & Sebastian**): just the pointless mitherings of a bunch of kids with a club house (the bus). Tiger (Debbie Russ) was the little gal conjoined to her teddy. The rest were Billie (Gillian Bailey), Brains (Michael Audreson, but see also **Brains**), Doughnut (Douglas Simmonds), Scooper (Peter Firth), Sticks (Bruce Clark) and Brinsley Forde as Spring. *Here Come the . . .* is remembered fondly by some, but this encyclopaedia is of the opinion that any show that would let Clive Dunn on it—even as a guest star—is worthy of suspicion (see **Grandad**).

Hergé's Adventures of Tintin

BBC TV. A BBC1/Tele Hachette production. Produced by Peggy Miller. Created by Georges "Hergé" Remi. UK-France, 1962-64

Tintin, boy reporter, and his dog, Snowy, found themselves caught up in a poor TV adaptation of their excellent comic strip adventures. By the time Peter Hawkins had finished narrating the story so far, there was little time for any action, so both major plot point and minor colour was ignored in favour of the credits. Some very bad cockerney accents for the bungling Interpol boys Thomson and Thompson provided the scant entertainment. A surprising 50 five-minute episodes were made, but all in all it was a wasted opportunity. A popular choice for padding out the summer holidays morning slot, the show had the odd effect of making you pleased to see **Why Don't You**.

Hickory House

ITV. A Granada Production. UK, 1973

Children have fertile and unfettered imaginations. It is one of the jobs of pre-school television to stimulate that sort of imagination. The idea, however, that the very cushion on your sofa might grow a face and start talking to you is not the sort of scenario you wanted to encounter in your own kindergarten reveries. Enter Humphrey. No, not Humphrey, the candy-striped drinking straw with a mind of its own which '70s milk adverts warned might just creep up steal your milk. Rather, **Humphrey Cushion** the upholstery-derived star of *Hickory House*. This rather lame show appears to have been Granada's answer to Thames' **Rainbow** and ATV's dismal **Pipkins**, neither of which were short of identity or rich content, whatever you may think of them. Like those shows, *Hickory* was set in a pretend house—just like the one you live in, children—but with added hazards: if Humphrey Cushion didn't get you, **Dusty** the walking, talking mop would. But the proceedings always seemed slightly forced.

The show—perhaps poignantly—was presented by Alan Rothwell, who came from *Coronation Street*, and Amanda Barrie, who ended up there. Mr Rothwell could also be seen treading the boards on **Picture Box**, although the author would not personally recommend a double bill of *Hickory House* and *Picture Box*, unless you're a glutton for spookiness.

Hillbilly Bears

A Hanna-Barbera production. USA, 1968

A family of bears, were drawn and voiced as caricature country hicks. Hilarious. A tame cartoon filler for The **Banana Splits Adventure Hour**, the show is worth noting for the names of its characters. They were: Paw Rugg (voiced by Henry Corden); Ma Rugg (Jean Vanderpyl); Floral Rugg (Jean Vanderpyl) and Shag Rugg (Don "**Scooby Doo**" Messick).

Honeyman, Mrs
See Camberwick Green

Mrs **Honeyman** was the village busybody. She wore a dress with a skirt down to the floor and appeared to float over the ground, and walked a troup of miniaturized dogs.

————

Hong Kong Phooey
ABC. A Hanna-Barbera Production. Produced by William Hanna, Joseph Barbera, Iwao Takamoto. USA, 1974.

You were watching **Tiswas**, but you knew that **Swap Shop** was about to show *Hong Kong Phooey*. Twitching with excitement, covered in Lego and yellow with Golden Nugget cereal abuse, you would switch back and forth, back and forth, catching horrific glimpses of Cheggers and Noel Edmunds as you went. Then, at last, it came. He was number one super-guy. He was quicker than the human eye. When the going got rough he was super-tough, with a Hong Kong Phooey chop. You waited a lifetime for the show in which he would take on that blob man with the net in the title sequence, a show which never came.

But who was that clumsy Kung Fu canine . . . that mediocre martial arts mutt? Was it—"Ooh. Ooh"—**Sergeant Flint**, long of body, short of leg, shorter of temper? Nope. Was it "Hello, hello?" **Rosemary the telephone operator** with the owl eyes and the bronx accent to cut through glass? Uh-uh. Was it **Penry**, the mild-mannered janitor?

Yes—Penry. It was short for Penrod, that well-known name. Penrod Pooch (voiced with perfect comic timing by Scatman Crowther) was a small, scuffy dog with long, tatty ears. He was also an incompetent police station janitor in a red cap and Chaiman Mao tunic. But what no one knew—except for Spot, his stripy cat and foil—was that the pup doubled up as revered super crime-fighting idiot Hong Kong Phooey, the judo Jack Russell. Into the filing cabinet he would go. And there he would stay, until the yawning Spot gave it a half-hearted nudge. Then— with a Hiiiiii-ya—forth would the Kung Fu king spring. Onto the ironing board, down the laundry chute and into the trash can, from which he emerged in the **Phooeymobile**, a Chinese pagoda on wheels, the engine sound of which was all done by bongos.

Sergeant Flint was not an ambitious man. If you were the only police officer on the force, wouldn't you make yourself a commissioner? He was no good at anything except chastising Penry for his janitorial misdemeanours and watching his favourite TV show, *Super Sergeant*. It is possible he had trouble catching up with ne'erdowells and gangsters because his legs were the same length as his hands. Whatever the reason, Flint (voiced by Joe E Ross of Bilko fame [see also **Botch**]) left the trickiest cases, such as mirror theft and sweet shop hold-ups—to the Tai Chi terrier.

Away that canine crusader would go, panting in pursuit of criminal cretins (and aided by a script rich in Hanna-Barbera alliteration), he would fail to recognise and only aprehend by accident. Cornered, they would cower patiently while their mongrel nemesis took advice from that dubious tome, the *Hong Kong Book of Kung Fu*, flicking through its pages for a move to subdue them. "Hmm. It says to use . . . the Hip Hop . . . Chip Chop, no wait . . . the Right Angle . . . Dingle Dangle." Spot (ably voiced by Don "**Muttley**" Messick) would shake his weary head in resignation as the fumbling fido went into an uncontrollable spin. The cat saved the day as Phooey picked himself up, gazed in disbelief at the bound bandits and barked: "Hey . . . I'm better . . . than I even know . . . myself." Spot slapped his forehead and muttered.

"Oh Penry," Rosemary (Kathi Gori) would shake her head back at the station. "Why can't you be maw like my favourite dream boat Hawng Kawng Phooey?"

But he knew, and you knew. And Spot wished he didn't. "Ya! Hoo! And a rinky dinky doo! To you! Too!"

Hooded Claw
See Penelope Pitstop

Penelope-hating alter ego of **Sylvester Sneekley**. He wore a Homberg hat and a long coat, which matched his long nose. He failed in all his attempts, which made him all the more bitter. It was hard to believe that—despite having no brain at all—Penelope could not discern that the Claw was none other than trusted guardian Sneekley. He made no attempt whatsoever to disguise his grating and distinctive voice, which should really have given him away in an instant.

———————

Houdi Elbow
*See **Tiswas***

Basically Bob Carolgees in his jimjams, escapologist Houdi Elbow (as opposed to Houdi Knee?) appeared in **Tiswas** with a bandaged head and gave his "expert" escapological advice.

———————

How (and How 2)
*ITV. A Southern production. Directed by Anthony Howard. Researchers: Sue Dyer and Lowri Garland. UK 1966. **How 2**: ITV. A TVS/Meridian/Scottish TV production. UK, 1990*

Do a deep, booming native American voice and say: "Howww!" Originally created and fronted by Jack Hargreaves, *How* began its unaccountably long life as a daytime show for pre-school viewers, in 1966. It was made by Southern Television and its broadcast was limited to the southern area. But the programme was successful and *How* muscled its way into the ITV network in a new format with four presenters, wearing a selection of the worst shirts and tanktops known to man (see also **Magpie**). Jack Hargreaves was joined by Fred Dineage, king of sideburns, Jon Miller and someone called Bunty James. Bunty was later replaced by Marian Davies. It might have been a name thing—would *you* trust anyone whose name was really a comic for girls, copies of which were always lying around when it rained and you weren't allowed out to play?

The brief of *How* was simply to explain how stuff worked, in an accessible manner. How does the jam get in the doughnut? That sort of thing. But, given the fact that each programme lasted 25 minutes, the team could often be seen to stretch a point, asking some fantastically contrived questions in order to work in a nifty pub-trick. Sometimes the viewer might be given the answer to a burning question he or she had never formulated in his or her wildest dreams, viz: How can corduroy be turned into an energy-saving irrigation system using only a Kit-Kat wrapper and a catapult? Well, I sent it in, but they never used it. The hows were then explained by good old-fashioned "here-comes-the-tricky-bit . . . whoops" studio demostration (see also **Blue Peter** and **Why Don't You?**).

Retrospective mockery aside—if only briefly—the ratings must have been good, since *How* carried on, undaunted by the challenge of "how" to fill the show, until 1981. At that point Southern Television disappeared into a tiny white dot, never again to reappear. But not even that could put the kibosh on the tenacious programme. A former *How* researcher, Tim Edmunds, had graduated to become a producer at TVS and in 1990 the show rose again, under his stewardship, as *How 2*. This time, veteran presenter Fred Dineage was joined by Carol Vorderman—the thinking man's **Johnny Ball**—and someone calling himself Gareth Jones. Gareth Jones, of course, turned out to be none other than poor old Gaz Top in disguise. Say what you like about Gaz, but I will always be grateful to "Gareth" for demonstrating "how" to get the perforations on two-ply toilet roll to match up. Ta Gaz.

TVS died the death as well—in a freak franchising accident—but *How* soldiered on. It was snapped up by Scottish Television and has not yet been dropped. "How," you might ask, can I come up with a TV format as successful as that and retire to Tunisia? The answer, of course, is that I can't, which is why am still here, writing this book. Next.

Huckleberry Finn, The New Adventures of
A Hanna-Barbera production. USA, 1968

As in all cartoons, for "new" read "worse". This inferior Huck Finn bash, featured live actors chromakeyed onto animated backgrounds. It originally aired as part of the **Banana Splits**, along with all the other cartoons bastardised from old books. Tom Sawyer (Kevin Schultz), Becky Thatcher (Lu Ann Haslam) and Huck (Michael Shea) were unaccountably stuck in a time-warp (see **Valley of the Dinosaurs**), while Injun Joe was plotting their demise. Rum.

Author Mark Twain may well have turned in his grave had he watched episodes such as: All Whirlpools Lead to Atlantis, The Curse of Thut and The Gorgon's Head. A salutory lesson for publishers and agents who sell rights indiscriminately to the highest bidder.

Huge Mobile
See Inch High, Private-Eye

Large car for a small man. Somewhere in there is humour.

Hughes the Gasworks
See Ivor the Engine

He ran the gasworks and hid elephants. Normal stuff for north Wales, if creators Peter Firmin and Oliver Postgate are to be believed.

Humphrey Cushion

See Hickory House

Nasty soft furnishing with mouth and grumpy disposition. Built and operated by the late Barry Smith, this grim puppet appeared with **Dusty**, a talking mop, on **Hickory House**, a pre-school show made by Granada for ITV in 1973.

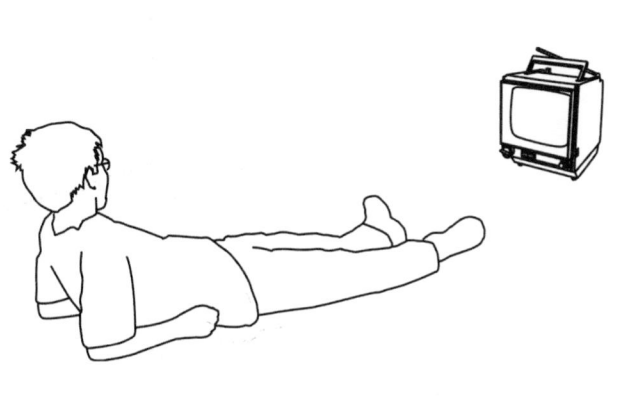

Idris the Dragon
*See **Ivor the Engine***

Pint sized red flame-thrower, fond of steam engines, kilns, bakers' ovens and anything red hot. Welsh.

Inch High, Private Eye
ABC. A Hanna-Barbera production. USA, 1973

If everyone was named after their most noticeable physical characteristic, the world would be a very different place. Most of us can forget our physical shortcomings as long as we don't look in the mirror. But this was not the case for Inch High, "the world's biggest little detective". He was the hero of this 1973 Hanna-Barbera shrinky-dink themed cartoon, and he had a secret fomula. The formula gave him the handy knack of becoming the size of a slug (see also **Arabian Knights, The**). Sadly, the formula was flawed and the midget sleuth would expand without warning in the most inappropriate circumstances. Imagine, kids, being trapped in your own pencil case.

As is normal in these circumstances, our semi-sized Sherlock was aided and abetted by some bungling buffoons. Lousing things up amiably for Inch High was his niece **Lori**, along with her doofus boyfriend, **Gator**, and their dog **Braveheart**, who was like all cartoon dogs, a coward (see also **Scooby Doo, Buford files**). Comedy simply oozes from this set-up, but contain yourselves, for there is more. They had a car: the **Huge Mobile**, in which they sallied forth to fight crime on behalf of the **Finkerton Organization**. According to *The Boxtree Encyclopaedia of TV Detectives*, it was "short on stature, short on entertainment," but in fact, it was no worse than any other Hanna-Barbera offering of the period. Such a review probably owes more to the fact that each episode was thirty minutes long—a luxury for kids, a trial for grown-ups. Thirteen episodes, with names like "Diamonds Are Crooks Best Friend" and "Super Flea", were aired in the US between 1973 and 1974, and UK showings were not far behind. The voicing was mercifully Daws Butler-free, although Hanna-Barbera pet regular Don Messick got a look-in as Braveheart the dog (he also did **Muttley**, **Spot** and **Scooby Doo**). Inch High was voiced by Lenny Weinrib, Kathy Gorias supplied the voice of Lori and Bob Lutell "was" Gator.

———————

Inigo Pipkin
See Pipkins

ATV's pre-school show began with this title, but it was soon shortened to **Pipkins**.

———————

International Rescue
See Thunderbirds

Secret organisation of clandestine samaritans headed by multi-millionaire former astronaut Jeff Tracy.

———————

Issi Noho
ITV. A Thames Television production. Produced by Ruth Boswell. Directed by Stan Woodward. Written by Keith Chatfield. Illustrated by Edward C. Standon.

Gentle stories about Issi Noho the Panda bear, accompanied by static illustrations, also of the gentle kind. He ate bamboo, he lived in a tree. It was all about magic.

Itsby and Bitsy
See Paper Play

They were a pair of hairy spider puppets who dropped down from above to "help" make neat stuff out of bits of paper, which you had no hope of reproducing yourself without tears and at least one cut, plaster and magic Smartie.

Ivor the Engine
A Smallfilms production. Made in black & white and shown by Associated Rediffusion, 1960–68. Written and produced by Oliver Postgate. Pictures by Peter Firmin. Music by Vernon Elliot. Narrated by Oliver Postgate. 40x5-minutecolour episodes remade by Smallfilms and shown by BBC, 1975–77. Credits as above, but narrated by Tony Jackson, Olwen Griffiths and Oliver Postgate. UK

The Merioneth and Llantisilly Rail Traction Company—a little-known railway in the top left-hand corner of wales—ran through Llaniog. Llaniog station was supervised by a character called **Dai Station** (possibly not the name his parents gave him). Under him worked **Jones the Steam**, a mild mannered man in glasses. Under him worked in turn Ivor the Engine and deep inside Ivor was **Idris the Dragon**. Railway antics ensued, in Welsh accents, through the barely disguised **Ffestiniog** valley and the dark wilds of Snowdonia. The landscapes reminded you of the scenes you used to see on tins of coloured pencils—perhaps because that is what they were drawn with. And why not? The pictures were charming, but the real thrill was the sound of Ivor's engine. It consisted of Oliver Postgate, saying: **Pishdy cuf**, pishdy cuf, pishdy cuf, pishdy cuf, pishdy cuf, pishdy cuf, pishdy cuf, pishdy cuf, pishdy cuf, pishdy cuf, pishdy cuf, into a microphone. These things stay with you . . . partly through nostalgia and partly through repeats: the show ran and re-ran for thirty years.

Not content with his own show, Ivor—as he pishdy-cuffed blithely through Grumbly Town and Tan-y-Gwlch—entertained notions of joining the choir, with **Evans the Song**, the choirmaster of the Grumbly and District Choral Society. He could only do three notes—through pipes eventually found for him from Morgan's organ—but that did not deter him from joining in. Timetables had to be altered to accomodate his vocal ambitions. Not that it mattered to the M&L railway: they rarely had any passengers. Other characters meandered through the episodes, such as **Hughes the Gasworks**, who was keeping an elephant under his tarpaulin, and Mrs Griffiths, chair of the Antiquarian Society, who regarded Jones and his fire dragon with buttoned-up bourgeois contempt. Bluebell the Donkey was also a friend—she and Ivor stood motionless and enjoyed each other's company in mute contentment.

That, at least, is one reading of the show. Oliver Postgate—*Ivor's* writer and producer—remembers differently. "I have never been to Ffestiniog. There was no managerial hierarchy apart from Mr Williams the Head Office. The pictures were not drawn with coloured pencils. Mr Hughes did not meander. Mrs Griffiths was not bourgeois, she was posh, and she didn't regard Jones with contempt, she just thought he was a bit mad, until she found out he wasn't." Mr Postgate adds that the correct spelling of pishdy-cuf is pss-t-koff, and that "there are no dark wilds in Snowdonia". Mr Postgate's assertions—undeniably authoritative—highlight the way this show, like so many of the Smallfilms productions, inspired the imagination of its young viewers. That, this encyclopaedia would like to suggest, is what children's television is all about.

Like all the Postgate/Firmin creations, *Ivor the Engine* was imbued with a charm and appeal all its own. Why else should we have fallen for that bleak, forsaken top left-hand corner of Wales? "It wasn't a very long railway or a very important railway, but it was called The Merioneth and Llantisilly Rail Traction Company Limited, and it was all there was." Apart from the Kendal mint cake, doilies, **Fenella** hats and old shortbread, that is. Or is it? "There was no shortbread or Kendal mints," Mr Postgate argues. Having some years ago purchased a particularly delicious Kendal mint cake in Portmadog, shortly before pishdy-cuffing into the highly romantic dark wilds of Snowdonia on the Ffestiniog railway, dreaming fondly of Ivor and Jones the Steam, the author begs to differ.

Jackanory

BBC TV. A BBC production. Executive producer: Anna Home. Produced by Angela Beeching. Directed by various, including Angela Beeching and Paul Stone. UK, 1965-96

"I'll tell you a story about Jackanory. And now my story's begun, I'll tell you another of Jack and his brother. And now my story's done."

So went the rhyme which gave this *Jackanory* its name. The rhyme itself does anything but deliver on its promise; but luckily there was the show. The premise was very simple. Take a good, engaging book or story and just read it to children—much like their parents would if they weren't still at work trying to raise the cash for the TV license. As for the kids: why waste your time reading a book when you can sit gawping at the telly with your face stuffed with Fruit Salad 1/2p chews. Killjoys rasped away in such a style, saying the show allowed children to shirk actual book reading, but they missed the point, as killjoys will, by definition. *Jackanory* was excellent, simple stuff and gave reluctant readers—such as the author of this encyclopaedia—an interest in books.

The story tellers ranged from actors to authors, and from the well known (Bernard Cribbins, Arthur Lowe, Martin Jarvis ...) to the obscure (John Grant and his Littlenose—stories of a decidedly high-pitched Scottish cave-dwelling boy, his family and his dual-eyed pet mammoth, er, Two-Eyes); but each drew the viewer in, as the camera switched seamlessly from studio to illustrations by artists such as Quentin Blake.

There is nothing quite like being read a story. *Jackanory* delivered an intimate and memorable dose of fiction into living rooms the country over, inspiring and stimulating children (and their parents) for a stunning 31 years of more or less continuous broadcast. Any good story was fair game, from Voltaire's *Zadig* (read by Jeremy Brett) in 1976, or Kipling's jungletastic *Just So Stories* (read by Michael Hordern) in 1973, to Penelope Lively's spooky Lyme Regis novel *A Stitch In Time* (read by Geraldine McEwan) in 1977.

A drama spin-off—*Jackanory Playhouse*—adapted a few

stories between 1972 and 1976, including the (in retrospect) ominous **Lizzie Dripping** *And the Orphans* in 1972, written by Helen Cresswell. *Jackanory* proper continued happily and assuredly under the stewardship of executive producer Anna Home (see also **Grange Hill**), until 1996 when reading to children suddenly became old hat. Perhaps there was not enough gunge (see **Tiswas**). Whatever the reason, *Jackanory* has long since been consigned to the archives. Shame.

Jamie and the Magic Torch

ITV. A Cosgrove Hall/Thame Television production. Directed by Keith Scroble and Chris Taylor. Written and narrated by Brian Trueman. UK, 1978

Like many boys, Jamie had a secret under his bed. But in Jamie's case it was not a dissected mouse, a caterpillar in a matchbox or an abandoned sandwich. It was a torch. But not any old torch. It had funny buttons, not found on ordinary torches. When Jamie shone it at the carpet, a hole appeared and, accompanied by his dog **Wordsworth**, he shot down a giant helter skelter into Cuckoo Land.

Cuckoo Land was an *Alice In Wonderland* style alternative world, reminiscent mainly of that bad acid you took in 1971 (I don't mean you personally, I wouldn't dream of suggesting ...). The characters and settings recalled **The Magic Roundabout** and **Noah and Nelly** and predated **Doctor Snuggles** (in terms of eventual transmission dates) and writer Brian Trueman's own **Chorlton & the Wheelies**, all of which were of a type: psychedelic.

Whether it was **Officer Gotcha**, the strangely-truncheoned unicycling policeman; or the elderly, rollerskating **Mr Boo—** who took the Snuggles role, floating about in his submachine; or **Bully Bundy the Show Business Rabbit** ("Is this a lettuce I see before me?"); or Jojo Help, the long-hatted handyman, things took a distinctly surreal turn. The trees were mauve and the grass was yellow. Luckily Jamie was there in his jimjams to fix things up with his torch, before sliding back up the helter

skelter and into his dreams. Actually, weren't they all his dreams? "Settle down now, Jamie" his mum would call from outside the bedroom door. "Come on Wordsworth, out of there." Remembers one viewer: "I wanted a magic torch. It was unbearable to watch someone go down that helter skelter into their own world. Mind you, I thought I'd probably stay there."

Thirty-nine 10-minute films were narrated engagingly by Trueman (**see Danger Mouse** and *Chorlton & the Wheelies*)— very much in the Eric Thompson vein—and broadcast by Thames for ITV, where they grabbed ratings away from FilmFair's **Simon in the Land of Chalk Drawings**.

Jana of the Jungle

BBC TV. A Hanna-Barbera production. UK Tx 1980. USA, 1978

Today's fans of Lara Croft should have no problem remembering Ms Of The Jungle (if that *was* her real name). Sinewy blonde posh girl-turned-Amazon with a range of animal skin bikinis? Thrashing through the underbrush, the sun glinting through shiny beads of sweat on her hot skin? Taking on whole gangs of rough sub-Aztec warriors? Gripping tree trunks with her muscled thighs and subduing giant snakes. How could you forget!

This hormone-heavy jungletastic jape for juveniles was almost certainly no more than an attempt by animators Hanna-Barbera to jump aboard the Tarzan bandwagon—particularly after the success of Filmation's, **Tarzan, Lord of the Jungle**. And what better way to compete than with a bit of all-girl action in the South American rain forest? Jana certainly pulled it off. But was this jungle Jane aimed at girls or boys? Either way she proved—in a cynically-produced-for-money sort of way—that girls could grow up to be Greystoke too, if they wanted, and allowed boys of a more sensitive bent to identify with an all-action star with better nails. The perfect badly-drawn antidote to Tarzan's butch blitherings and indeed to the stereotypical feminity of that other dubious Hanna-Barbera role model, **Penelope Pitstop**.

Jenny

*See **Chorlton and the Wheelies***

She had blonde hair, she had freckles, she had wheels. She also had something of a crush on Chorlton. Not that the vacuous Happiness Dragon would ever have noticed. He seemed to be more preoccupied with **Fenella**. The character was voiced by Joe Lynch.

Jigg

*See **Jigsaw**, below*

Pedantic floating jigsaw piece, irritatingly voiced by John "K9" Leeson.

Jigsaw

BBC TV. A BBC Production. Produced by Clive Doig. Music by Martin Cook and Richard Denton. UK, 1979-81

Work-it-out mystery word show from Clive "**Vision On**" Doig. Clues to each letter were delivered by sketches, mimes and other jiggery-pokery and went together, why, like the pieces of a jigsaw. Studio-based presentation was delivered admirably by **Jigg** the creepy floating jigsaw piece, **Ptery** the creepy floating pteradactyl, Biggum the giant and Dot the invisible dog. They were hampered by useless comedy puppet extras Janet Ellis (see **Blue Peter**) and Adrian Hedley in his "wacky" dungarees. Or was it the other way around? John Leeson—the voice of **Doctor Who**'s K9—was also there providing the voices. The show featured the Prof in the white coat from *Vision On*, who starred as spoof detective Cid Sleuth in "zany" films shot on location in the car park, or some field. *Vision On* mime stalwart Sylvester McCoy and David Rappaport (see **Tiswas**) appeared as the "O Men", whose questionable presence could be avoided by not using words with an "oo" in them. Such as goon or palooka or bufoon. Night terrors were stimulated courtesy of the alarming **Noseybonk**—a kind of Mr Bean (but funnier) in a white frightmask and ill-fitting comedy trousers. Really not bad as improving, educational shows go, but could not hold a candle to **Think of a Number**.

Jim'll Fix It

BBC TV. A BBC production. Produced by Roger Ordish. Directed by Stanley Appel. UK, 1975

Your letter was only the start of it. "Dear Jim'll, please will you fix it for me to appear on a rubbish TV show, love Amy age 8 from Knutsford." Well. Now then, now then. What have we here, what have we here, guys and gals? Here we had a scary old cigar-waggling man in a tracksuit dressed like a New York pimp, seated in a magic chair, making every little girl and boy's most fervent fantasy (appear to) come true (using the "magic" of television). The pensioners' own B.A. Baraccus, former Radio 1 DJ, marathon runner and loony Sir Jimmy Saville OBE might have been too heavily weighted with gold chains, rings and bracelets—or indeed too old—to stand up, but from the comfort of his magic throne—whence came those gleaming badges with the bright red ribbons—he worked miracles with a BBC budget.

Some odd requests came in: please fix it for me to visit a Toby jug factory, for example. What was the world coming to when a child's wildest dream was to observe ceramics? Most were fairly standard kid ambitions: sing-with-Showaddywaddy, go white-water-rafting, go "behind the scenes" of **Swap Shop**. The author's own request ("please fix it for me to live comfortably from a private income and sit in a room grumbling") was sent, but sadly never fulfilled. The BFI catalogue reveals some stunning episodes. What horribly misguided childish fix-it, for example, could have been behind the cryptic 1978 entry "Arthur Negus"? A fantasy more readily imaginable might have spawned 1980's "Legs & Co" entry, and readers who are also parents may recognise the heartfelt desire which gave rise to

1979's "Boy made invisible" episode. The odd viewer got to play football with assorted mullet-headed heroes, but a lot of fix-its ended in chromakeyed disappointment for the hopeful kids, as they stood before a blue screen in the studio and had their fantasy pasted on afterwards.

Jim'll—not his proper name—chose the request, showing the actual hand-written letter on camera, while he, himself, read it out in a guileless monotone, where every word had equal emphasis (scrapingly familiar to those who had heard their own children trying to read aloud, or had ever heard a dalek speak). Viewers were then treated to a gruelling film of said child, numb with shyness, attempting to lip-sync to Depeche Mode's "Get The Balance Right" or bungee jump off the Forth road bridge, supervised by kind grown-ups on their best behaviour. Then it was back to the studio in their best blouses for the overly formal presentation of the Jim'll Fix It badge, the atsmosphere tense with Saville's stilted and wooden delivery (delicious, awkward silences, the like of which live on even today in episodes of *Countdown*). He grilled the kids with moronic questions: "Now then, did you really jump out of that aeroplane?" He grilled the grown ups too: "Did this young man behave himself in your aerodrome, Mr Red Arrows squadron leader, Sir?" "Absolutely, Jim." "Good. Now then, now then will you please present this very special Jim'll Fix It Badge ..." etc *ad nauseum* until axed.

Joe

BBC TV. A Q3 London production. Illustrated by Joan Hickson. Stories by Alison Prince, told by Colin Jeavons. Music by Laurie Steele. UK, 1970

"Shhh," said Joe's mother. Seventies pre-school series, engagingly illustrated by Joan Hickson with lots of ink-penned swirls, painted over in washes of burnt umber and deep orange. Joe was a little boy. And that was pretty much that. He had a helmet haircut, a pair of dungarees, a resigned expression, and a range of t-shirts. He also had a duffel coat, which was constantly being put on him.

Joe followed the fairly average life of a little boy, looking out on a big world, full of adults who didn't listen properly. A new baby? What's that all about then? Moving house? Why's that then? Are we nearly there yet? Full of long car journeys in the blue VW Beetle, questions with confusing answers, impatient adults and kid's-eye views, *Joe* was adept at conveying the semi-mute powerlessness of the pre-school years. In that—and through the reassuring tones of narrator Colin Jeavons (see also **Barnaby**)—it spoke directly to its viewers, with especial poignancy in episodes such as "Joe And The Goulash". There were gentle jokes for the adults too, ensuring they stayed put for its "Watch With Mother" slot. It was made by Q3 London, the production company which also brought you **Fingerbobs** and **Crystal Tipps and Alistair**. Retro fans will appreciate the quintessentially '70s illustrations and groovy period music by Laurie Steele, although the show scores nil for pioneering animation genius: the illustrations might have been still but the camera wasn't. Wobbly fun not withstanding, *Joe* was subtle, gentle and charming. Its like is gone. "'There's my mum with Uncle Eric,' said Natasha." Ah, the lost innocence of childhood.

Joe 90

UK tx: ITV, 1968. A Century 21 production in association with ATV for ITC World-Wide. Created by Gerry and Sylvia Anderson. Executive producer Reg Hill. Produced by David Lane. Directed by Desmond Saunders, Alan Perry, Leo Eaton, Ken Turner, Peter Anderson. Written by Gerry and Sylvia Anderson, Shane Rimmer, Tony Barwick, David Lane, Pat Dunlop, Donald James, John Lucarotti, Keith Wilson, and Desmond Saunders. Music by Barry Gray. USA, 1968

Victory at last for the four-eyed. Joe (voiced by Len Jones) was just a nine-year-old marionette—until BIG RAT (Brain Impulse Galvanoscope Record and Transfer) swapped his brain information and turned him into an invincible super boffin secret agent with glasses. BIG RAT was the invention of Joe's guardian Mac McLaine (Rupert Davies). But when Mac showed BIG RAT to the World Intelligence Network, they suggested he use his helpless orphan ward Joe as a guinea pig. The specs—thick-framed and chunky—were special BIG RAT specs for transfer-ring brain stuff from other people. It was a style used later by Morrissey. Joe, now as special agent Joe 90, kept his electric glasses in his school bag, along with a pistol. He was despatched to save the world from despots and free-thinkers.

The sixth of Gerry and Sylvia Anderson's Supermarionation series (see also **Thunderbirds** and **Stingray**), *Joe 90* was a top watch for small boys, who instantly ran off to pack their own school bags with glasses, their secret agent badge (made from Cornflakes packet cardboard and felt-tips) and the all-impor-tant loaded weapon, a spud gun.

———

John Craven's Newsround
BBC. A BBC production. UK, 1972–82

Although a show called *Newsround* is still broadcast, the origi-nal Craven-branded product is most remembered by retro fans. It was a scaled-down version of the day's news, with simplified, digestible stories, suitable for a child audience—although it was equally appreciated by adults who didn't really know what was going on. The show also delivered a neat précis of the back-ground to any given story: Rhodesia, Middle East, Northern Ireland. Mr Craven appeared, serious-faced and avuncular in a series of alarming shirts and jumpers (see also **Magpie**), before a backdrop revealing the day of the week: wednesdaywednes-daywednesdaywednesday. Space correspondent Reg Turnbull was always on hand to explain the minutiae of NASA's latest exciting extra-terrestrial project, which dates the show better than any shirt. Mr Craven's appearance as a presenter on light entertainment travesty **Multi-Coloured Swap Shop** might have softened his image for myriad mums, but ate his credibility in the eyes of young news lovers.

"And finally," a bit of soft news to sweeten the dose. Timmy the lost tortoise found hiberbating in old man's hair; woman lives to 300 by eating shed; good night. **Xylophone hammering** at the beginning told you *Newsround* meant business. Viewers were warned the show was about to go down the pan when it ran a news "feature" of the new composer making up the new blippy bloppy theme tune on an old analogue synthesizer. Mr Craven was replaced by Richard Whitmore, Roger Finn, Helen Rollason and a succesion of pretty young boys, who must have been off sick for the autocue skills seminar.

————————

Jones the Steam
See Ivor the Engine

Softly-spoken John Denver lookalike, who drove Ivor and chucked coals into his furnace, where **Idris the Dragon** ignited them with his breath. Tolerated Ivor's desire to sing with admirable stoicism.

————————

Josie and the Pussycats
CBS. A Hanna-Barbera production. USA, 1970-72

"Cool it, Alexandra. There's probably an electronic device or electric eye, controlling a secret entrance." Yes, probably. If only all the world were like Hanna-Barbera. If it were, then all good men would have 70-inch chests, all evil men would be physically repulsive—and easily distinguished by their bloodcurdling laughs—and all women, good and bad, would run about with their arms straight out in front of them, wearing nothing but baby-doll nighties. It might not be a better world, but at least it would be easier to predict.

Meet Josie (voiced by Janet Waldo), flame-haired beauty on guitar and vocals; Valerie (Barbara Parriot), dark-skinned intellectual sophisticate (tambourines); and the inappropriately-named Melody (Jackie Joseph), a stereotypically vacuous blonde, whose tongue, when not stating the obvious, was usually sticking out (drums). Nominally a band—although any fool could have told them that guitar and tambourine does not a band make, unless you are born-again Christians, in which case the lyrics carry it anyway—Josie's Pussycats travelled the world "doing" gigs, with their idiot manager Alex, a grinning hipster doofus who was little more than **Shaggy** in disguise. He was even voiced by the same "artist": DJ Casey "Zoinks" Casem.

Josie never travelled without her impressively-torsoed blond chunk of a boyfriend **Alan** and, for some dark reason best not explored, Alex never travelled without his badger-haired sister Alexandra. Alexandra was riven with jealous hatred of Josie. She was envious of her looks and she was envious of her band-leader status, thinking she could do better if the band were named after her. But most of all—seeing as how all she had for company was a demonic cat called Sebastian (see **Belle and Sebastian**)—she wanted Alan. Constantly contriving to be alone with the man, she would jump into his lap at the slightest opportunity. If Alan was completely oblivious to her efforts and her charms it was probably more from stupidity than from decency. One disturbing factor of this set-up was that the so-called "Alan" was clearly **Freddy** from **Scooby Doo**, in exactly the same clothes. He was even still bossing everyone about, with his "plans". Where does **Daphne** think he is now? you found yourself asking. Did he tell her he was staying with his uncle? And did he never put that smock and neckerchief in the wash? Grisly.

Even more grisly was the band's costume. Tiger ears and hot pants with tiger tails. Not even vaguely demeaning. No wonder Alex was always grinning. Perhaps he should have taken his eyes off the talent and gotten some decent personnel. The author is no expert but surely the way to get the best out of a tambourine is not to bash it against another one. That's just wasteful.

You might think all of this would be enough to fill out 22 minutes of badly-drawn time-wasting, but no. There were mysteries to solve—104 of them. These followed the usual format: the ugly man you meet at the beginning, gurgling with satanic laughter and brandishing an axe, turns out to be the bad guy after all. It is his sole aim to mercilessly control all plant-life (yes, an actual plot-line)—how can there be such unmitigated evil in the world? Shame those meddling pussycats had to get in the way. Cue running about with arms straight out. But since the mystery plots were lamer than the lamest *Scooby Doo* episode, thrill-seekers revisiting this '70s piece would do better to focus their attentions on the swirly pseudo-psychedelic backgrounds and incedental music which had been given a hefty, if calculated, dose of da phunk, coutesy of Hoyt S. Curtin (see **Battle of the Planets**).

Josie and the Pussycats was a pretty limp offering from Hanna-Barbera, not in the same class as The **Hair Bear Bunch**, or even **Jana of the Jungle**. Watching again such gruelling episodes such as "The Swap Plot Flop", in which Valerie, an African American, is obliged to pose as a kidnapped Arab princess because they are "almost twins", the author has been struck dumb with the senseless banality of it all. There is, for some, kitsch appeal in this kind of thing, but even knowing sniggering won't hold the viewer for a prolonged visit, unless the viewer is one of those people who pays to be stepped on by women in stilettoes. The reason this cheesy old chestnut warrants such a big entry is that, sadly, a Deborah Kaplan-directed film version—*à la* **Flintstones**—is scheduled to hit our movie theatres, via Universal, thrusting this dated trash into the mainstream limelight. The girls' singing voices were provided by Cathy Douglas, Cheryl Ladd (going under the name of Moore) and Patricia Holloway.

Just William

ITV. An LWT production. Executive Producer: Stella Richman. Produced by John Davies. Written by Keith Dewhurst. Based on the characters created by Richmal Crompton. UK, 1977

Sunday teatime was the wrong slot for this TV emetic. A child Bonnie Langford as the histrionic Violet Elizabeth promised: "I'll scweam and scweam and scweam until I'm sick." No such televisual amusement was delivered forth. She merely acted and acted and acted until *you* were. Adrian Dannatt played William Brown, the standard-issue schoolboy tyke who led a band of **Famous Five**-style well-spoken tearaways, The

Outlaws. Also featured the comely Diana Dors as Violet Elizabeth's mother, Mrs Bott. All in all enough to put you off your sarnies and cake. If the TV show was a little hard to swallow, it was probably not the fault of the production team and actors; it was a fair and faithful adaptation of the idiots in the books. A total of 26 30-minute traumas were aired, along with an hour-long extravaganza. There were other versions, before and after, but this is the one you remember, thanks to Bonnie.

K

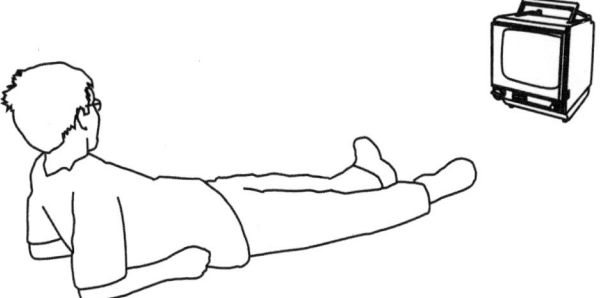

Keith Harris and Orville

Step away from the book. If this is your idea of a cult, you are clearly a menace to society. So step *away* from the book, and no one will get hurt.

———

Kids From Degrassi Street, The
CBC. Canada, 1979–85

Learn to pronounce about, "a-boat". *The Kids . . .* was a Canadian soap for children in the *Neighbours* vein, although it predated the Australian canon and more likely provided the inspiration for such programmes. The Degrassi Street kids learned hard, valuable and schmaltzy lessons a-boat life, love and studying at elementary school in a Toronto "neighbourhood". They talked to each other openly a-boat their emotions, while a nation of UK kids watched **Grange Hill** instead. The show was actually filmed on the streets of Degrassi Street and Queen Street in Toronto, Ontario, giving it a parochial realism only matched by The **Littlest Hobo**. A hefty 26 episodes were made, before the kids got too old. Spin offs at junior high etc, followed as did a higher snog quotient, the inevitable teenage pregnancy and AIDS. Those who credit the show with the quality of "gritty realism" should perhaps re-read the theme song: "Wake up in the morning, feeling shy and lonely / Gee, I gotta go to this school / I don't think I can make it, don't think I can take it / I wonder what I'm gonna do / But when I look around and see / That someone is smiling right at me / Wait, someone talkin' to me / Hey, I got a new friend". Life was harsh in Toronto. Nevertheless the format has stuck around, notably in the form of *Heartbreak High*, where all the "kids" are at least 25 and pay the rent on their converted lofts by working nights at the bar. That's the life.

Degrassi Junior High

King Rollo

BBC TV. A BBC/King Rollo Films production. Written by David McKee.Animated by Leo Belltoft. UK, 1985

Married to Queen Gwen, the pretty redhead girl from the palace next door, Rollo ruled with childlike whimsy, despite his square beard. Aided by a droopy nosed magician in a stripy tunic, by Hamlet (bit of a dark reference, that, for pre-schoolers) the dancing cat and by his cook, a sturdy blonde woman, Rollo attempted to grow up on television. The king began his life in the books by David "**Mr Benn**" McKee, and enjoyed a stint as a comic strip in *Buttons* magazine, before coming to animated life. King Rollo films made 13 episodes of this animated short for the BBC, while Ray Brooks provided the narration. *King Rollo* had all the charm of *Mr Benn*, thanks to McKee's inspired illustrations, but perhaps lacked something of the earlier show's imagination.

Kizzy

BBC TV. A BBC Birmingham production. Produced by Dorothea Brooking. Directed by David Tilley. Script by John Tulley. Adapted from the novel The Diddakoi, by Rumer Godden. Music by Peter Gosling. UK, 1976

Fun with Romany prejudice as Kizzy, a young gypsy girl, ventured forth from her gran's caravan and tried to mingle with the hoi polloi at a new school. Predictably, protracted bullying followed, as her odd habits were mocked and ridiculed by Prudence, an upper-class nit without the brains she was born with. A blood-filled fight dénouement lead to a new understanding, when Prudence realised it probably wasn't okay to actually kill someone, just because you don't know where they're coming from. For an extension on the bullying theme, try **Lizzy Dripping**, or **Grange Hill**. For social tolerance and understanding, avoid **Diff'rent Strokes**. Verdict: worthy but depressing.

Knut
See Noggin the Nog

Small son of Noggin, King of the Nogs. Destined to grow up with a chip on his shoulder, no doubt.

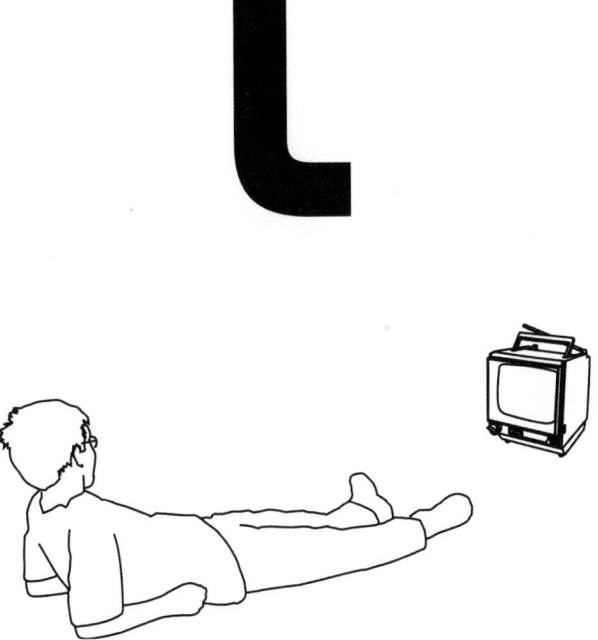

Lady Penelope
*See **Thunderbirds***

She was supposed to be an aristocratic English lady but was actually a stiff marionette with (often) visible strings, permanently fagging it with a long cigarette holder. Wore headscarves and reminded you of Joanna Lumley. More hinterestin' was her clapped-out driver **Parker**, who always looked as if he'd had one too many to be on the road. Chic sophisticate Lady Penelope is not to be confused with the turbo-charged sophisticate **Penelope Pitstop**.

Larry the Lamb
ITV. A Thames production. UK, 1972-74

Wobbly-voiced puppet animation, featuring chunky square lamb and chums, living in **Toytown**. Larry was permanently falling foul of the law, the mayor in particular. Why didn't they just eat him? Over-long, horribly voiced, and rather too fixated on local politics, *Larry the Lamb* was something of an ordeal. Thames, happily, was to learn from this and go on to produce some of our best loved shows (see **Chorlton & the Wheelies, Jamie & the Magic Torch** and **Rainbow**).

Lavender Sheep
*See **Doctor Snuggles***

All you need to know is in the name. They were looked after by **Woogie The Freckled Camel**. They sang lullabies

Lazy Luke
*See **Wacky Races***

Verandah-dwelling dungareed driver of the **Arkansas Chugabug**, along with **Blubber Bear**, a large mammal with claws. A bear, in fact. Both characters were voiced by John Stephenson.

Let's Pretend
ITV. A Central production. Produced by Michael Jeans. UK, 1982

Infinitely less sophisticated (and cheaper-looking) than its predecessor, **Pipkins**, *Let's Pretend* was a prop-led make-believe show for pre-school age children. Ooh, look—a mop. Let's pretend it's a horse. Here's a story about a horse. Now let's act it out. That sort of thing. Not bad but, frankly, rather tame compared to the full-on manky puppet lunacy of *Pipkins*.

In 1982, when ATV morphed into Central Independent Television Plc (see also **Tiswas**), *Pipkins*—which ATV had produced at its Elstree studios—was axed and the studio sold. Even though *Let's Pretend* was developed by *Pipkins* creator Michael Jeans, something about it suggested his heart might not have been in it. Not awful by any means and often engaging, it simply had a hard act to follow. *Let's Pretend,* then: a pared-down **Play School** but a lunchtime godsend to students and truants (see **Stepping Stones**).

Li'l Gruesome
*See **Wacky Races***

Big Gruesome's smaller half behind the wheel of the ghoulish **Creepy Coup**. Together they were the **Gruesome Twosome**. The character was voiced by Don Messick.

Lippy the Lion (And Hardy Har-Har)

NBC. A Hanna-Barbera production. USA, 1962

The concept was common enough . . . take two savannah-dwelling animals, in this case a lion and a laughing hyena, and make them con-artists. It happens all the time. Lippy, as his name might suggest, had the gift of the gab. Or thought he had. His sidekick, **Hardy Har-Har**, was a confirmed pessimist. Lippy would come up with a scam. Hardy would predict that the plan would bring doom. Doom would arrive on cue and Hardy would laugh in grim satisfaction:"We're falling into the snake pit—a-har, a-har-har."

The two creatures went together like chalk and cheese. Chalk and cheese, though, might have made a more convincing double act. Otherwise it was the usual Hanna-Barbera schtick with, by now *de rigueur*, voice work by Daws Butler for Lippy (see also **Snagglepuss**, **Wally Gator**, etc) and, er, Daws Butler for Hardy. Mel Blanc also provided back-up voice on Hardy. Talented and in-demand voice artists they may have been, but why were they always shouting?

First aired in 1962, this animated short surfaced as part of the *Hanna-Barbera New Cartoon Show*, and UK showings had fizzled out by about 1976. The piece was shown in the UK on its own or doubled with other H-B fare such as **Wally Gator**; although in that scenario, a full ten minutes of unabridged Daws Butler voice "work" might prove more than even the average child—with its robust capacity to endure, and indeed create, noise pollution—could stand.

Little My

*See **Moomins, The***

Basically a goblin, My (short for Mymble, whose daughter she was and to which species she belonged) was very tiny, and given to disparaging comments and provocative gestures. She was fiercely independent, enjoyed her own company, mocked everyone, especially the sensitive **Moomintroll**, and wore her orange hair in an enormous bun. Her role was to provide caustic commentary on the buffoonery of her friends. For some reason, she had quite a few.

Littlest Hobo, The

CTV. Glen-Warren productions. Series producer: Simon Christopher Dew. Song by Terry Bush. Lyrics by John Crossen. Littlest Hobo created by Dorrell McGowan. Canada, 1979-85

"There's a voice, keeps on calling me . . ." Special guest star: Patrick Macnee.

The Littlest Hobo (London the dog—actually several dogs) was a slightly soiled Alsatian stray who made a habit of befriending hick town Canadians in imminent moral peril and saving them. The doomed ones would generally try to get rid of him, using local vernacular: "git gawn mutt". But the know-how bow-wow was not to be shoo-shooed—at least not yet.

Using only highly refined dog powers and a good set of gnashers, the hobo hound would prove its worth, outsmarting villains, hoods and bamboozlers galore, and delivering a neat moral message (viz: do not kill daughter for money/do not steal from own dying mother), causing the now undoomed to repent and try to adopt him as some form of pet. "Hey, li'l buddy. I'll call you Smoke/Einstein/Scout/Mr.Magic/Lucky/Shadow/Buddy/Slapshot/Roamer/Crusoe/Ulysses/Hercules/Sinbad/Gulliver."

But—whoosh—was that freight train fido ever outta there, leaving his new "friend" standing on the sidewalk, scratching his head and looking first one way, then the other, a-wondering where his goddam dawg had done gawn. Hazy light and singular colour representation—oddly reminiscent of suburban summer camcorder footage—coupled with a sub-Waylon Jennings theme song (sung by Terry Bush) gave this show a down-home—some might say home-made—predictability that could not be matched by *Lassie*, of which it seemed to be a cheesy pastiche. But was it?

The Littlest Hobo was originated by one Dorrell McGowan

for the eponymous 1958 Allied Artists (black and white) film, directed by Charles Rondeau. The BFI library synopsis reads: "Dog rescues boy's pet lamb from slaughterhouse". Some readers may think that plot a little thin to spread over the duration of an entire feature, but people took notice. Canadian producers Storer Programs Inc thought the dog had legs, and ran with it. A black and white series aired from 1963 to 1965, delighting British Columbian audiences with its caring canine capers. Syndication took it further afield in the USA and Canada, where it became a fixture until 1979, when Canada's CTV network remade the show—to the tune of 114 episodes—on colour videotape for a prime-time slot. The show was, again, syndicated, bringing it crooning and barking to UK screens. Patrick Macnee did indeed appear, as a magician, as did a then unknown Mike Myers (as a paraplegic frisbee thrower's friend). The show was indeed shot in the summer in the suburbs on a camcorder, in the Toronto area.

But what gave the dog its special powers? A two-part episode called "The Genesis Tapes" suggested that our hairy hero was the first of a new breed of telepathic "Meta-canine" (see also **Tomorrow People, The**). The idea, however, was not pursued. Maybe tomorrow …

———

Lizzy Dripping

BBC TV. A BBC production. Produced by Angela Beeching. Directed by Paul Stone. Novels by Helen Cresswell. UK, 1972–75

Lizzy Dripping, Lizzy Dripping, don't look now, your skirt is slipping. What did that mean? In this lame and nebulous fashion the berated, be-anoraked Lizzy Dripping was taunted by school hoodlums, causing her to consult with a witch and have them all cursed. This bully-phobic boreathon was brought to you by **Jackanory** stalwarts Angela Beeching and Paul Stone, who should have known better. Hapless Lizzy was played by the girl who was to become pregnant **Blue Peter** presenter Tina Heath. The "witch"—clearly a hallucinatory manifestation of Lizzy's entirely understandable persecution complex (also clearly a man)—shot up from behind clumpy bushes on Lizzy's way home from school, when she was alone and her troubled mind was wandering. This device was a cruel touch: after all, what child doesn't pass a hedge or two on the way home from school? Despite the appealing self-indulgence of the witch-fulfilment fantasy, you cannot help but feel that Lizzy—as a role model for unfashionably-coated children—would have done better to stand up to those creepy classroom cowards. Tsk.

In one form or another, Ms Dripping spent more time than was strictly necessary gracing our screens: in her own series, as a *Jackanory* story and as a *Jackanory Playhouse* drama. And just when you thought she had gone, up she popped once more in the series *Lizzy Dripping Again*, whose title had a touch of the inevitable about it. The character and stories were based on the novels by Helen Cresswell.

Lord Belbrough
See Chigley

Monied landowner and guardian of **Bessie**. Like all monied landowners, Lord Belborough was loved, respected and valued by the workers at the local factory, who were forced, at the blowing of a whistle, to waltz in formation to the tooting sound of his restored barrel organ.

Lori
See Inch High, Private-Eye

Normal-sized niece of abnormally-sized cartoon sleuth. Also, girlfriend to **Gator**.

Ludwig

BBC 1. Created by Mirek and Peter Lang. Storylines by Jane Tann and Susan Kodicek. Narrated by Jon Glover. Musical arrangements by Paul Reade. Music by Ludwig Van Beethoven.

There was something strange going on in the woods. A giant egg was playing Beethoven violin concertos and traumatising the birds. Mechanical arms came out of holes in its body and performed bizarre acts. Animals got into scrapes and the egg's auto-helicopter mode would save the day. No one knew what it was and no one knew where it came from. But every move was being spied on by a mysterious man in a deerstalker with a pair of binoculars permanently attached to his face. A sinister 25 5-minute animated films were made by Mirek and Peter Lang and aired on BBC 1 in the post **Blue Peter** slot. Creepy. European. Gone.

M

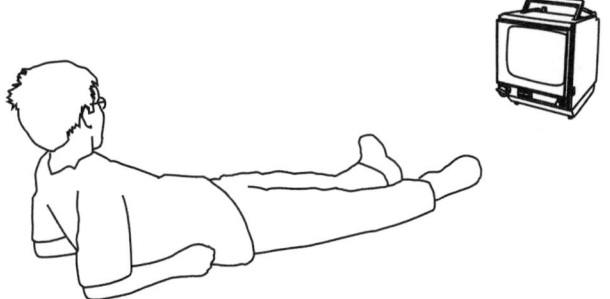

Madabout

ITV. A Tyne Tees production. Executive producer: Crispin Evans. Produced by Diane Campbell. Directed by Barry Crozier. UK, 1981

Unremarkable series on people and their hobbies, revealing far too much about the dark underbelly of the collecting instinct. Weak lemon drink not pictured (budget constraints probably). It was originally presented by the well-meaning Michael Bentine (see **Potty Time**) and Matthew Kelly, before *Stars In Their Eyes* made him a star in the nation's eyes, although the episodes which immediately preceded its axeing were presented by hairy DJ Dave Lee Travis (DLT) and, strangely, fashion designer Zandra Rhodes.

———————

Madame Dumpitoo
*See **Doctor Snuggles***

Pipe-smoking woman. She had a greyhound called Lord Louis.

———————

Madeleine
*See **Bagpuss***

A rag doll, who sat in a chair and was a dab hand at all sewing and knitting activities. She generally fixed up Emily's new toy a treat.

———————

Magic Roundabout, The
BBC 1. Created and directed by Serge Danot. English scripts and narration by Eric Thompson. UK tx 1965. France, 1963

"'Crazy,' said **Dylan**, yawning." A theory circulated in webrings and internet chat rooms that *The Magic Roundabout* was actually a complex satire of French politics—and that **Dougal** was plainly De Gaulle—would appear to be niftily scotched by the revelation that, in the original French version of the series, Dougal was called Pollux and spoke with an English accent. Other theories, circulated around student common rooms, that each character represented a different drug, probably represented no more than youthful wish fulfilment. Students do theorize, especially when they are taking drugs. But the point is that the theories are indeed put about. Created in 1963 by French animator Serge Danot, *The Magic Roundabout* (*Le Manège Enchanté*) has become a byword for cult television. When—as in the case of **Captain Pugwash**—a 5-minute animated film for children becomes the subject of adult urban myths, it can be deemed to have been a success.

Just to recap, the roundabout in question was stationed in the psychedelic garden of one Mr Rusty. The garden bore the colours of the French flag—blue, white and red—and was the domain of several preternatural characters. Florence was the wide-headed little girl with enormous sneakers. Dougal—who looked like a mobile Shredded Wheat—was actually a kind of ill-bred and churlish dog. He was hooked on sugar lumps and actually mined them out of the ground. He had a very wide nose. Dylan, the blissed-out bunny, was usually to be found strumming his guitar. Presumably he kept the garden free of the weed. "I'm a rabbit who sleeps . . . I'm not the hopping kind." Zipping in and out were Brian the Snail and **Ermintrude**, an old cow, permanently chewing on a flower. Cycling by on his tricycle was old and bearded (see **Fingerbobs**) Mr MacHenry the gardener, himself partial to a flower or two. And of course there was **Zebedee**. Zebedee was half-tomato, half-industrial spring and had an impressive handlebar moustache. He sprung down from the sky at the end of the show and said: "Time for bed".

The show went out around 5.30 on BBC1 in the pre-evening news slot. This guaranteed it a viewing figure of around eight million, half of which was made up of adults (believe it or not, in those days some adults got home before 5.30). With lines like "'I feel like lighting up,' said the star," it is easy to see how, as adults, we have been seduced into believing the whole thing was about drugs. But how much of our mythologising truly belongs to Danot's show? Arch FilmFair animator Ivor Wood certainly had an input into the show. He worked on it with Danot in Paris, before returning to England and launching his own company. The line from *The Magic Roundabout* to FilmFair's **The Herbs** is a fairly easy one to draw.

But more important to the UK perception of Danot's films are the English scripts, written by the late Eric Thompson. Thompson ignored the French scripts and created his own unique world out of Danot's animations. Only then does Pollux become Dougal, and only then does he take on the boorish persona we know and love. As for Dylan, Danot christened his rabbit Flappy and, far from the tripped out hippy Bob Dylan caricature we know, Flappy was a lazy Spaniard. Thompson— father to the actress Emma—wrote *The Magic Roundabout* from an old cottage in Argyll, and imbued Danot's creation with a subtlety and sophistication it had not known before. The jokes, the clipped repartee, the dry narration: these were all Thompson's additions and the show was better for them. Channel 4 aired a new series of previously unbroadcast French episodes in 1992. By that time Thompson had died, so Nigel Planer, who played Neil the hippy in *The Young Ones* took over scripting and narration duties. Bloomsbury published Eric Thompson's scripts in 1998.

Magpie
ITV. A Thames production. UK, 1968-80

One for sorrow, two for joy, three for a girl and four for a boy, five for . . . er . . . Basically a **Blue Peter** bandwagon magazine show, *Magpie*—presented by Tony "living sideburns" Bastable, Peter Brady, Susan Stranks (see **Paperplay**), Jenny Hanley, Mick Robertson and Dougie Rae, although not all at the same time— lasted a fairly respectable 12 series, plumbing the depths of the Thames wardrobe for killer-collars and tanktops. Items included

"miltary uniforms and their past" and "how television works": both gripping in their way. Not a patch on Blue Peter's 43 years, though. *Magpie* was produced by the estimable Thames Television, which brought you the far more noteworthy **Rainbow** and **Chorlton & the Wheelies**.

Marina
See Stingray

Naughtical but nice mermaid daughter of Aphony, ruler of the peaceful world of Pacifica, which was in turn beset by the warring world of Titan. She was mute, and harboured a love for the sturdy-jawed **Troy Tempest**, which dared not speak its name. Well, not so much *dared not*, as *could not*. Not to be confused with **Neptina**.

Marine Boy
BBC TV. A Japan Tele Cartoons/Seven Arts International production. UK, 1969

Unusually for a Japanese *anime* show, *Marine Boy* premiered on BBC TV. The corporation's willingness to showcase the cartoon may have had something to do with its right-on ecological stance—also unusual for *anime* (see **Battle of the Planets**). Like many shows of its kind, *Marine Boy* raised as yet unsolved child labour issues. Marine Boy himself—small of stature, wide of eye—was the offspring of one Professor Mariner, benevolent boss of Ocean Patrol, and appeared to be in continuous employment at the age of nine. The patrol's mission was to keep the seas trouble- and pollution-free , and its chief foes were not aliens of the **Titan Terror Fish** variety (see **Stingray**), but—look out—Man himself. That said, there was the occasional sea monster to subdue as our boy patrolled the depths in his vessel, P1, with crew members Piper and Bolton.

One excellent feature of the show was the device by which

Marine Boy was able to breathe plausibly under water: Oxy-gum, invented by the improbably-nosed **Professor Fumble**.Thrillingly, the gum device gave cause for many action close-up shots of Marine boy chomping furiously. Fantastic. It was the dramatic equivalent of Superman delaying his pursuit of villains while he put on his cape and pants.Also, the effects of the gum wore off after a bit, adding in a vital time constraint. If ever that happened (and it always did) Marine Boy could up the ante via use of his propellor shoes (take a bow again, Professor Fumble).The show's superfluous cutesy element was provided by **Splasher** the dolphin, in association with **Cli Cli**, a useless but well meaning child.The bit of tail was provided by **Neptina**, the mermaid.

————

Marmalade Atkins

See Educating Marmalade

————

Mary Mungo and Midge

BBC TV. A John Ryan Production. Pictures and movement by John Ryan Studios. Stories by Daphne Jones. Filmed by Bob Bura and John Hardwick. Narration and voices by Richard Baker, with Isabel Ryan. UK, 1971

"Do you live in a town?" **Captain Pugwash** creator John Ryan produced this animated series which told the stories of a little girl, Mary, her pompous old dog Mungo (a little on the **Hector**ish side) and an irritating little flute-playing mouse called Midge. Pleasingly urban after the idyllic village life of the **Camberwick Green** trilogy, *Mary . . .* was based in a busy town "full of buildings, some tall, some short, some wide, some narrow". Mary herself lived in a flat on the top floor of a high rise block. She lived in the flat with the flowers in the window box. She was careful to shut the door and press the right button in the lift when going out with Mungo. Midge was supposed to stay at home, but usually tagged along and made an ass of himself. Mary had a large sunny room to play in and always had something to do. The show followed her exeats into the outside world, full of (uniquely creepy) people and busy streets.

The show was adept at portraying the detail of urban life, even if it was a little slow moving. This aspect may have had something to do with Ryan's animation technique. Developed for *Captain Pugwash*, his method involved a highly sophisticated system of arms and levers which worked flat elements on a flat background. The scenes were shot in real time by *Camberwick Green* animators Bob Bura and John Hardwick as Ryan and his team wiggled the levers. Eyes moved. Hands moved. Less eerie than *Pugwash*, but still a little disconcerting, Mary Mungo and Midge was helped by the dreamy seventies music of Johnny Pearson, which was nostalgic even in 1971. The stories were narrated in BBC English by Richard Baker, while Mary was voiced by Isabel Ryan.

Master Bates
See Captain Pugwash

Mathilda Junkbottom
See Doctor Snuggles

Basically a slave, Mathilda was a poorly constructed robot girl with pigtails. Her creator Jeffrey O'Kelly, who designed her for his show **Dr Snuggles**, claims her role was to perform "various useful and enigmatic roles". She was made out of tin cans.

Mean Machine
See Wacky Races

Pointy-nosed vehicle owned and driven by the evil—i.e. moustachioed (see **Mr Pimoulu**)—**Dick Dastardly** and his sentient, cynical dog **Muttley**. It was installed with a host of automated evil, such as an oil spill facility, saws on wheels; that sort of thing.

Miss Nettles
See Doctor Snuggles

Miss Nettles was the formidable matriarchal power (i.e. house-keeper) behind the portly inventor and loon, Dr Snuggles. Portly creator Jeffrey O'Kelly uses the epithet Miss Nettles to describe his own wife, at www.doctor-snuggles.com.

Moomin

This was the Japanese cell animation adaptation of the Moomin books. It did well, so well that you cannot move on

Helsingfors 1878 3.1

The Moomins

the Internet for well researched and informative sites about it. Japanimation, *anime*, manga: call it what you will, Japanese animation has a huge cult following all of its own and in deference to those who for some reason love this clumsy pastiche, I am passing over *Moomin* for the more obscure Polish adaptation, which I believe was truer to the whimsical and haunting nature of the Tove Jansson children's novels (see *below*).

Moomins, The
Film Polski/Jupiter Films, in association with FilmFair. UK tx ITV: Watch It, 1983. Poland

The Moomins was a delightful (to some, but to many others, gloomy) Polish adaptation of the excellent (to some, but to many others, dark and sinister) children's novels written and illustrated by the late Tove Jansson, a Helsinki-born native of Finland. Everything from the movements and gestures of the characters, to the colour schemes and the haunting theme

The Moomins

207

music exactly replicated the elegiac atmosphere of the novels. Keenly sensitive to the passing delights and secret worries peculiar to childhood, Jansson articulated her insights via a host of woodland creatures, who lived in a kind of parallel Finland paradise; along with goblins, spooks, creeps, weirdoes and dysfunctional tuba playing bores, who were always hanging around the verandah in the hope of jam.

The plots of the television series, as of the novels, centred around a family of plump white trolls—Moomins—the balanced parental figures for a host of rejects (see above). Moominpappa was a slightly distant old egotist in a top hat, perpetually pondering the meaning of life and given to bouts of dissatisfied melancholy. The latter had him sailing off after the mysterious and silent **Hattifatteners**, ghostly white creatures which became energised during electric storms; trying to rehouse his family and their hangers-on in a lighthouse, so he could protect them and discover the meaning of the sea; or simply writing his memoirs in an attempt to recapture his lost youth.

Moominmamma was the archetypal matriarch: discreet, wise and concilliatory in her apron. She held everyone together with raspberry juice, such that poor Pappa had little to do. Like all mothers, she had a flair for the making and storing of preserves and always knew exactly what to say. Moomintroll, their child, was a sensitive creature, forever caught in the no-man's-land between boyhood and young adulthood. He was driven to acts of clumsy heroism by the feminine charms of the **Snork Maiden**, whose penchant for bows, ribbons, jewellery and mirrors beguiled him. He looked up to the enigmatic **Snufkin**, a wandering, tent-dwelling, musician and free spirit. Snufkin wore a trusty old green felt hat and a smock, and smoked a pipe. In the novels he played a harmonica, but the animation had him evoking melodies on a tin whistle. Snufkin seemed to know all the answers but only imparted his wisdom to Moomintroll on a need-to-know basis, preferring to let his young *protegé* take his own path and make his own mistakes. He hated authority and rules and—unlike most jobless drifters—was entirely self-sufficient. Despite this independence, he always returned from his wanderings to pass some time with Moomintroll—or perhaps it was the lure of

Mamma's preserves. In any case—and again, unlike most aimless workshy loafers—he politely declined offers of hospitality and slept outside the Moomin House in his tent—a squat ridge tent in the novels but a nifty teepee in the animation.

Also on permanent loan was **Little My**, one of the Mymble's many tiny offspring. She wore her orange hair in a tall bun, passed sarcastic and cynical comment on proceedings, and was usually able to get a rise out of the malleable Moomintroll. Sniff (a kind of porcine beast) made up the set. He was a small, jittery idiot and the only son of The Muddler. He loved shiny things and was constantly aflutter with selfish neurosis.

In the wider Moominvalley one might also come across **Hemulens**. These were brash, boisterous, clumsy but well-meaning creatures. More a class of boring person than anything else, they were forever making rules, playing tubas, having vacuous parties, networking or talking loudly and confidently about nothing at all. There was the Fillyjonk: a frail, willowy old woman with too many trinkets; the Gaffsie, a pasty-faced woman with clinical depression; Too-Ticky, a robust tomboy in a beret; Toft, a shy frightened little boy in a macintosh with a yen for electricity and ... well the list goes on.

The forests which bordered Moominvalley were peopled by Creeps and Woodies and the whole area was traversed and surveyed by the Groke. The Groke was a large, lonely creature with a long skirt. She was so cold she burnt the grass where she sat, and was doomed forever to seek warmth and company, only to extinguish the lamps and frighten away the people. That the characters and storylines were such skillfully executed archetypes and allegories has been the key to the lasting appeal of the Moomins, and hence the considerable interest in this respectful adaptation.

The Film Polski animation series mixed and matched storylines and characters from the novels and did not set out simply to present the stories in their original form. But its respectful attention not only to the detail and nuance but to the general spirit of the books made it a highly successful adaptation. It spoke of magical summers and long evenings, with the paraffin lamp burning safely and steadily on the verandah, the crystal ball glowing gently in the garden. And freaks in the shadows.

But what you really want to know is whether the Snork Maiden was "doing" Moominpappa. Having been asked to examine the question, the author can conclude that the circumstances were certainly ripe for it. Pappa was enjoying a classic mid-life crisis. The supreme parenting and all-pervading efficiency of his spouse clearly emasculated him, so he was in constant search of a scenario which would prove and justify his moominsculinity. This encyclopaedia does not suggest that Mamma was no longer "up for it", but sexuality did not exactly ooze from her apron strings. Her youthful devotion to Pappa had evolved into a kind of stoic acquiescence. Meanwhile, the Snork Maiden—all youth and beauty in her anklets and earring—was finding Moomintroll a bit immature. Nothing substantial developed between that pair. With her own patriarch out of the picture, the Maiden was missing a father-figure. While Moomintroll tried hard to be a man for her, his naïve efforts foundered. Pappa, by contrast, could build a whole house and had his own top hat. He was the voice of reason and exploit. The encyclopaedia cannot confirm that an affair actually took place, but if it had, it would certainly explain a few things around Moominvalley. Pappa never stepped in, for example, to teach his son the ways of manhood, and they did leave for that lighthouse in a bit of a rush . . .

Central TV bought the Polish films for ITV, whereupon they were fixed up for UK transmission by FilmFair (of **Wombles** fame). The latter company edited and added narration by Richard Murdoch and an excellent theme tune by Steve Hill and Graham Miller. Two series of the animations were shown on Children's ITV, when it was called "Watch-It" for a short while, starting in 1983, but the programme disappeared thereafter. Its hand-made idiosynchrasies—a mix of 2D Fuzzy Felt technology and 3D puppets made out of bits of raffia and string—may well have seemed a bit old-fashioned at a time when children were demanding ever more sophisticated entertainment. In any case, it gave way in terms of UK showings to *Moomin*, a far less subtle but arguably more accessible Japanese cell animation. Sadly—one might say criminally—the episodes were never released commercially.

Link: There are many Moomin links on the Web, but this is the most pointless:

www.dcs.gla.ac.uk/rooms/f111/moomins.html

––––––––––

Morph
*See **Take Hart***

Plasticine, basically. He was a man, a ball, a paintbrush. In a way, he was the **Barbapapa** of stop-frame animation. He was animated and created by Peter Lord and David Sproxton. In later episodes of **Take Hart** he acquired a buddy, Chaz, who was a bit aggressive. Later still he bagged a short run in his own show *The Amazing Adventures of Morph*.

––––––––––

Mouse Organ
*See **Bagpuss***

Ornamental organ upon which the ornaments were mice. Since they were only ornamental, when they came to life they were no bloody good at anything. They faked up everything they put their hands to, whilst squeaking "we will fix it, we will fix it" and "we will stick it with glue, glue, glue": charlatans and cowboys you wouldn't employ to sweep the floor.

––––––––––

Mr Benn
BBC 1. A Zephyr Films/BBC Production. Created by David McKee. Directed by Pat Kirby. Written by David McKee. Music by Don Warren. Narrated by Ray Brooks. UK, 1971

Mr Benn was a man in a suit and bowler hat who lived alone at number 52 Festive Road and had a fetishistic relationship with a mysterious shopkeeper. He would visit his "special costume shop" where the shopkeeper would appear "as if by magic".

There, discreet in his purple fez, the shopkeeper would allow Mr Benn to try on one of his costumes, even though Benn never bought one of them. With a nod and a wink, he would direct Mr Benn to the changing room, where the suited man would strip down to his vest and pants and try on the costume. When he walked back out of the changing room door, he would find himself transported into some strange land where we would experience a colourful and elaborately-contructed scenario based on his costume and various events of the day.

He might have been in a balloon race, or visiting planet after planet in search of the perfect place. He was, chronologically: Red Knight, Hunter, Cook, Caveman, Balloonist, Zoo Keeper, Diver, Wizard, Cowboy, Clown, Arabian Knight (magic carpet epsiode), Spaceman and Pirate. The end of each of his 13 adventures would always be signalled by the sudden appearance of the shopkeeper who would guide him back to normality, through a door which mysteriously appeared and led back to the changing room.

Benn could not afford to buy a costume in any case, since he never worked. He was most likely a care in the community case, which would explain the shopkeeper's patient indulgence of his child-like ways. Living all alone in that house, putting on his suit every day, as if he were going to work ... When Benn started to become divergent, imagining rich fantasies, all somehow linked back to things he had seen on his journey to the shop, it took the shopkeeper to bring him down.

Mr Benn was created by children's author and illustrator David McKee (see **King Rollo**), whose books include *Not Now Bernard* and *Mark and the Monocycle*. McKee based Mr Benn's residence on his own, at 52 Festing Road in Putney. The show has been shown every year since its release on BBC television which puts it second only to **Blue Peter** for length of service. Its colourful episodes encouraged imaginative play and contributed to its status as one of the most remembered cult children's shows.

Mr Boo
See Jamie and the Magic Torch

Red-haired portly midget on roller skates. He drove a submachine, with a brolly on top, sometimes disappearing into the protective earth of Cuckoo Land. Bore more than a passing resemblance to **Dr Snuggles**.

Mr Peevly
See Hair Bear Bunch, Help! It's the

Officer Dibble-style keeper of the Wonderland zoo. He would "get those bears one of these days" and send them back to the north woods, while they contrived to stay in the zoo, in the lap of luxury.

Mr Pimoulu
See Barnaby the Bear

Alarmingly moustachioed circus boss, and ringmaster. He got top value out of his acts by forcing them to multitask endlessly. He did his own magic act in which he subdued a large cat.

Mr Rossi
Created and directed by Bruno Bozzetto. Italy

"Viva viva happiness" Excellent animated films about the squat, middle aged Mr Rossi who—the victim of a mid-life crisis (see also **Moomins, The**)—travelled the world in a series of costumes with his neighbour's dog Harold (in the UK, Gastone in Italy) in search of happiness. Up and down the hills his little car went as the beguiling two-dimensional man got lost in his dreams. The excellent tv.cream.org—run by Phil Norman and his team of dedicated noastalgia buffs—remembers that Rossi's ability to "jaunt" through time and space (see **Tomorrow People, The**) was helped by a magic whistle donated by a fairy godmother called Fata.

It's hard to be totally happy when both your eyes are set into one side of your giant nose, but the music might have helped. The "groovy" theme tune—"Viva La Felicita" by Franco Godi—was probably one of the finest ever given to an animated short. With its bossanova flutes, bongos and choir of beat girls it was reminiscent of some of the best Italian soundtrack work from the sixties and seventies (as produced by Morricone, Micalizzi, Marchetti *et al*). Although Rossi was sold into the UK and Germany the distribution seems to have run into problems somewhere along the line. Two 80-minute features—*Mr Rossi Looks for Happiness* and *Mr Rossi's Dreams* were produced in 1983—but the films are not available to order and there is definitely no one at home at the web page of his creator, *Allegro Non Troppo* animator Bruno Bonzzetto. Come back, Rossi.

———————

Mr Trimble

ITV. A Yorshire Television production. Produced by Bill Cole, Irene Cockroft. Animated by Paul Vester. Puppets by Chris Somerville. Music by Peter Gosling. UK, 1973

Early pre-school affair involving avuncular presenter and the, by now, familiar mix of puppetry, story telling and animation. At the time it was pretty new. *Mr Trimble* was Yorkshire's contribution to the rearguard action against **Sesame Street** commissioned by the IBA, which also included Granada's **Hickory House**, Thames' **Rainbow** and ATV's **Pipkins** (originally **Inigo Pipkin**). It didn't last as long as *Rainbow*, though, or even *Pipkins*, but had its place in the history of things.

Mr Twiddles
*See **Wally Gator***

Zoo keeper to giant, hat wearing, awful-voiced alligator called Wally. His job was to put Wally back in his pen after the leviathan reptile had nipped out in a bid to live as a human. Thinking about it, his job was presumably to keep Wally *in* the pen in the first place, but he wasn't very good at it—something that could have been guessed by the use of the name Twiddles. The incompetent keeper was voiced by Don Messick (see **Scooby Doo**).

————

Multi-Coloured Swap Shop, The
*BBC TV. A BBC production. UK, 1976–81. See also **Swap Shop***

Jamie from Ipswich will swap one pair of roller skates and the *Blue Peter Annual 1976* (with **Bleep and Booster** coloured-in over the edges in brown felt-tip) for Bionic Man Action Man (with liftable whole engine). Noel Edmunds, Cheggers and every mum's favourite John Craven (see also **John Craven's Newsround**) chaperoned a nation of square-eyed juveniles still in their jimjams through three hours of Saturday morning filler material before showing **Hong Kong Phooey**. You were, frankly, watching **Tiswas**. Edmunds was helped during the more tricky autocue moments by a purple stunt-dinosaur called **Posh Paws**—why surely that's just Swapshop spelled backwards! Cunning. Also showed **Valley of the Dinosaurs**.

Hold on a minute, though. Surely this was entertainment as you had never seen it before. Episode two boasted both **Basil Brush** *and* Eddie And The Hot Rods. Episode six promised a riot with Rod Hull and **Emu** *and* Nerys Hughes in the same studio. Series four kicked off enticingly with Lindisfarne and Delia Smith, but had—after only 25 weeks of Mud, Showaddywaddy and Cheggers doing his own record—resorted to that old tried-and-tested Suzi Quatro/Magnus Magnusson combination. Never forget that the *Multi-Coloured Swap Shop* was the show that launched its own supergroup, featuring Cheggers, John Craven and Alan Price. Who's Alan Price? Ask Georgie Fame. Who's Georgie Fame? I don't know I'm five. Winning stuff. But the hardest thing to fathom was the premise on which the entire show was founded. Swapping stuff. It was like watching your peers' rites of passage televised, their tender growing pains scribbled cheaply and fleetingly with magic marker onto a piece of BBC cardboard, and held in front of the camera for the whole country to gawp at. Louise from Whitley Bay would like to swap Fantasy Hairbrush Barbie for anything to do with Shakin' Stevens . . . poignant, but also chilling. Or, alternatively: seminal interactive TV first. You choose.

Multi-coloured . . . was the show that launched a thousand Saturday morning shows hosted by Radio 1 DJs who were not as pretty as their voices. It was also the show that launched the careers of Noel "Mr Blobby" Edmunds and Keith "**Cheggers Plays Pop**" Chegwin. Sobering stuff. Perhaps fearing the format was getting tired, in 1981 BBC producers changed the name to the more snappy **Swap Shop**. The show died a year later, leaving nothing but identical formats in its wake (*see **Fun Factory**, Going Live, Live and Kicking, Get Set For Summer*, and all other Saturday morning shows[not covered]).

Mumfie
*See **Here Comes Mumfie***

The Muppet Show
Syndicated, A Jim Henson production. USA, 1976

Groundbreaking family variety show, with special human guests, showcasing the Muppet talents of the late Jim Henson and Frank Oz. **Sesame Street**'s Kermit the Frog took the central role of producer of a theatre show whose cast included Fozzy Bear, the dire stand-up comedian; Gonzo the rubber tyre eating vulture; the Swedish Chef; Sam The American Eagle; the amorous Miss Piggy (who liked a bit of Frog); Dr Teeth and his band the Electric Mayhem, featuring Animal on drums and Zoot on sax. Statler and Waldorf were the two senile old hecklers. Rowlf the dog played a bit of piano and had his own soap Animal Hospital. Scooter was the hired gofer.

Although *Sesame Street* had been a children's show, *The Muppet Show* proved Henson's creations could work in a mainstream light entertainment slot. Notable other Muppet creations included **Fraggle Rock** and the *Muppet Babies*. Jim Henson died in 1990 after a short illness.

Musky
See Deputy Dawg

Musky the Muskrat was the lazy, drawling Mississippi thorn in the side of Deputy Dawg. Did he like a bit of egg-snatching from the nearby coup? "It's possible ... it's possible."

Mustard Bush
See Doctor Snuggles

The old **Treacle Tree** should not have complained so much about his lot. At least he had this bush to keep him company.

Muttley
See Wacky Races

Grim-faced dog, owned by **Dick Dastardly**. He hated his master, but still stuck around to watch him fail, whereupon he would laugh like this: sheeeschsheeeschsheeeschsheeeschsheeeesch. The famous laugh was created by voice artist Don Messick. The character may have provided the inspiration for another Hanna-Barbera animal sidekick: **Spot**, from **Hong Kong Phooey**, also voiced by Messick.

Mystery Mob

See Bailey's Comets

Yet another team striving to beat Barnaby Bailey's band of teenage, roller skating all-American clean-guys in the De Patie-Freleng answer to Hanna-Barbera's **Wacky Races**. They may have owed a little to the **Scooby Doo** squad, but that was OK since the creators of *Baileys Comets* also created *Scooby Doo* for Hanna-Barbera.

Mystery Machine

See Scooby Doo, Where Are You?

It was the pyschedelic bubble-shaped microbus or van driven by **Fred**, **Daphne**, **Velma**, **Shaggy** and **Scooby**. Unlike most cartoon vans it was capable of breaking down, leaving the "gang" stranded in a spooky place where spooky things happened.

N

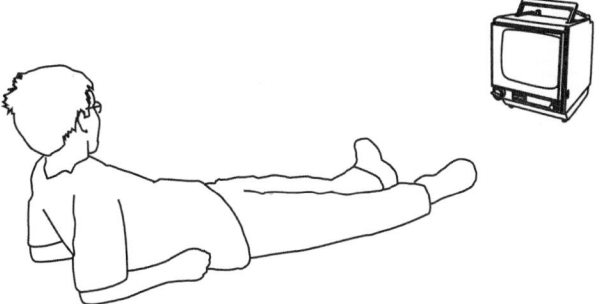

Neptina

See Marine Boy

She had class, she had looks, she had scales and a tale. She was **Marine Boy**'s fishy love interest from the deep.

New Shmoo, The

NBC. A Hanna Barbera production. USA, 1979

There was not much to distinguish this aimless **Scooby Doo** pastiche from all the others. Nonetheless it is often recalled in the form of a question: "What *was* that white thing?" By 1979, Hanna-Barbera had been banging out tired formula pieces like this for what seemed like an eternity. In *New Shmoo*, Scooby was replaced by a metamorphosing blob of white called a Shmoo. The Shmoo could change shape. That was a handy device which eliminated the need for decent scripting. Kids are stranded? Have the Shmoo turn into a car. Someone in a burning building? Have the Shmoo turn into a trampoline. Shaggy was replaced by a tubby couch potato in a loud shirt. The rest was pretty much standard crime-fighting fare (see **Scooby Doo**, **Inch-High, Private Eye, Josie and the Pussycats**, **Buford Files**, **Goober & the Ghost Chasers**). The general idea was that crime—which had confounded the nation's police forces—would be solved in an instant by a raft of pizza-eating doofus teens. In this case they all worked for "Mighty Mysteries Comics" and found that life was more mysterious than fiction. The Shmoo was voiced by Frank Welker, who "was" **Freddy** from *Scooby Doo*. Nita was voiced by Dolores Cantu-Primo and Mickey was voiced by Bill Idelson, while Chuck McCann provided the vocal tones for Billy Joe. New Shmoo was released in 1979 in the US. Syndication brought it to the UK in 1981. A white **Barbapapa**, basically.

Newsround
See John Craven's Newsround

Although *Newsround* continues to be broadcast by the BBC, this encyclopaedia is concerned with the original Craven-branded product.

Noah and Nelly in Skylark
A Roobarb Enterprises production. Produced and directed by Bob Godfrey. Created and written by Grange Calveley. UK, 1976

Richard Briers narrated this oft-forgotten cartoon from the team that brought you **Roobarb** and **Henry's Cat**. Noah (not the exact same one who begat Japheth, Shem and Ham, you imagine) and his wife Nelly donned their capes and sou'westers to steer their craft, the Skylark, through uncharted territory, for no good reason other than to combat boredom. Destinations were picked from a blank map, and off they went. "All aboard the Skylark!" The animals went, not exactly two by two. They were all push-me-pull-yous. One head manic, the other depressed, the beasts—such as Achmed the Camels and Rose the Elephants—would poke fun at themselves, rub themselves up the wrong way, get under their own feet and generally give themselves a stern talking to. As the Skylark went speeding through skies full of watering cans and lanscapes full of sweeties, Nelly would knit their way out of all problems, her eyes invisible beneath her waterproof hat. The show was written by *Roobarb* scribe Grange Calveley and animated—on cells this time, instead of paper—by award-winning *Roobarb* wobblemeister Bob Godfrey, which meant it did not wobble. Fans of *Noah and Nelly*'s unabashed trippiness generally found a lot to like about **Jamie & the Magic Torch** and **Dr Snuggles**.

Nobby Mouse
*See **Doctor Snuggles***

Small rodent and mischief-centre.

Noggin the Nog, The Sagas of
BBC TV. A Smallfilms production. Created by Peter Firmin. Written and produced by Oliver Postgate. Music by Vernon Elliott. Narrated by Oliver Postgate and Ronnie Stevens. UK, 1959–65

"In the Lands of the North, where the black rocks stand guard against the cold sea, in the dark night that is very long, the men of the Northlands sit by their great log fires and they tell a tale…"

You might think a man would have to be fairly crass to name a child **Knut**. But Noggin, King of the Nogs, was a peaceable soul. Writer Oliver Postgate remembers: "Noggin himself is the antithesis of the decisive, bloodthirsty Vikings of history, in that he is gentle, friendly and very often doesn't know what to do next." Mr Postgate also counters that, in some parts of Scandinavia, Knut is a very ordinary name. He's right, of course—only a facile smart-alec after a cheap gag would laugh at it.

Mr Postgate goes on to tell me that viewers might recall "Olaf the Lofty, who, with Graculus the great green bird, invented the ill-fated flying machine. They will remember Grolliffe, the dragon whose breath was not fire but ice, and how he fought the black genie in the sky and blew him into an ice cube. They will remember the King under the hill and the giant crows, the sword of the sorceror and the stone giants." But most of all, says Mr Postgate, viewers will recall Nogbad the Bad, "the vilest of all wicked uncles". Nogbad was a ne'er-do-well, more akin to those pillaging "Vikings of history". In most cases, Nogbad's villainy nearly prevailed, Mr Postgate recalls, but he was foiled in each saga, sometimes more by good luck than good judgement.

The saga-inspired cartoon series was the first of many animated legends to come from the creative partnership of Peter

Firmin and Oliver Postgate, as Smallfilms. Firmin came up with the idea after being beguiled by a set of Norse chessmen in the British Museum, and Postgate wrote the scripts. The series of 30 10-minute films—"crudely animated on a shoestring budget"—was commissioned by the BBC and the rest—including The **Clangers**, **Bagpuss**, **Ivor the Engine** and **Pogles Wood**—is history. *Clangers* scoremeister Vernon Elliott provided the music while Postgate narrated with Ronnie Stevens.

Oliver Postgate adds: "These films are legends, a part of television's folk history." He points out that, although the films were apparently "lost for years" they are now available again via the internet. I am particularly grateful to Mr Postgate for his memories and extensive contributions.

Link: www.smallfilms.co.uk

———————

Noseybonk
See Jigsaw

A kind of bungling Mr Bean in a horrible white mask with a pendulous snout. Actually **Jigsaw** presenter Adrian Hedley in an ill-fitting suit. He attempted—through the media of bad visual gags and mime—to give viewers a clue to the mystery letter which formed that week's mystery word. He was accompanied by comedy tuba. If he didn't freak you out you were already weird.

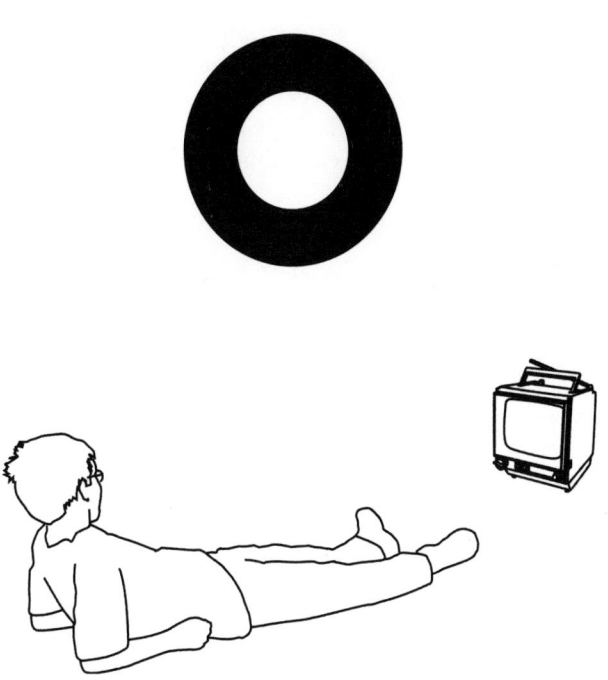

Oddball Couple, The

ABC. A De Patie-Freleng production. USA, 1975-77

If, by chance, the reader has been searching for a way to illustrate cultural decline, then the encyclopaedia suggests he or she look no further than this entry. One of those "lost cartoons", *The Oddball Couple* was an attempt by **Pink Panther** animation house De Patie-Freleng to jump on the *Odd Couple* bandwagon.

First, there was the 1965 Broadway play by Neil Simon, which introduced that chalk and cheese divorcee theme, with Walter Mathau as Oscar Madison and Art Carney as Felix Unger. Then there was the 1968 feature film in which Jack Lemmon took the Felix role. Taking its own cue from the 1970 ABC television series—which had by now replaced Mathau and Lemmon with Jack Klugman as Madison and Tony Randall as Unger—De Patie-Freleng went one or two steps futher and replaced both with bad drawings of a finicky cat (see also **Baggy Pants and the Nitwits**) and a mangy dog (see **Hong Kong Phooey**), called Spiffy and Fleabag.

The duo shared a flat—one half palace, one half midden—and an office. They also shared a profession. They were both freelance reporters. Paul "**Dick Dastardly**" Winchell lent Fleabag his voice and Frank Nelson took the Spiffy role, while Joan Gerber (see **Wait Till Your Father Gets Home**) voiced Goldie, their secretary. Airing in the same year that the TV series was axed, *The Oddball Couple* failed to capture an audience and lasted a mere two seasons. Episodes such as: "To Heir is Human", "Who's Afraid of Virginia Werewolf?" and "Do or Diet" are probably best forgotten. De Patie-Freleng made a better job of **Doctor Snuggles**.

Officer Dibble
See Top Cat

Voiced by B-movie thug actor Allen Jenkins, the beleagured beat cop Dibble obsessed over TC, a cat—probably a sign that he'd been walking that beat too long. His human heart was usually his downfall, as he allowed TC's treacly tones to smooth-talk his way out of one impending arrest after another. He was emulated— in look and voice—in a later Hannah-Barbera character: **Mr Peevly**, in **Help! It's the Hair Bear Bunch**.

Officer Gotcha
See Jamie and the Magic Torch

"Ooh, that's upset me that 'as. I shall 'ave to tek a truncheon for me nerves." Yorkshire-voiced Gotcha travelled on a unicycle with a siren and ate his own truncheons (cucumbers), replacing them from a store under his hat.

Oscar the Grouch
See Sesame Street

Dishrag in a dustbin. Not to be confused with **Top Cat.**

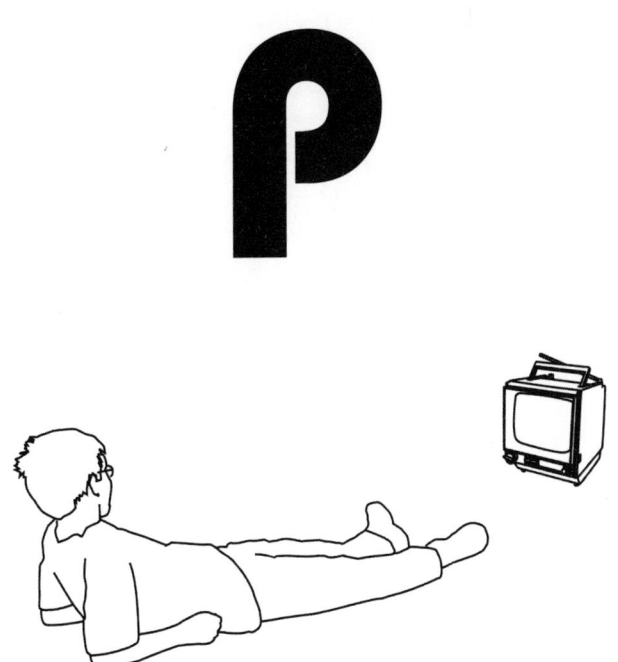

Paddington

BBC TV. A FilmFair production. Directed by Ivor Wood.
Written by Michael Bond.Animated by Ivor Wood. UK, 1976

Paddington Bear was created by writer Michael Bond, whose
"Monsieur Pamplemousse" books are published by the same
prestigious house as this encyclopaedia. Leaving shameless
product placement aside for a moment, Paddington was a
rather charming character. Found on a platform at Paddington
station, this beguiling bear had allegedly travelled from darkest Peru—where his Aunt Lucy was in a home for retired
bears—with only a duffel coat and a small brown case, marked
"wanted on voyage", which mostly contained marmalade
sandwiches.

The bear having been abducted by the Browns and kept
in their suburban semi, the episodes focused on the humorous inability of the bear to fit in with English society, and his
exasperation at our illogical ways. He gave idiots and rude
people short shrift with his hard stares and caused a great
deal of chaos at Mr Gruber's antique shop. Tolerated by
the community at large, loved by his adoptive family, but
hated for no reason by his miserable neighbour Mr Curry,
Paddington Bear and his show work quite well as allegories
for immigration the world over, although this encyclopaedia
is loath to assert that social satire was Mr Bond's intention.

Paddington was made by Ivor Wood and his FilmFair, the
company which brought you The **Wombles**, The **Moomins**,
The **Herbs**, **Simon in the Land of Chalk Drawings** and
others.

Paperplay

ITV. A Thames TV production. UK

Former **Magpie** presenter Susan Stranks fronted this late-
morning pre-school show about making stuff with old toilet

rolls. In a cunning mix of tweeness and creepiness, the show had Stranks call on the assistance of two puppet spiders called Itsby and Bitsy. They descended from the ceiling in all their hairiness (see **Fingerbobs**) and added their helpful questions into the mix. You tried to concentrate on the toilet rolls, but the spiders held you transfixed with childish fear. *Paperplay* may have unnerved the arachnophobic toddler, but it was nothing compared to the full-on nightmare of **Rainbow**, which followed it, in its original schedule.

_____

Parker
See Thunderbirds

Lady Penelope's driver. Those heavy bags under the careworn eyes, that forelock-touching deference, that poor command of the Hinglish language. Class sterotypes haint what they used to be. Had a hipflask under the coat, this encyclopaedia suspects.

_____

Parsley the Lion
See The Herbs

A character in **The Herbs** and also the title of his spin-off show, which relegated the other Herbs to bit-parts and focused on the comedy double act between its pompous old eponymous hero and **Dill** the breathless dog. Witty, eccentric and tastefully understated.

_____

PC McGarry
See Camberwick Green

He was a "big, friendly policeman". He had a motorbike and a number: 452.

Penfold
See **Danger Mouse**

Danger Mouse's "asinine assistant" Penfold was voiced by the inimitable comic actor Terry Scott, whose *Carry On* voice lent the hapless mole an appropriate Boys-Own innocence. "Cripes, DM! What are we going to do now?" "Penfold . . ." "Yes, Chief?" "Shush." Classic comedy, really.

Penelope Pitstop
See **Wacky Races**

Willowy blonde woman in a flying hat and tailored clothes. She was classy, she was beautiful, she was chic, but that counted for nothing as her creators made her stupid as well. Supposedly weak and defenceless, she was protected by the **Anthill Mob**, a bunch of Bugsy Malone-derived hoodlums, all voiced by Mel Blanc. She drove a car called the **Compact Pussycat**—a word combination which says it all—and had an interest in make-up. In fact she was generally putting on a bit of slap when she should have been watching out for **Dick Dastardly**. She was voiced by Janet Waldo and was not a positive female role model. Hanna-Barbera was so taken with the interplay between this talent-free It-girl and the useless, dithering mobsters that it span off a new show, *The Perils of Penelope Pitstop*, as a vehicle for the two parties. In this show, which could seem contrived unless you had first seen *Wacky Races*, Ms Pitstop was in constant danger from the **Hooded Claw**. The Claw was none other than her guardian **Sylvester Sneekley**, who stood to gain in life insurance and inheritances from her death. Coming to her aid, in Buster Keaton-esque slapstick, was the Anthill Mob, one of whose number chuckled uncontrollably as a kind of nervous tic: "Ha-ha-ha-haaa-ha-haaaa, Penelope's going to die! Ha-ha-ha-haaa-ha-haaaaa." **Hardy Har-Har** has a lot to answer for.

Penry Pooch
*See **Hong Kong Phooey***

The canine Clark Kent. This dimwit dog, voiced by Scatman Crowther, invariably upset his bucket as police station janitor. But as **Hong Kong Phooey**, the Kung Fu crime fighter, he saved the city, using moves like the Two For One Super Run, from the pages of his bunglers bible *The Hong Kong Book Of Kung Fu*. Or did he? His striped cat **Spot** kept the myth alive by doing all the work for none of the credit.

———

The Perils of Penelope Pitstop
*See **Penelope Pitstop**, above*

———

Peter Perfect
*See **Wacky Races***

Narcissistic, impressively-chinned driver of the **Turbo Terrific**. He would have loved to have stopped to woo the winsome **Penelope Pitstop** (above), but winning that Wacky Race came first.

———

Pfeiffer, Paul
*See **Wonder Years, The***

Best friend, and foil, of **Kevin Arnold**, 12 year-old hero of *The Wonder Years*. Paul was geeky, Paul was bespectacled. Paul looked a little like Morocco Mole (see **Secret Squirrel**). Paul was a decent kid who had none of the social advantages of his buddy. He was not handsome, he was not good at sports, he did not attract good luck or girls. Nevertheless, Kevin would use him as a dumping ground for his woolly thinking concerning his troubled love-life with his demure, pastel-clad neighbour Winnie Cooper, whose name was surely a kind of old car.

Phantom Flan Flinger
See Tiswas

Masked marauder in trenchcoat and hat. Flung flans randomly to up the pace when the unrehearsed mitherings were flagging, covering all around in shaving foam.

Phooeymobile
See Hong Kong Phooey

Wobbly car, hidden in the police station trash can and driven by Kung Fu super hero wannabee Hong Kong Phooey. It looked like the pagoda in Kew Gardens and made the sound of a bongo. Weirdly, given the mediocre mutt's numerous incapabilities, his car could change shape, into a helicopter, boat or aeroplane.

Picturebox
ITV. A Granada production. UK, 1971

In the title sequence, a questionable choice of funereal organ music washed over a rostrum camera shot of a spinning crystal, out of which rose, in a spooky, mystic way, a perfectly harmless film about differently-cultured people far, far away. This encyclopaedia understands the films were very good and instructive too, but the author would not have known, since by the time they kicked in he was well established behind the sofa. The Granada-produced schools programme was presented by Alan Rothwell, formerly David Barlow in *Coronation Street*.

Pigeon Street

BBC TV. A David Yates production. Produced by David Yates and Alan Rogers. Animated by Peter lang. Design by Alan Rogers. Music composed by Beeni Lees, performed by Soulyard. UK, 1981

Big-handed bonanza from the house of Yates and Rogers. Bird fanciers, lured by the title of this show into expecting a concentrated dose of all-pigeon action, will have been disappointed by this colourful, multicultural, cut 'n' paste animation series. All the chacters had massive hands, a characteristic which seems to have stuck in many viewers minds. There was Long Distance Clara, the truck driver and her role-reversing husband Hugo the chef. No pigeons there. Then there was Mr MacAdoo, the pet shop owner. No pigeons there, either. Dr and Mrs Glossop had three children, Gerald, Polly and Molly (distinguished by the P and M on their jumpers), and no pigeons. Astronomy-mad Mr Jupiter had a telescope and a dog named Flash (see **Fingerbobs**), but no pigeons. Sleuth-like Mr Baskerville had a hound, called Watson. He had a magnifying glass but no pigeons. Rose and Daisy the dotty old women, were fairly active, keeping fit and amusing themselves with arguments. They had no pigeons, but sometimes used to scare them off their windowsills. William and Betty had a boy called Jim and no pigeons, while Reg and Doreen liked a bit of a ballroom dance. No pigeons there either. Bob owned the bike shop. *He* had a few pigeons—"booo, booo"—but by then it was too little, too late. The voices were supplied by George Layton and John Telfer.

Pink Panther

MGM [film titles] NBC [animation shorts]. A De Patie-Freleng production. Created by Friz Freleng/Hawley Pratt. USA, 1964

"Don't say *sí*, say *oui*, Deaux-Deaux." He was thin, pink, and very, very hip. He got into a kind of space-age racing car, driven by some grinning catamite in a crash helmet, who ran him around the corner to the TV studio, where he got out. So what was that all about, and just who was that crazy pink guy? "It's as plain as your nose". He was the Pink Panther. The "rinky-dink panther", if you will. Either way he was the "one and only truly original Panther pink from head to toe".

He was the ultimate in cool sophistication. Far too hip even to speak (the author can relate to this, especially at 7.30 in the morning), he inhabited an exquisitely inked world of minimalistic graphic design, at the vanguard of early '60s chic. Where did he come from? He came from an unlikely, if eminent, source. The Pink Panther character was created by one Friz Freleng in response to a commission from director Blake Edwards to provide the title sequence for his 1964 comedy film *The Pink Panther*.

Freleng, an Oscar-winning Warner Brothers senior director, had been a mainstay of the cartoon business for some 30 years, directing *Bugs Bunny*, *Daffy Duck*, *Tweety*, *Sylvester*, *Porky Pig* and *Yosemite Sam*. All worthy stuff, but nothing there—except parhaps the laid-back bunny—could be seen as a precursor to the cool cat. Perhaps Warner's commercial requirements drove Freleng to supervise such formulaic crowd-pleasers. But Warner shut down its animation department in 1962 and Freleng went into partnership with another cartoon producer, David DePatie, to create the surprisingly named DePatie-Freleng Enterprises (see also **Bailey's Comets** and **Baggy Pants and the Nitwits**).

The movie, which starred former Goon Peter Sellers (see also **Michael Bentine**) as the bungling Inspector Clouseau, was a hit but—according to Freleng—the titles received better reviews than the film. As a result, a series of animated shorts was made. The contemporary design, laid-back jazz score from Henry Mancini and high production values of the films set this "groovy cat" a cut above the rest of its contemporaries. Episodes with titles like: "The Pink Phink" (which won its creators another Oscar), "Dial 'P' For Pink", "Pink Pajamas" and "Pinkfinger" swiftly became cult classics. The secret was that Freleng and co-director Hawley Pratt considered that they were making cartoons for adults. Rearing its head once again was the notion some producers and directors seem to have that children do not want, understand or appreciate anything remotely sophisticated (see also **The Moomins**). Regardless of the directors' intentions, the decision to pitch the pink one at grown-ups resulted in a unique and unforgettable quality show which delighted kids as much as their parents.

When Edwards made a film sequel, *A Shot In The Dark*, the following year, Freleng created a cartoon Inspector Clouseau character for the titles. Once again this was rolled out into a series of spin-off shorts called *The Inspector*. The animated Clouseau starred with his dim-witted sidekick, the uniformed *flic* sergeant **Deaux-Deaux** (pronounced Dodo). He appeared to be Spanish, or, at least, he had trouble with the language. He kept saying the wrong words, to the Inspector's eternal frustration. The segment was voiced by Pat Harrington, in both roles.

Although they were originally made for the cinema, the Pink Panther shorts aired on NBC TV in the US between 1968 and 1973, before fanning out into the wider world. In terms of UK showings, we mostly saw *The Pink Panther Show*, a triple bill which sandwiched an episode of *The Inspector* between two Panther shorts. The rose-coloured hepcat usually came into contact with a funny little big-nosed generic man, who turned up in every place, in every guise. Sometimes he was a meddling member of the public, sometimes a policeman, hunter, ranger, shopkeeper. Whoever he was, he would get caught up in the Panther's episodic life and get dragged along into the plot. Or he would be the ignominious cause of it. If the author remembers rightly, a piano once fell on his head.

Surprisingly, the chic design of the Freleng-Pratt cartoons has not been much emulated. Notable exceptions are the excellent, retrospectively stylised *Ren & Stimpy* and the obscure and vaguely psychedelic Italian-produced **Mr Rossi**, who was himself a sort of advance on Generic Man.

But things change. Formats tire, directors stagnate, artists move on or ratings fall, and networks demand novelty. Whatever the reason, the *Pink Panther Show* became the *New Pink Panther Show*. For "new" read: "not as good as the old one" (qv. *New* Avengers, *New* Seekers, *New* Labour) in 1978 something rather tawdry called *The All New Pink Panther Show* emerged to replace the old new format. In its souped-up state, Pink's backgrounds became homogenised with the bulk of mainstream cartoon shows. Gone were the groovy stylised sets and graphics. In their place, pseudo-realistic brushwork, muzak and—anathema to cult followers—eventually a talking Panther. Clouseau was out too. He was replaced by a blue aardvark in *New* and a worthless offering called **Crazylegs Crane** in *All New*. Crazylegs (voiced by Larry D. Mann) had an ongoing love-hate relationship with a dragonfly (voiced by Frank "**Freddy**" Welker). Where do these ideas come from? It is likely that the new formats resulted from a decision finally to pitch the show at children. But in any case, it seems surprising that DePatie-Freleng—still credited as producers of this banality—could have countenanced such a pointless bastardisation of their winning formula.

Despite extensive panther research, no explanation has been found for the catamite with the sturdy helmet. But a clue, perhaps, may be found in the cat's unprecedented disco dancing at the end of the show.

Link: if you are at all interested in this cult classic, avoid **www.pinkpanther.com**—despite a cursory "history" of the character, it appears to be a humourless exploitation of merchandising rights and a way to sell branded goods and services to teenage girls. It's also worth noting that the keyword "crazylegs", when typed into a certain search engine, delivers a site called Impotence Online.

———

Pipe Cleaner Family, the
See Pogle's Wood

Additional **Pogle's Wood** characters. A father pipe cleaner, a mother pipe cleaner and their two infant pipe cleaners lived in a wooden pencil box and sometimes came out to play. They formed an occasional story telling segment in the bilberry wine-drenched Postgate/Firmin woodland animation.

Pipkins

ITV. An ATV production. Created, produced and directed by Michael Jeans. Music by Chris Hazell. UK, 1973-81

One man alone, marooned for hours at a stretch in festering shop, talks to the old, mildewed toys, as though they are his friends. "It's time . . . (bong, tick, tock, whirr, ding, proot, toot, bong) . . . for a story."

Welcome to *Pipkins*, the hospice for decomposing puppets. Based in a mouldy shop—supposedly a puppet shop, like the kind you see on every high street—*Pipkins* (formerly known as **Inigo Pipkin**) was another pre-schooler featuring a cast of wobegone glove-puppets in varying states of wet rot and decay. The ringleader was **Hartley Hare**, a pompous rodent in the advanced stages of mummification, quivering with fleas and myxomatosis as he laid down the law. Prone to the worst kinds of childish behaviour, Hartley craved attention and notoriety, and sulked if he did not get it. If he had had a friend, it woud have been **Zippy**. Also in attendance were Topov the monkey with cinnamon whirls for ears; Octavia the ostrich; Pig the pig, complete with Brummie accent; Tortoise, the tortoise; Moony the Badger and various human presenters. The original Inigo Pipkin was played by George Woodridge, who was sadly and unexpectedly despatched to that great Poundstretcher in the sky after getting only one series in the can. After that the presenters became more motley. Stories were read, puppets were inspired to play, and indeed put on a play or two. Preschool children everywhere fell asleep and dribbled yoghurt down their fronts as Hartley and his cronies pretended to run their own company, appointing the mirthless Tortoise treasurer.

Actor Nigel Plaskitt was the man with his "hand up Hartley Hare" for nine years. He remembers his time crouched in agony operating puppets: "It never stops hurting." Having trained as an actor, Plaskitt was not keen to "do" puppets at first. But puppet maker Jane Eave, with whom he had worked at Islington's Little Angel theatre, persuaded him to come on board. "They said 'can you do funny voices? You can? The job's yours.'" Even though he went through a period of depression while filming *Pipkins*, Plaskitt says that it was a great job to do. "You don't realise, *then*, that you will eventually have conversations with the audience, the viewers who have grown up." He cites the testament of one such viewer, now a theatre designer, who attributes his career to an episode of *Pipkins* which inspired him to start building model theatres. "It might be one little thing in a programme which sparks things off," says Plaskitt. "It's very important. It shapes the imagination."

The show was filmed at ATV's Elstree studios. ATV's owner Lew Grade apparently "put his money where his mouth was" and funded the show's high production values. Where **Rainbow** was recorded "as live", *Pipkins* could afford post-production and on-location shoots. Work became less cramped after producer Michael Jeans watched Jim Henson assembling the sets for his **Muppet Show** in the studio next door. Henson built up the stage so that puppeteers could stand upright and move about freely underneath the action. Jeans followed suit. Plaskitt's pain abated.

Along with *Rainbow* and **Hickory House**, the show was commissioned by the IBA, rather hopefully, as a rival to **Sesame Street**. Somehow, somewhere, someone missed the point. It's not that *Pipkins* was bad. But where *Sesame Street* was worldly, colourful and outward-looking, *Pipkins* was like being locked in a cupboard with the mildewed hymn books at the church hall. When ATV mutated into Central (see also **Tiswas**), the Elstree studios-produced *Pipkins* was axed and replaced with the more sanitary looking, but blander, **Let's Pretend** which went out at the right time for those older children on home dinners to catch and turn into a kitsch favourite. But don't waste time hunting down *Pipkins* memorabilia. There was no merchandise.

Link: the official *Pipkins* site exists at **http://freespace.virgin.net/greg.taylor1/pkpig.htm** Hold your sides together as you read those original scripts ...

Pippin
*See **Pogles Wood***

Not really the natural offspring of Mr and Mrs Pogle, but some child they seemed to have abducted from the King of the fairies. He was a tyke and played with a stripy squirrel called **Tog**. Had his own comic and annual.

Pippin fort
*See **Camberwick Green***

Every village needs a fort. In the case of **Camberwick Green**, Pippin was it. The fort housed **Sergeant Major Grout**, **Captain Snort** and their troops.

Pishdy cuf
*See **Ivor the Engine***

The sound made by Ivor's engine. The unique sound effect was cunningly created in Peter Firmin's cowshed by saying it into a microphone. The correct spelling, as supplied to the encyclopaedia by Ivor creator Oliver Postgate, is pss-t-koff.

Play Away
BBC2. Produced by Cynthia Felgate and Anne Reay. Written and directed by Anne Gobey. UK, 1971–84

Play Away was the source of this encyclopaedia's favourite joke. Here it is: "Knock knock." (Who's there?) "M-A-B it's a big horse." (M-A-B it's a big horse who?) Sings: "M-A-B it's a big horse I'm a Londoner ..." (watch those sides).

A step up from **Play School**, *Play Away* (give us a P, give us an L, give us ...) was a proper variety show for kids, shown at teatimes on the weekend on BBC 2. A studio audience of chuckling tots bore ecstatic witness to sketches, music and stand-up from former *Play School* presenter Brian Cant and his cast of helpers.

Jonathan Cohen was permanently "at" the piano, hammering out plinky plonky accompaniments as jobbing actors like, oh, Jeremy Irons (in 1975) and others looned about in dungarees, eyes crazed with ambition and cheeks shiny with greasepaint. Derek Griffiths, Floella Benjamin, Carol Chell, Toni Arthur and the rest of the **Play School** cast were regulars, while the avuncular Brian Cant played the jolly ringmaster. Other participants included Spike Heatly, Alan Rushton, Chloe Ashcroft, Julie Covington and Tony "Baldrick" Robinson. Jonathan Cohen is (at the time of writing) still actively tickling those ivories on Channel 5's *Havakazoo*. The *Play Away* graphics were supplied by Hilary Hayton, who also brought us **Crystal Tipps and Alistair**. Born in 1971, the show ran for 13 years, then died. Brian Cant still tours today.

Play School

BBC TV. A BBC production. UK, 1968

"Come on Jemima, let's go shopping. Are we walking? No we're hopping!" Why talk when you can sing? Ridiculous rhymes and manky teddies apart, *Playschool* was the mother of all children's programmes. You *owned* this show. It was yours. Floella Benjamin was yours, as were Brian Cant, Toni Arthur, Fred Harris, Derek Griffiths, Carol Chell, Johnny Ball and all the many other young actors for whom this banged-together pre-school shambles was good money. You were, understandably, less keen to claim ownership of Hamble, the deformed baby doll, complete with eyes that went up into their sockets, or of Humpty, that ne'er-do-well nursery school ninny. Big Ted and Little Ted were fooling no one by pretending to whisper into the presenter's ear and Jemima was always hopping.

But you believed the presenters. They were talking to you, in your own after-school show, about issues in your life, like learning to whistle and sharing. The best thing was going "through the round window" or indeed "through the arched window" (the square window was a bit run of the mill). And just what *was* through the arched window? Why, a film of milk bottle tops being put on the bottles in a "big factory", or baked beans being put into cans in a "big factory". It was educational and useful, especially when you left school and ended up working in a "big factory".

Each day—today is *Wednesday* (say very slowly)—the

Brian Cant: by kind permission of Amanda Howard Associates

244

presenting duo would say hello and find out what was on the clock. Whatever it was you could be sure you had to get a grown up to help you make some kind of approximation of it. Then off they would go, singing and dancing about, before forcing you to tell the time. When the big hand pointed straight up you knew it was something o'clock. All you had to do was work out which. Luckily, they told you. A quick shufty out the window and then it was back to the studio to commune with Bit and Bot the goldfish, or Katoo, the white Cockatoo with the yellow mohican, or the toys in all their mildewed glory. Don't forget Dapple, the rocking Horse: "Ride a cock horse to Banbury Cross ..."

Presenters came and went, some dimly remembered, some sadly forgotten. Here's a quick memory jog. Brian Cant (see **Play Away, Camberwick Green** etc), Toni Arthur (see **Play Away**), Chloe Ashcroft, Johnny Ball (see **Think of a Number**), Floella Benjamin, Derek Griffiths (see **Bod**, also **Heads and Tails**), Fred Harris (see **Chock-A-Block**, **Ragtime**), Maggie Henderson (see **Ragtime**), Carol Leader (see **Chock-A-Block**), Don Spencer, Ben Thomas (see **Take Hart**), Delia Morgan, Gordon Rollings, Iain Laughlan, Eric Thompson (see **Magic Roundabout**), Ben Bazell, Julie Stevens, Carol Ward, Judith Hann (see **Adventure Game**) and many many more ...

Jonathan Cohen (see **Play Away**) and William Blezzard were "at" the piano.

Pob's Programme
Channel 4. A Rag Doll Production sponsored by Cb4. Produced by Anne Wood. Directed by Douglas Wilcox. UK, 1985-88

"Puh—Aww—Buh . . . Pob," said Pob, a pug-nosed TV-set-dwelling puppet, drawing the letters of its name in its own spit on the camera lens. That is how the show started and it set the tone. Dark at best, the show the author first saw had Spike Milligan as special guest, whose humour made it positively sepulchral. He told a joke: "Why did the squirrel fall out of the tree? Because it was dead." The author fell off his seat, but not through laughing.

Presented by the likes of esteemed children's author Dick King-Smith, *Pob* was supposed to inspire intellectual pursuits, such as reading. Enjoyed by some, the show was avoided by many.

––––––––––

Pogle's Wood

BBC TV. A Smallfilms Production. Wrtten by Oliver Postgate. Puppets and settings by Peter Firmin. Music by Vernon Elliot. UK, 1964-68

"Here comes master Hedge-pig," said Oliver Postgate, as the hedgehog scampered over the moss and up to the door of the house of Pogle. For "deep in the middle of a wood"—or more precisely, inside the hollowed-out and ivy clad root of a tree— lived the Pogles, a family of beguiling yokels with spooky black eyes and cod West Country accents. Mr Pogle was a rugged man's man, fancied himself as some form of leathery-handed master craftsman, built all manner of things, led blackberry picking trips and called his wife "woife". It is possible that he had an under-developed sense of his own masculinity. According to creator Oliver Postgate, in his autobiography *Seeing Things* (Pan Macmillan, ISBN: 0330390007), the boy Pippin was not Pogle's real son. Rather, Pippin was the "son of the king of the fairies". He had to come and stay with Aunty and Uncle Pogle while who-knows-what went on at home. The Pogles had no progeny of their own, but Pippin found a play- mate in the small, elfin Tog, evidently some kind of squirrel (the striped kind) crossed with a ferral sprite (the elfin kind). He had a notable speech impediment, a barely intelligible glottal mess not unlike the Taunton accent.

Mrs Pogle wore her hair in a bun, and wore her bun in a doily—like the lid of a jar of toxic jam, sold at a country "fayre". She may have stayed at home cooking up such natural woodland recipes as bean cake and beechnut milk while her men clowned around in the copse, but everyone knew she wore the trousers. She sent the boys off to collect things—mainly ingredients for their own supper, to which she devoted her whole day—and delivered doses of morality as well. Mr Pogle was proud of his wife, or at least, he approved of her: "You are a good wife, for you can bake bread," he said. Together they lurched around in glorious stop motion like a coven of Woodcraft Folk (see **Fingerbobs**), guzzled bilberry wine and talked to a magic plant called Plant (pronounced plarrnt).

The plant itself was a giant flower, a bit like the original celluloid manifestation of the Triffids. When the pogles "watered" it with bilberry wine it launched into a stream of educational anecdotes. It had learning value. It could play the fiddle. It truly was a magic plant. *Pogle's Wood* also showcased the Pipe Cleaner family, who lived in a pencil box and formed an occasional segment. A total of 26 charming episodes of the woodland show were cobbled together admirably in Peter Firmin's barn and aired on BBC television between 1964 and 1968. Those who remember the show remember it fondly and vividly.

Oliver Postgate, however, comments: "The stuff about Mrs Pogle's alleged dominance has no basis in fact or film." He adds: "Jam you buy at country fayres is not toxic. It's usually rather good." He is, or course, correct. Once again (see The **Clangers**, **Ivor the Engine**, **Bagpuss** and **Noggin the Nog**) Mr Postgate has unveiled the smug and facile nature of this alleged encyclopaedia (as if it needed any unveiling), in which mere fact has been all too readily built upon in the pursuit of comic material. The author extends his thanks to Mr Postgate for his time and his corrections.

Link: **www.smallfilms.co.uk**

Portland Bill

A FilmFair production. Executive Producer: Graham Clutterbuck. Produced by Barrie Edwards. Design by John Grace and Barry Leith. Music by John Grace. UK, 1986

This pleasant FilmFair also-ran told the seaside stories of lighthouse keeper Portland Bill and his two little chums (see also **Cockleshell Bay**). FilmFair made 13 10-minute episodes of the stop-motion animation series, narrated by Norman Rossington. Nice but not in the same league as FilmFair's earlier successes with The **Wombles** and The **Herbs**.

Posh Paws
See Multi-Coloured Swap Shop

Just one of many dinosaurs who presented the BBC's staid Saturday morning rival to **Tiswas**. This dinosaur, though, was made of haberdashery. Would have come off worse in a fight with **Spit The Dog**.

Postman Pat

BBC1. A Woodlands production. Produced by Ivor Wood. Created by John Cunliffe. Music by Brian Daly. UK, 1981

Village postman Pat delivered his load around the houses of Greendale, along with Jess, his black and white cat. The show hit the mainstream with an onslaught of merchandise tie-ins. *That* song was sung by Ken Barrie, who also narrated the episodes. Despite the input of Ivor "**The Herbs**" Wood, *Postman Pat* did not have the subtle wit of his previous shows (see also **Wombles, The**). In many ways, it was a substitute **Chigley**. But, given the fact that only 13 short films were made, Pat achieved fame rapidly and mercilessly. But within Postman Pat, we saw the evil blueprint for Fireman Sam and Bob The Builder. A further 13 episodes were added later, where Pat had a teenage son.

Potty Time, Michael Bentine's

ITV. A Thames production. Produced and directed by Leon Thau. UK, 1973-80

Former Goon Michael Bentine CBE devised and presented this hairy puppet-led edu-comedy with a history and literature theme. The puppets looked like a cross between **Dusty** from **Hickory House** and **Captain Caveman**: all hair with a pug nose sticking out. Not without its own sense of irony, *Potty Time* seems to have been quite a laugh for its actors, puppeteers and crew; Bentine himself presented with an expression of slightly amused and quizzical surprise, which belied the fact that the mayhem was all his own making. The show ran for 7 years. Bentine did a similar series in the 1950s called *The Bumblies* and his *It's a Square World* won the Montreux International TV Press Prize in 1963. In addition, he presented *Madabout*, an ITV hobby show, and may also have had a seminal—but non-creative—role in the story of **Doctor Snuggles**, if that show's creator is to be believed.

Prince Turhan
*See **Arabian Knights**, The*

Young, just like you, kids. Got usurped by the evil **Bakaar**, a grown-up. He was voiced by Jay North.

Princess Nida
*See **Arabian Knights**, The*

"Siiiiiize of an earwig." Nida (voiced by Shari Lewis) was mistress of many disguises. By use of the cunning "size of ..." invocation she could transmute (see **Battle of the Planets**) into any living beast. It had a limited use. Someone might have been coming at her with a sabre; she would give it "size of a seagull" (surely Eagle?) and swoop up into the air away from danger.

Once in the air, as a bird, you are pretty much committed to a retreat, unless you can succesfully take out a marauding Mongol with sheer guano-power. Nevertheless, the scripts required that she prevail, so prevail she did. Enemies obediently stood still and waited for their lame doom (see also **Hong Kong Phooey**).

Private Meekly
See Wacky Races

Along with his boss **Sergeant Blast**, he drove the **Army Surplus Special**.

Professor Emerald
See Doctor Snuggles

Evil magician and megalomaniac nemesis of the benign, interestingly-trousered inventor, and part time messiah.

Professor Fumble
See Marine Boy

Exceptionally nosed creator of Oxy-gum.

Professor Mariner
See Marine Boy

Progenitor of Marine Boy, and patriarch of Ocean Patrol.

Professor Pat Pending
*See **Wacky Races***

Crazy, science-driven loon and driver of the versatile **Convert-a-Car**. The character was voiced by Hanna-Barbera stalwart Don Messick.

Professor Yaffle
*See **Bagpuss***

Pompous old teacher and woodpecker bookend. He came alive when Bagpuss woke up and told everyone what to do.

Ptery
*See **Jigsaw***

Pronounced: puh-terry. He was a pteradactyl prop with a pompous tone voiced by John "K9" Leeson.

Puddle Lane
ITV. A Yorkshire production. Produced by Mike Harris. Directed by David Turnbull. Stories by Sheila McCullagh. UK

Neil Innes presented this fine storytelling and wizardry show which featured the supremely-named Mr Gotobed. Another lunchtime favourite with students and truants (see **Stepping Stones**).

Pugh, Pugh, Barney McGrew, Cuthbert, Dibble, Grubb

*See **Trumpton***

Collectively they were Trumpton's fire brigade, as directed by Captain Flack. But their real talent was waltz playing in the bandstand, every afternoon, during which there were no fires.

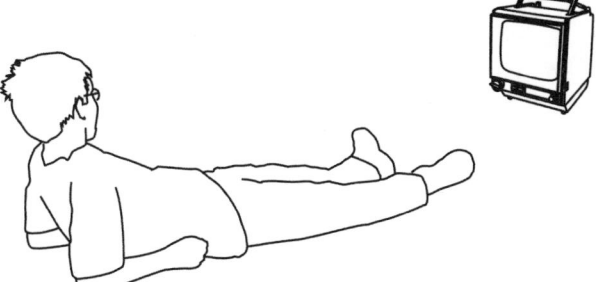

Ragtime

BBC 1. A BBC production. UK, 1973-75

Fred Harris (see **Play School**) and Maggie Henderson (see **Play School**) presented this basic blend of stuffed toys and wooden spoons, with silly accents.

Rainbow

ITV. A Thames Television production. Produced by Pamela Lonsdale. Directed by various, including Roger Price and Robert Reed. Created and written by John Kershaw. UK, 1972-95

What were they thinking? Up above the streets and houses... the theme (by Telltale, the original Rod Jane and Freddy) encouraged us to envisage an average town, filled with average houses. But what filthy dens of iniquity lurked behind those closed doors? Let's choose the house with the rainbow on its door, what do you think is inside? A pink hippopotamus cross-dresser—on valium, judging by his blissed-out, passive state—fluttering his lashes and angling his head coyly to one side; a man-sized bear with the temperament and skirt-wearing proclivities of a spoiled six-year old girl, and a bitchy spoilsport alien with SM overtones. Plus one grinning man old enough to be, why, their big daddy.

George, **Bungle** and **Zippy** (for it is they) made for an unhappy band of bedfellows, forever arguing with each other and vying for the attentions of Geoffrey Hayes, their affable and long-suffering (22 years) guardian. Zippy was a naughty boy. He always talked over everybody else and said bad, thoughtless things, causing him to be punished by a bondage ritual in which his mouth was zipped up. Oh, he could protest, but who would hear him? "Do you want the zip?" the warning would be delivered. "Oh no, Geoffrey, I don't want the zip, I'm very sorry, I won't do it any more." Bungle, by contrast, was an insipid little tattle-tale, standing

GEOFFREY HAYES

Geoffrey Hayes: by permission of Qdos Entertainment

with his hands on his hips in righteous indignation, his hairy bear lips permanently forming the phrase "It's just not fair".

George, spineless and fey, swung which ever way the wind was blowing, but usually came out on the side of Bungle when it looked as though Zippy was about to get zipped. (George actually replaced the original glove puppet duo Sunshine and Moony, in which Sunshine was a kind of proto-Zippy and Moony was, seemingly, an unfortunate cross between a potato and a mole.) The pets (if that is what they were) used to be

258

kept in the garden, and showed themselves by peeping through the window at Bungle, like guilty voyeurs. Eventually they were brought inside, where they sprang up from behind a desk (see also **Lizzy Dripping**) without warning.

Their mitherings were interspersed with primitive animations and jarring sound effects from Cosgrove Hall (see also **Chorlton & the Wheelies, Dangermouse** etc) in which thick black lines rattled and squeaked their way into the shape of a pram or similar pre-school artefact. There were also little films about going to buy milk with your mummy, or waiting for the postman.

There were high points and low points. If the zenith was Geoffrey's reading of a story (at which he was damn good, even though he was constantly interrupted with idiot questions from the "children"), then the undisputed nadir was the song from Rod, Jane and Freddy, a trio of hairy swingers from next door (surely "singers"). This strange *menage à trois* might always have been changing its line up—indeed, the Freddy position was up for grabs at various stages and was filled for a short time by Matthew "**Sooty**" Corbett—but the songs were of a consistent quality: awful. It was as though the black notes on the piano were never there. Rod, Jane and Freddy span off into their own show eventually, but Geoff and the boys soldiered on until 1995 when enough was clearly enough.

It might seem facile to put such a sniggering, nudge-nudge slant on a show which was, after all, aimed at pre-school children. Indeed it is; you might think we had learned our lesson with **Captain Pugwash**. But when the producers turned out such classic episodes as the Jack and Jill re-enactment, the joke seems at least partly justified. In case you missed it, this particular show had the team staging a mini-musical. Bungle threw a flouncing fit until he was allowed to be Jill, complete with grass skirt. Every line or so, our man Geoff—narrating—was interrupted with nagging questions such as: "Geoffrey, Geoffrey. What's a pail?" To which the reply came something like: "Well, George , a pail, well that's just another word for a bucket." Which was fine until the second verse—which the author has to admit never being taught as a child—was delivered: "Then Dame Dob did wrap his nob in vinegar and brown paper."

Instantly interrupted, Geoffrey aquitted himself admirably: "Jack's nob?" he grinned innocently. "Well that's just another word for ... his head." Indeed it is, but not one in common usage, nor one you would immediately think of teaching a child. But then, churning out this stuff year on year, you have to do something to keep yourself amused.

However, the episode above pales into insignificance in the light of one untransmitted show which was made as a joke for a Thames Christmas tape, but which then fell into the wrong hands (ie mine). The episode opens as Zippy is peeling his banana: "One skin, two skin, three skin ..." George interrupts him, but can do nothing to stop the onslaught of double entendres that follows. "Bungle's playing with his twanger," says Geoffrey. "I've only got a small twanger," George mopes, as Zippy has a quick look under the desk to check. Etc ad infinitum. Much use of the word banging, as Bungle gets his hammer and pegs out, while Rod, Jane and (possibly not the actual) Freddy arrive to bang out a tune. The cast keep up professional straight faces at all times, making it one of the best bits of comic footage this encyclopaedia has seen for some time.

Watching *Rainbow* now, it seems hard to imagine that the show was commissioned by the Independent Broadcasting Authority (in 1972, along with **Hickory House, Mr Trimble** and **Pipkins**) as a rival to the USA's mighty **Sesame Street**. It pottered along for a year with presenter David Cook, Bungle, Zippy, Sunshine and Moony, before finding its feet with the acquisition of Geoffrey and George. The IBA's aim was to create a portfolio of shows for under-fives which provoked imagination ... the author thinks it's safe to say the goal was achieved, if not in the way the IBA envisaged. If *Rainbow* was a million miles away from the stimulating and unpatronising fun of the American show, then at least it had a camp charm all its own and, in its way, unique to Britain.

Stanley Bates, the man inside Bungle—if you will permit the author to float that image just for a second—was reported as having been involved in an alleged road rage incident, after the show was axed. It is not clear whether he was in costume at the time of the alleged rage, but it may well have been 23 years of being Bungle that did it. The puppets were voiced by Roy

Skelton. My thanks to Geoffrey Hayes for his enthusiasm and help.

Razzamatazz
ITV. UK, 1981–86

The ITV tots' *Top Of The Pops*, *Razzamatazz* ran from 1981–86. The first series began with Chas 'n' Dave and the last ended with Feargal Sharkey. Given this context, the author believes the reader will—unusually—agree that budding starlet Vanessa Paradis' performance of "Joe Le Taxi" was the show's zenith point. The author has unearthed no evidence of a *Razzamatazz* cult following, so this entry is just in case.

Razzmatazz, Algernon Winston Spencer Castleray
See Tiswas

An unknown comedian from Dudley by the name of Lenny Henry treated those smart enough not to be watching **Multi-Coloured Swap Shop** to condensed milk chaos as this spoof Rastafarian in an elongated hat. He said: "Ooooooooooooooooooo—kaaaaaaaaaaaaaaaaay" and had a "ting" for "De Condensed Milk" (**DCM**). The Jamaican japester appeared on **Tiswas** between 1977 and 1982 and his demonstrations of exactly how to make bread and condensed milk sandwiches always ended with the requisite plastering. Note: Mr Razzmatazz is not to be confused with **Razzamatazz**, above.

Rebel
See Champion, The Adventures of

Ricky's little pedigree chum.

Record Breakers

BBC TV. A BBC production. Produced by Alan Russell. UK, 1972

Dynamic domino-toppling rave-on brought to you in (tenuous) association with Ireland's most famous stout. Dedication was what you needed. The late great Roy Castle carried this show, and when he moved on, the show died.

The perfect foils to Mr Castle's all-singing, all-tap-dancing, trumpet-blowing showmanship were Norris and the late Ross McWhirter, twin compilers of the *Guinness Book of Records*. Always on hand—like the charismatic lexicographers in *Countdown*'s dictionary corner—to deadpan those hard record-breaking facts, the sibling duo (and mono, after the shock killing of Ross, reportedly by the IRA) were also called upon for on-the-spot, off-the-cuff, one-on-one memory tests. A kid would say: "What's the tallest tree?" Norris would reply: "Well, the tallest *species* of tree, Daniel, is the American Giant Redwood . . . the tallest *individual* tree, however . . ." and the child would look on in rehearsed fascination, battling the irresistible urge to look into camera and gurn.

The show was, undoubtedly, a trivia turn-on for genuine fact fans. But it also had great scope for those with an eye for the absurd. In the first series alone, viewers bore possibly ecstatic witness to such events as the flea highjump and tallest aspidistra (see also **Adventure Game, The**). By 1973 we were onto more solid ground with the world handshaking record, while 1976 brought us the now legendary peanut pushing contest. But there were other thrills to come. The slowest typewriter was identified in 1977, along with the most expensive turkey. The frenzied coin-snatching bid of 1979 was eclipsed only by 1981's lowest hill. The idea could be seen to be running a bit thin when, in 1991, the record for the most concerts in the shortest space of time was won by evergreen pub rockers Status Quo. Finally, the artistic demise of the show, if not the actual demise, was signalled by 1997's documentation of the world bog-snorkelling record attempt.

At times little more than a politically correct excuse to stare at freaks, *Record Breakers* introduced viewers to a world of diverse fanatics, driven by the sheer—and ultimately laudible—determination to succeed. At anything. It didn't matter if you were a weakling, or couldn't run, jump, ski, dive or play sports. There was always sneezing. You could always be best at that. Unsporting or sickly types watched in the continued hope that there might be a facial tics extravaganza, a dermatological complaints convention, or an award for the most corduroy owned by a single person. Goldfish-laminating, silk-eating, moth-stroking: they were all accolades waiting to be heaped upon the strong-willed. Dedication was all you needed. With such gripping content it is not hard to see why the format survived for so long.

The classic show ran for a stunning 27 series, after which Roy Castle finally lost his running battle with cancer. His premature departure left the show to be relaunched in 1998—perhaps in error—as *Linford's Record Breakers*. Mr Christie notwithstanding, a further tragedy befell Castle's memory when former Bucks Fizz "performer" Cheryl Baker took the reins, munching and chomping her lines as you might a Curly Wurly bar, and hammed it up along with Kris Akabusi for a further two series. Castle may have gone, but he passed the baton of hope to us all. Let's run with it. If you can't run, walk. If you can't walk, hop (see **Play School**).

Red Max

*See **Wacky Races***

Baron Von Richtoven-style driver/flyer of the **Crimson Haybailer**. He was voiced—in Germanic caricature—by Daws Butler, of **Snagglepuss** and **Wally Gator** "fame". He was not featured that often on *The Wacky Races*, as he was rather dull.

Reilly
See *Chorlton and the Wheelies*

Fenella's one-eyed telescope. He spoke like Val Doonican doing "Paddy McGinty's Goat". He was voiced by Joe Lynch. Reilly, that is, not Doonican.

Rentaghost
BBC TV. A BBC production. Produced by Paul Ciani. Directed by David Crichton. UK, 1975-84

"An apparition ripped from deep inside a crypt—that's Rentaghost."

As a masterpiece of low production values, *Rentaghost* stands up as one of the all-time cult favourites. The creation of—possibly misguided—writer Bob Block (see also **Grandad**), *Rentaghost* followed the hammily-acted machinations of a group of ghosts who decided to set up in business renting themselves out.

It started evenly enough when the straight, if feckless, Charlie Mumford (Anthony Jackson) fell off a cross-channel ferry and came back as a ghost. But it wasn't long before things started to go pantomime with *faux*-medieval jester Timothy "Hods bodkins" Claypole (Michael Staniforth) and the cod-Victorian Hubert Davenport (Michael Darbyshire). Over the years (nine years, to be precise) various other over-acting luvvies appeared, such as the Scottish Hazel McWitch and Dobbin the pantomime horse, whose main role was falling over (possibly not scripted). Add in Miss Nadia Popov, whose nasal congestion informed her entire personality, and things went from bad to worse. Mumford's evil landlord Mr Meaker (Edward Brayshaw) took on a central role—as did Claypole—when Jackson and Darbyshire sensibly ran off.

The script consisted mainly of the kind of jokes **Crackerjack** rejected, and when those fell flat—as they always did—actors were presumably told to "go large". And large it they did. Foam pies were thrown, soot dislodged and jets of water issued amid theatrical shrieks and silly voices, even when the projectiles missed their targets. Where slapstick failed, ridiculous, overblown costume and bad makeup tried to bridge the gap. The all-pervading awfulness of the show was mitigated in part by its theme tune, penned by Michael Staniforth.

Rarely in the course of television history has there been such an ill-advised and embarrassing marriage of poor scripting, poor acting and poor directing (take a bow *Crackerjack* director Paul Ciani), and if there had it would owe a lot to *Rentaghost*, the master of the art.

Rickety Rick
See Doctor Snuggles

A shed. Christened Richard.

Ricky and Dicky
See Barnaby the Bear

Monkey denizens of **Mr. Pimoulu**'s Circus. They played the instruments in the band. Actually, they *were* the band. They also perfomed—appropriately enough for primates—a trapeze act, during which drum duty was delegated to **Sara the Seal,** who could always match their rhythm.

Rock 'n' Rollers
See Bailey's Comets

Music-centric competitor, striving to beat Barnaby Bailey and his roller-skate derby team.

Roobarb

BBC TV. A Roobarb Enterprises production. Produced and directed by Bob Godfrey. Created and written by Grange Calveley. UK, 1974

Commissioned for the BBC by Monica Simms, the nation's favourite wobbly green dog arrived on television screens in 1974 for the just-before-tea slot, introducing viewers to a host of wobbly birds and bird-brained schemes, banged out by Roobarb in his wobbly shed and laughed at by the wobbly birds. No one laughed louder, however, than Custard, the wobbly pink cat from next door. Caleveley's scripts were oblique at times, but always witty, full of wry word play and existential musings, making them a wobbly winner with adults. The wobbling, of course, was a "deliberate" animation technique caused by punitively low budgets. Godfrey was given so small a loan from the BBC that he was forced to make the animation on paper, rather than cells, giving them a kind of funky, post-modern white background. The characters were banged out with magic markers, giving them their chunky feel. But Godfrey's inventiveness in the face of minimal funds was to his enduring credit; *Roobarb* broke the mould. The groovy brushed drum and bass jazz-out soundtrack was provided by Ted Heath band bass-man Johnny Hawksworth. Despite not making any money (*Roobarb* was not to break even for 10 years), Godfrey next took his magic

Roobarb: by kind permission of Mike Hayes/Roobarb Entreprises

markers to the excellent **Noah and Nelly in Skylark** two years later, moving onto the better-known **Henry's Cat** in 1983 and—no one is perfect—*Wicked Willy* in 1990. He was awarded an OSCAR for *Great*, a film about Isambard Kingdonm Brunel.

Episodes—which numbered 30 in all—included "When Roobarb made a spike", "When Roobarb was being bored, then not being bored", "When it wasn't Thursday" and "When Roobarb found sauce". Classic stuff, brilliantly and breathlessly narrated by Richard Briers.

Rosemary, the telephone operator
See Hong Kong Phooey

"Hello, hello? This is Rosemary your ravishing receptionist. You don't say! You don't saay! You don't saaaay!" "Ooh—ooh. What is it?" asks **Sergeant Flint**. "I don't know. He didn't say." Cue comedy trumpets: wah, wah, wah, waaah. Although Rosemary, voiced by Kathi Gori, was in love with her "favourite dream boat" **Hong Kong Phooey**, she failed to notice he was none other than bungling bucket boy **Penry Pooch**, the mild mannered janitor. Doh (see **Crackerjack**)!

Rufus Ruffcut
See Wacky Races

Driver of the **Buzz Wagon**, along with **Sawtooth**. He was voiced by Daws Butler (See **Snagglepuss**, **Wally Gator**, **Lippy the Lion** etc).

Runaround

ITV. A Southern Television production. Produced by John Coxall. Directed by Terry Bryan. UK, 1975–81

Diamond geezer Mike Reid always looked like he might "do" your kneecaps if you messed him around. Pity the poor sheep that relieved itself on the *Runaround* studio floor during episode one. "Mr Reid is not a very happy man," you imagined the hired goons explaining. Not even the fantastic prizes—piles of the kid-friendly tat, such as Shakermaker, Big Badge Factory, Soda Stream, Spirograph, Race 'n' Chase, advertised remorselessly between children's programmes on ITV—could tempt this encyclopaedia compiler into competing on the TV quiz. The format was simple enough, though. Mike would ask an easy multiple choice question: What's the longest river in South America? Is it, A, Amazon; B, Marvelon, or C, Marathon? Then he would snarl "G, G, G, G, GO!" Children would sprint forth to stand by the letter they thought in their childish brains corresponded to the answer. Decisions, decisions, was it A, B or C? You had to choose one. Feeble-minded children who had stopped on one answer, but wanted to change it to what their friend had chosen, could do so when Mike growled, "Runarahnd nah!" Ooer, I thought it was Marathon, but now I think it's Marvelon. Come on, come on, I want that Spacehopper. The multitudinous prizes ensured the show's contestants were motivated solely by greed for erzatz entertainment (Were any masterpieces ever created on an Etch-A-Sketch?) and so it was most probably to appease the exacting requirements of the IBA (see **Tiswas**) that "interesting and informative" segments were slotted into the middle of the show, where someone would come in from the real world with their sheep and have it soil the studio . . . And that's how we get woollen jumpers. Now back to the prizes.

Runaround was sinister in its own right, but more so for the inclusion of host Mike Reid. The comic and actor's eventual move to *EastEnders* ensured he continued to haunt viewers long after they had grown up. *Runaround* itself was not to lie down and play doggo either. The format resurfaced in the late-night effort *God's Gift*, where *Big Brother*'s Davina McCall cut her presenter's teeth. Hordes of precocious Leeds teeny-boppers in bra tops ran around at the behest of slimy Stuart Hall in voiceover, with the vague intention of picking one of the five male show-off contestants to be God's gift to woman, but mainly for the excuse to be seen on TV having their toes sucked by an idiot. It doesn't get better than that.

s

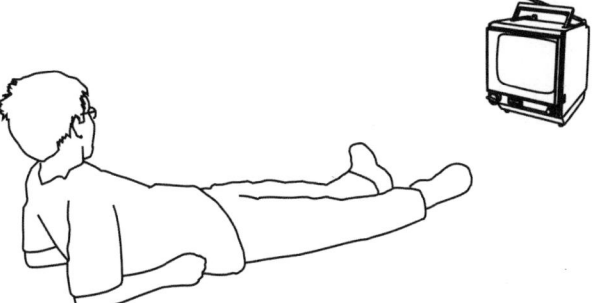

Sally and Jake

ITV. A Thames Television/Cosgrove Hall production. UK, 1973

Sally and Jake, and their mother and father and Granny and Harry and Sly the cat too: all of them lived in a village called Dimbledale, where—like in all villages—there were always lots of things to do-oo-oo. Sally and Jake enjoyed each day (it says here) . . . Presumably, that is, until they left school and realised there was no work in the village unless they wanted to run the sub-post office or work at the Spar, selling old shortbread and doilies (see also **Ffestiniog**) and that they would have to buy a car and commute to Dimbleton (near Dimbledale) just to keep a roof over their head. Not to mention the lack of fresh genes to mingle with. For Jake this would probably mean coupling either with Sally or with the girl from the Spar, although the latter may already be some way down the food chain, judging by the glazed look in her good eye and the dribble on her chin. For Sally it would probably mean one emotionally scarring experience in the car park of the Dimbledale Arms and nine months later the appearance of a mewing infant with whiskers. Sly was never far away. Meanwhile, for at least another ten years, everything was cosy. And that pretty much sums up this animated pre-school series, produced by arch British animators Cosgrove Hall.

It was of the type that began with **Camberwick Green** and eventually spawned **Postman Pat**: kids owned it and parents liked it for its utopian view of an idyllic and tranquil middle England where everyone had enough to eat and no one ate Tesco economy bread. Popular in its time (I mean specifically the show, not the bread).

Sara the Seal
See Barnaby the Bear

Elegantly-flippered mammal and minor star of Pimoulu's Circus. Like all seals, she was also a competent drummer and doubled for **Ricky and Dicky**, twin monkey-musicians, when they loped off to perform their trapeze act.

Sawtooth
See Wacky Races

Partner to **Rufus Ruffcut**, and co-driver of the **Buzz Wagon**. Also a beaver.

Scooby Doo, Where Are You?
ABC. A Hanna-Barbera production. Created by Ken Spears and Joe Ruby. UK first transmission BBC1 1970–2. USA, 1969

"Raggy?"

Four 30 year-old teenage snitches and a talking dog the size of a small cow (see also **Doctor Snuggles**) drove about on a perpetual holiday in a small, bubble-shaped VW microbus, painted with hippy flowers—the **Mystery Machine**. More like mystery magnet really, as wherever they went in it, heavy kooky spooky scenes, like, happened. But despite cursory and random use of the word "groovy", those fuzz-loving meddling kids could not less like hippies have been.

Daphne, the flame haired beauty in the purple dress, was a fully paid-up member of the straight squad (see also **DeNuccio, Jennifer**) and had an hourglass figure way beyond her tender years: "What a run-down and creepy place for a weekend of skiing", she would observe in that one-line scene-setting sort of way she had.

Freddy, the blond chunk in the orange beat-poet neckerchief, had a 60-inch chest and was clearly a preppy sports jock and natural leader, rather than the beat poet his outfit suggested: "Okay, gang—let's split up," he would suggest in a way that invited obedience. **Velma**, the dumpy frump in the heavy-framed spectacles, the thick orange turtleneck, and the pleated miniskirt, looked like a retired librarian and was—obviously—the brains of the outfit: "Hm, I think I'm beginning to figure out this kooky deep-freeze mystery." **Shaggy**, the cowardly, tufty-chinned hunchback scruff with the eating disorder, was to all intents and purposes a doofus, but as such was the only one of the gang who could honestly claim hippy status: "Like, zoinks, Scoob". Far out. He was lazy and liked to eat junk food: giant milkshakes and multi-layered burgers the size of traffic cones.

But it was the dog who stole the show. Here's how legend has it. CBS daytime programming boss Fred Silverman had commissioned the spooky show from Hanna-Barbera. The arch animator had duly delivered the gang we know and love, in their bus with a sidekick dog in the style of **Inch High Private Eye**'s **Braveheart**. Silverman remained unconvinced by the format until he reportedly heard Frank Sinatra crooning the immortal phrase "Scooby dooby doo" on "Strangers In The Night". He made a suggestion, Hanna-Barbera ran with it and are still running.

The dog took on a character of its own in the hands of HB veteran voice artist Don Messick, who gave him his trademark laugh and doggy diction. The hound formed a doofus double act with the scraggy Shaggy and together the pair goofed off, stealing giant hamburgers from each other and jumping into each other's arms. This lily-livered duo was invariably sent off by the authoritarian Freddy down the darkest passage in the whole Gothic mansion to encounter the "ghost" and engage in slapstick comedy. Where are they hiding? Why, in those giant flowerpots of course. Look, here's a restaurant, we'll call for service by tugging on this cord which we believe to be a bell, but is actually the tail of this episode's ghost, who is standing behind us. "Like, zoiks, it's the ghost!" "The roast? Rooby rooby roo." Cue **xylophone hammering** and a swift exit down a long corridor lined with the same bookshelf over and over again.

Meanwhile Daphne and Freddy unearthed clues, such as a

barely-hidden set of explicit instructions: "Tuesday—deliver stolen mirrors to Mr Jeffries the hotel owner who is fencing them for me, signed Mr Ho the suspicious Oriental gentleman with the unconvincing Chinese accent and gurgling laugh whom you met in the first scene" (I might have made that up). Velma lost her glasses with comforting regularity, crawling grimly around on all fours, and usually unwittingly up the leg of that episode's groovy ghoul. Yoiks.

And what ghouls! Of course there were no ghosts. Typically, Mr Jeffries the hotel owner would be involved in some desperate scam like garlic smuggling or mirror theft (see also **Hong Kong Phooey**), but felt the need to scare off snoopers with an elaborately contrived ghostly mock-up with a basis in local legend to lend it credence. Using nothing but an enormous network of wires, pulleys, TV cameras, projectors, tape loops, pyrotechnics, electronic voice-altering devices, make up, prosthetic limbs and latex masks, the heavy hood would hoodwink everyone. Everyone, that is, but Scooby's gang. For the same money he could have paid to have them shot. The disingenuous dastard would inevitably end up tightly bound and ready for an unmasking in front of grateful local police officers, while Velma and Freddy stood proudly by like school keeners with their hands up. And he would have gotten away with it too if it hadn't have been for them meddling kids. Like, groovy: that's what I call anarchy!

Scooby Doo was a hit and was syndicated all over the world. But such ratings-grabbing success could only mean two things: endless merchandising and spin-off shows. Let us pretend for a moment that we do not remember Scrappy Doo, Scooby's pugnacious nephew. He shouted "puppy power" in a grating high voice before running into certain death which, sadly, never came. He joined Shaggy and Scooby for the lame *Scooby and Scrappy Doo*. Theme tune: "Scooooby—Scrappy dappy doo." Indeed. Let us also forget Scooby Dum, the Great Dane's inbred country cousin and the female Scooby Dear, both of whom appeared on spin-off show *Scooby's All-Star Laff Olympics*. A less obvious spin-off was the pseudo-psychedelic chick-fest **Josie and the Pussycats**, in which a barely-disguised Shaggy appeared as the clean-shaven hipster manager of the very lame eponymous girl-band, while Freddy appeared—in the same clothes—as Josie's boyfriend **Alan**.

Freddy was voiced by Frank Welker, Velma's vocal came courtesy of Nicole Jaffe; Daphne was voiced by Heather North and Shaggy's scraping drawl was donated by DJ Casey Casem, the smooth-voiced host of America's Top Forty. The format was created for Hanna Barbera by Joe Ruby and Ken Spears (see also **Bailey's Comets**)—with a little crooning help from Fred Silverman.

Screen Test

BBC TV. A BBC Manchester production. Produced by John Buttery. Directed by Des Sissons. UK, 1979

Watch carefully. You will never see this film in any cinema. Teams of eagle-eyed cinematic would-bes from opposing schools sat behind a BBC quiz desk with buzzers and quivered with anticipation. They were then tested on their special film buff observation powers, after being shown an unmemorable clip from Disney's *Fantasia* or—more often—some obscure Children's Film Foundation flick, or grim Eastern European masterpiece like **Danger on the Danube Delta**, which had only ever aired on BBC 2 six years previously on a Sunday afternoon. Was it just you, or were those Disney "clips" remarkably indentical to the publicity trailers they showed as film news three months previously?

Michael Rodd (who was simultaneously presenting *Tomorrow's World* to your mum and dad) sat in the question master's chair, wearing John Craven's hair and your dad's shirt. When he mysteriously disappeared in 1979, without explanation, Brian Trueman (see **Chorlton & the Wheelies**, **Jamie & the Magic Torch**, **Danger Mouse**) took over. Once a year the show held a competition for viewers' own films. How—you wondered, muttering and cursing, to yourself—with no camcorders yet invented and no income, did these pre-teen Hitchcocks afford to make a celluloid film? Surely their rich, indulgent parents must have funded and indeed written, directed and shot the whole thing for the shallow reflected glory it would bring at the office. That's what you told yourself anyway, when your Cornflake-box and toilet-roll cine camera (formerly **Bessie**) failed to work. In any case the film-buff angle was redundant: the quiz was little more than a comprehension test. Trueman disappeared too, so Mark Curry was drafted in to see the flagging format through to its end.

Seaman Staines
See Captain Pugwash

Secret Squirrel
NBC. A Hanna-Barbera production. USA, 1965

Secret Squirrel was a rodent intelligence agent in a trenchcoat, whose fez-wearing sidekick Morocco Mole accompanied him on rodent spy-missions over the world. Two seasons and 26 episodes delivered the usual formulaic set of situations (eg. imagine what went on in the episodes "Masked Granny" or "Robot Rush"...) with predictable outcomes, but the rodent angle was inspired, and gave the espionage theme a winningly ludicrous air. The scripts were voiced by Mel "Bugs Bunny" Blanc for Secret Squirrel and Paul Frees for Morocco Mole. Originally part of a bigger show including the appeal-free *Atom Ant* and the grating *Winsome Witch*, *Secret Squirrel* was by far the most entertaining of the set.

Espionage has always inspired us. From James Bond to Anthony Blunt, spy work has had an intrinsic appeal, as we imagine dashing figures living double lives, talking in code and risking death for their countries (or someone else's). Having interviewed outspoken former MI6 officer Richard Tomlinson, on publication of his controversial book *The Big Breach: From Top Secret To Maximum Security*, I have no reason to suspect a squirrel might not have done the job any better.

The rodent/mole crime fighting combination was later

taken up by UK animators Cosgrove Hall in the superlative **Danger Mouse**.

––––––––

Sergeant Blast
*See **Wacky Races***

He drove the **Army Surplus Special**, aided by his wimpish underling **Private Meekly**.

––––––––

Sergeant Flint
*See **Hong Kong Phooey***

"Ooh. Ooh!" He was 3% head, 3% leg, 94% body and 100% dum dum. He railed against the janitorial jackass **Penry Pooch**, little knowing that the clumsy canine caretaker was none other than Kung Fu crime fighter Hong Kong Phooey. The sergeant was voiced by Joe E Ross, of Bilko fame.

––––––––

Sergeant Major Grout
*See **Camberwick Green***

Played a mean melodica. Readied the troops at **Pippin Fort** for inspection by **Captain Snort**.

––––––––

Sesame Street
A PBS/Children's Television Workshop production. Created by Joan Ganz Cooney. Bob: Bob McGrath. Susan: Loretta Long. Gordon: Roscoe Orman, Matt Robinson. David: Northern J. Callaway. Mr Hooper: Will Lee. Gina: Alison Bartlett. Luis: Emilio Delgado. Maria: Sonia Manzano. Uncle Wally: Bill McCutcheon. Lillian: Lillias White. USA, 1969-

Salida. Sa—li—da. It was good to have puppets teach you how to leave the room in Spanish. Much better than our own home-grown efforts, **Pipkins**, **Rainbow**, **Hickory House** and **Mr Trimble**. For this was *Sesame Street*, your favourite Harlem back alley, where a policeman was a person in your neighbourhood, which in turn was populated by giant yellow birds (the idiot Big Bird, taking the **Bungle** role), a green scourer called **Oscar the Grouch**, who lived in a "trash" can, a maniac in a white coat who had always "gotta paint a 5", and patient people, slow of voice, who talked benignly to camera and never seemed to do much work. Single-sex relationships were unproblematic: cue **Ernie** and **Bert**, co-habiting men in polyester tops, who taught you valuable lessons about human interaction. "Ah, Ernie, Ernie, I'm going *out* but I don't have my *key*. So I'm going to have to ring the *bell*." Uh, okay Bert. I'll just practice the *drums* while you're gone ...

Plenty of diverting animations kept wandering powers of concentration glued to the TV set, unaware that they were being taught the alphabet and basic numeracy. I'm a **Y**. I can be a **Y**oghurt, or a **Y**acht or ... uh-oh—here comes a **Y**ellow **Y**ak, I'm sure he's going to **Y**ell at me. Mini films, soundtracked with twangy '70s easy listening, told viewers about children of differing races, happily helping their parents prepare meals and do the washing up: "In my family we eat rice for breakfast and whole sugar canes for supper". Nothing was out of the ordinary in this superlative long-running (3000 episodes and counting) educational show for kids.

Kermit the Frog, the on-the-spot reporter, brought you the news on Rapunzel as it happened: "She's letting down her hair even as I speak, now back to the studio". Also present in Muppet form was the **Count**, who was, understandably, obsessed with counting, which gave him a slightly sinister thrill. One! One chocolate cookie! Ah—ah—ah. Two! Two chocolate cookies (cue lightning). Here comes the Cookie Monster, smashing the biscuits into his pretend mouth, sending crumbs flying. What was the difference between near and far? *Sesame Street* could tell you. What about big and small? It could help with that too. One of these things was not like the others—*Sesame Street* would help you ostracise it.

If the songs about co-operation, community spirit and mutual respect did not light your fire, there was always the man who could only talk in sound effects. Open mouth: sound of train. Or how about the duo who could only say one syllable each? "Ham!" "Er!" You want a hammer? But who could ever forget that pinball animation with its poignant lyric: 1, 2, 3, 4, 5— 6, 7, 8, 9, 10—11, 12?

The Muppets—provided by animatronics pioneers Jim Henson, Frank Oz and their team—went on to host their own series *The **Muppet Show***, a string of fairly routine gags, songs and celebrity appearances, given value by the strength of the puppet characters (see also **Fraggle Rock**). *Sesame Street*, meanwhile, went the way of all kids shows: hip hop theme tune.

But despite modernising, the show will always remain a bastion of basic values, where all races get along, where people sit on their porches and co-operate with their neighbours, where people take a genuine interest in the lives of the others around them in their urban community. The weather was always clement, the children were always happy, it was always late summer, where the echoes of some distant ball game and barking dog mixed with glowing feelings of safety, security and nostalgia. All of which leaves only one question. "Can you tell me how to get, how to get to Sesame Street?" It doesn't exist, of course, it's just a utopian ideal, brought to you by the letters C and Y and by the number 7, and made in association with the Children's Television Workshop.

––––––––––

Shaggy
*See **Scooby Doo***

Cowering, tufty-chinned hunchback scruff with eating disorder. Was to all intents and purposes a doofus, but as such was the only one of Scooby's supposedly mellow and groovy gang who could honestly claim hippy status: "Like, zoinks, Scoob". Far out. He was lazy and liked to eat junk food: giant milkshakes and many-layered burgers the size of traffic cones. Oddly, he was voiced by US DJ Casey Casem, the cheesy-grinned, smooth-talking host of America's Top 40 radio show. Yoiks.

Simon in the Land of Chalk Drawings

BBC TV. A FilmFair production. Directed and animated by Ivor Wood. Narrated by Bernard Cribbins. Music by Mike Batt. UK, 1975

Simon was a small child who had disappeared into his own fantasy world and actually believed that the drawings he made with his chalk could come alive and be his friends. There is not a clinical name for this condition, but **Moominmamma** had it as well, when her husband trapped her in a lighthouse where no plants would grow. The show—brought to you by FilmFair, who also produced **The Herbs**, **The Wombles**, **Paddington**, **The Moomins** (with Film Polski) and various others—was narrated by Bernard Cribbins, animated by Ivor Wood and scored by Mike "Remember you're a womble" Batt. A total of 26 charming episodes were made, but for some reason it did not have the pulling power of *The Wombles*. Perhaps it was too subtle, or perhaps it was because Thames' **Jamie and the Magic Torch** knocked spots off it.

Singing, Ringing Tree, The

Feature film. 70 minutes, colour. A DEFA production. Directed by Fransesco Stefani, Germany, 1957

If you looked this up specifically then you were probably as frightened by it in your childhood as the author was. In later life—after therapy—the author has identified a growing circle of friends, family and aquaintances who pale and shudder at the mere mention of its name. Quite apart from the giant goldfish with bulbous eyes, *The Singing, Ringing Tree* was the terrifying film of the equally terrifying Brothers Grimm fairy tale. The Grimms—unrepentant creators of Rumpelstiltskin and other goons—were not known for their anodyne fluffiness, and Stefani's 1957 film does colourful and dramatic justice to the other-worldly horror of the text. Stefani's vision was aided and abetted by cinematographers Karl Plintzner and Walter Roßkopf, whose etherial use of light contributed greatly to the atmosphere. It was shown on UK television regularly enough in the years following its general release to strike abject fear into the hearts of at least two generations of pre-teens. Now it is available on VHS video and DVD (details below) giving today's parents the chance to inflict it on their own unsuspecting off-spring in a choice of formats and languages.

The story—ostensibly a romance, although score nil for erot-ic intrigue, unless the sight of Christel Bodenstein straddling a giant fish in her smalls lights your fire, and it won't—starts with a typical token gift/grail quest. A prince (Eckart Dux) has a thing for a rather superior Princess (Bodenstein), herself a bit of a cold fish. *She* tortures animals; the *Prince* finds her hard to resist. But to win her love he must find the singing, ringing tree. The usual setbacks and hurdles follow and eventually, having enlisted the help of some kind of fairy, he finds it. Hooray.

But here is the twist: before the tree can be released, the Princess must love him back. Since she does not, the Prince is turned into a giant bear by an evil dancing gnome (Richard Krueger). In a surprise move which sets a dubious example for pre-teen romeos, the bear-prince then abducts Bodenstein and spirits her away to something called the Enchanted Forest. For "enchanted" read "ghoulish and filled with weird light and creepy animals". These animals (including the gruesome gold-fish, above) have not forgotten the princess's torturing ways, and they send her to Coventry. Her only friend is this bear, to whom she becomes gradually attracted. Just like in real life, the closer she gets to bestiality, the better the person she becomes. Now, just as it seems the bear-prince will get his girl, Krueger's gnomic wrath (are you still following this?) boils over and he tries to lure the princess away from the grisly forest and into deeper danger. What happens next? The animals help her, she gets the tree (remember the tree?), rescues the prince and they all live happily ever after. In a castle.

The moral of the story is not clear. At first it might appear to be "do not be cruel to animals", but that theory is nixed by the fact that the creatures end up helping their tormentor. Perhaps the moral is "form intimate physical relationships with animals and you will become a better person", but that seems more doubtful the more I think about it. Watching the film again, I am led to conclude that the true message is "do not eat forest toadstools before sitting down to write", a code I believe we could all live by, if pushed.

At the time of writing, *The Singing, Ringing Tree* is available to buy from icestorm-video.com in various versions. For the true retro-terror effect, I highly recommend the English dubbed version, with its chilling non-mastery of lip-sync technology, although there is a certain horror to be derived from the narrated version, which comes complete with the original German dialogue low in the mix like an insistent mad evil teutonic whispering, deep inside your head. Perfect, but again, not to be mixed with mushrooms.

Link: **http://icestorm-video.com/singing_ringing.cfm**

Slash, Johnny
See Square Pegs

Not punk but new wave. It was "a totally different head". He loved the snooty **Fennifer** DeNuccio, but was way too weird to woo her. Was known to own **Devo plastic hair** (wig substitute worn by members of USA's then most technologically geeky but hip new wave band).

Smurfs, The
First series produced by Hanna-Barbera. Second series produced by S.E.P.P. International. Created by Pierre "Peyo" Culliford. Belgium, 1979

Where are you all coming from? From Smurfland where we belong. And that, it goes without saying, is where they should have stayed. *The Smurfs* was a phenomenon. More than that, it was a marketing package. An animated series with tie-in figures and pop records, which span off into a feauture film plus other merchandise, *The Smurfs* was a profiteer's dream. The Smurfs themselves were a race of small blue proto-pokemons in white hats who lived in the forest, where they were tormented by a giant cat. Modelled, possibly, on the seven dwarfs, they all had names like Brainy, Clumsy, Lazy, Jokey, Grouchy and Tracker. There was a patriarch called Papa Smurf and a token bimbo called Smurfette. It was not clear whether Papa was her daddy or her sugar-daddy (see **Moominpappa** and **Snork Maiden**). Her fluttering eyelashes and minimal input told viewers where the woman stood in Smurf society. You could collect the set, if you were willing to nag your mummy until she caved in. The TV show, all things considered, can only have been done for money and not love, which renders it small fry in terms of cult viewing. Two series of animations were made to whet the tweeny spending appetites. The first was made by US arch animator Hanna-Barbera, which should have known better. The usual suspects were there on voice duties, notably Don "**Scooby Doo**" Messick and Paul "**Bubi Bear**" Winchell. The second series was made by Belgian production house S.E.P.P. International.

Journalist Louis Barfe reports that the Smurfs' records were released in the UK on the Decca label. "To think," says Mr Barfe, "they rejected the Beatles, but went for the Smurfs". But business is business. The Smurfs songs were the creation of one Pierre Kartner, a songwriter and producer who went under the name of Father Abraham. In another strange marketing deal or "strategic alliance", the Smurfs ended up endorsing National petrol in a series of advertisements. Petrol, Smurfs; petrol, Smurfs . . . the two don't immediately go together, until you imagine dousing one with the other.

According to the *Look-In Television Annual* 1981 (Thanks Phil Norman) The Smurfs were invented by Belgian artist Pierre Culliford. As he asked a dinner companion to pass the salt, he used the word *schtroumpfe*, meaning "thingy" in Flemish and in a flash of inspiration took it for the name of a band of blue midgets he had been working on. The name was translated to Smurf for anglophone territories. Gratingly, the "blue fuckers" —

as one of the author's survey respondents put it—inspired a host of mocking songs, which surely misses the point. Surely the Smurfs were mocking us? After all, we were the ones buying into it. The Barron Knights had a go at it, as did Jonathan King who released the memorable hit "Lick a Smurf for Christmas", under the *nom de disque* of Father Abraphart and the Smurps. S.E.P.P. and Peyo, according to their chum Jeffrey **"Dr Snuggles"** O'Kelly, still hold the rights and are going strong. So that's that. Next.

Snagglepuss
ITV. A Hanna-Barbera production. USA, 1961

"Heavens to Murgatroyd!" Snagglepuss—a self-consciously *outré* pink pussycat from US animators Hanna-Barbera—first appeared in January 1961 as part of *The Yogi Bear Show*, but span off into his own series, repeated for years. A total of 32 episodes of the Hanna-Barbera show were produced and Kellogg's sponsored the syndicated series, resulting in a string of Snagglepuss-endorsed cereal adverts.

Far too fey and far too cool to get mixed up in undignified pursuits, he would excuse himself from potentially rough stuff by saying, with a delicate flick of the paw: "Exit—stage left," before scramming, accompanied by Hanna-Barbera standard-issue **xylophone hammering** (Doodleoodleoodleoodleoodleoodle, Peeoww!). Snagglepuss was supposed to be a mountain lion but, since he was bright pink and wore a bowtie, this categorizing was obviously no more than a device to enable bungling oafs with blunderbuss guns to try and hunt him down like the jungle meat he was, so providing the plot for every show.

Snagglepuss seems to have been Hanna-Barbera's answer to the evergreen Bugs Bunny—with similar gun-escaping antics—but, in this encyclopaedia's view, he never had the charm of the buck-toothed one. This was mainly because he had a voice like breaking coke. Inflected like the dark love child of Truman Capote and Stephen Hawking, the voice was created by veteran voice artist Daws Butler who, when all is said and done, must have been a trooper to squawk 32 episodes of this stuff. You found yourself siding with the hunters. The only bit that made me laugh out loud was when, about to fall out of a tree, the pink one said: "Exit—stage down."

Snagglepuss, however, is not entirely without worth. In adult life, a good example of effective Snagglepuss use—which has the added value of compounding injury with insult—is the random insertion of his name in employment rejection letters:

> Dear Mr Lewis
> Thank you for your interest in the post of [anything senior]. We regret that we will not be able to snagglepuss your application at the present time. However we appreciate the effort you have made and would like to keep your CV on file ... etc

Link: **www.cartoonnetwork.co.uk/bts/snaggle-puss/index.html**

Video: Snagglepuss: *Major Operation* Hanna-Barbera

Snork Maiden
See Moomins, The

In terms of feminine beauty she looked a little like Miss Piggy, only more hippo-like. Nevertheless, she activated **Moomintroll**'s hormone centre, with her fringe and ankle-bracelet combo, and he was always trying a little too hard to impress her. Sadly, she was selfish and superficial. But in being so, she was permanently teaching Moomintroll to value personality over looks, which he never did, doomed as he was to endure her hot-and-cold game playing. The Moomins acquired her when Moomintroll rescued her from some beast and her father the Snork, seizing the moment, dumped his dumpy daughter on the doe-eyed troll and ran off, never to be seen again. My publisher has put it to me that the Snork minor was having a torrid affair with **Moominpappa**. For an in-depth probe please look at the **Moomins** entry.

Snufkin
See Moomins, The

Manky hat-wearing, tin-whistle blowing, tent-dwelling, all-knowing, ratrace-eschewing, free agent, friend, story-teller and mentor to **Moomintroll**. He prized solitude and calm, knew all the secrets of the woods and Moominvalley, smoked a pipe and had a dearth of material goods. In the novels by Tove Jansson he played a harmonica. He also named a small animal Teety-Woo, to his instant regret. He was the only son of the Joxter, as revealed in **Moominpappa**'s memoir. In another world he might have been a jobless charlatan, forever justifying his laziness and lack of mettle with high-minded anti-capitalist notions of freedom. But this was Moominvalley and he was a hero.

Sooty Show, The
ITV. A Thames production. Produced by Daphne Shadwell. Directed by John Rhodes. Presented by Harry Corbett. Latterly: Produced and directed by Peter Webb. Presented by Mathhew Corbett. UK, 1968–92

Basil Brush for beginners. Imagine the dewy eyed scene as Harry Corbett turned to his progeny and cried: "One day, son, all this will be yours." What the boy acquired was a mute orange teddy, who communicated in the **Play School** fashion pioneered by Big and Little Ted (pretending to whisper). What else? A grey dog who squeaked unconvincingly and, most alarming of all, a lady panda who spoke. It's not a whole lot to shout about, but don't knock it: the *Sooty Show* ran from 1968 to 1992. That's 24 years during which one or two people didn't have to look for a job. Apart from the positive employment aspect, though, it was unremittingly awful. Inane gags in the **Rentaghost** vein, with various Corbetts grinning to camera, like puppet-loving Jeremy Beadles (see **Fun Factory**) and—surprisingly—looking self-conscious while talking to teddy toys for money. If this is your idea of a cult show, then fine. But at least have a quick read of **Fingerbobs**, a quality show about talking to your hands. It may not be too late. This encyclopaedia could save you.

Spectra
*See **Battle of the Planets***

Alien adversaries of **G-Force**. They were led by an enigmatic fluffy-faced villain. He looked like one of those hairy pencil tops that got nicked out of people's pencil cases on day one after the Christmas holidays, appeared to **Zoltar** on a screen and gave him his evil orders, eg: destroy G-Force.

Spiderman
ABC. An ABC-Marvel-Grantray-Lawrence-Krantz production. Executive Producers: Robert L. Lawrence, and Ralph Bakshi USA, 1967-69

Peter Parker—after picking a radioactive peck of pickled pepper (surely, after being bitten by a radioactive spider?)—finds himself transmogrified into a crime fighting superhuman, capable of launching web at great speed from his arteries and sticking to walls with his sticky spider hands. Spiderman, therefore, did a lot of climbing up sheer walls and emitting web in the name of snatcher-catching. Villains were never far away, but woe betide the foe who dared get tangled up in Spiderman's wily web. It was all in the wrists, you see. And he could only use his powers for good. Spiderman/Peter Parker was voiced by two actors—Bernard Cowan and Paul Sols—over 52 half-hour episodes of uniform silliness. Gripping—insofar as adhesive was involved—but not as good as the live-action **Batman**.

Bob
Carolgees

Spikers, the
See Chorlton and the Wheelies

They were spineless, they were spiky balls with eyes and they did **Fenella**'s bidding. Mostly, this meant rounding up the Wheelies, that Fenella might harm them.

Spit the Dog
See Tiswas

ITV's very own punk pooch. It spat. That was its act. Could have had **Posh Paws** any day. It was attached to Bob Carolgees (see also **Houdi Elbow**).

Splasher
See Marine Boy

Minor character in sea-based Japanese *anime* cartoon. Type: dolphin. Colour: white. Uses: not many.

Spook
See Top Cat

Dibble-avoiding alley-cat also-ran, voiced by Leo DeLyon.

Square Bear
See Hair Bear Bunch, The

He was the big, pot-bellied one with the deep voice. His hat covered his eyes, and when he took it off, his hair was the same shape.

Square Pegs
CBS. An Embassy Television production. Created and produced by Anne Beatts. USA, 1982–3

Set in the fictional **Weemawee High** school, this sitcom for teenagers followed the futile efforts of unconfident freshmen

Lauren Hutchison (Amy Linker) and Patty Greene (Sarah Jessica Parker) to fit in at school and become popular. Their efforts went against the odds, since they were geeks and nonentities who did not "click with the cliques", wear the right clothes or come from the right sort of family. For instance, poor Lauren, with her less-than svelte figure and mouth brace, was far too uncool to be accepted into the privileged circle of popular girls, led by the snooty, rich **Jennifer DeNuccio** (Tracy Nelson). Despite efforts to gain approval, Patty and Lauren were doomed to while away their time with leftfield weirdoes like Johnny "Slash" Ulasewicz (Merritt Butrick). "I'm not punk, I'm new wave," he would protest. "It's, like, a totally different head." He spoke a little like **Snagglepuss**, but that was not his main problem. **Johnny Slash** harboured a fierce but enrequited love for Jennifer DeNuccio, whom he addressed as **Fennifer**, for no other reason than to provide the ice queen with yet another reason to spurn him. In one episode, overcome with love, he gave her the gift of a turtle. As far as the encyclopaedia can establish, her response was "Eww."

Just like in real life, of course, the geeks and rejects were the real heroes, and the viewer was invited not to sympathise with snobs and fashion-victims like Fennifer. Unlike almost any other high school show—especially the soft-focus chunk 'n' cheesecake of *Beverley Hills 90210* (not covered in this book; do you mind!), the characters were relatively well-drawn, the scripts were genuinely funny and the transient adolescent heartaches believable. Which is probably why it only lasted one season. The encyclopaedia has found no evidence to support rumours on the Net that reefer-tooting and backstage politics caused its demise: it seems more likely that the ratings just weren't there. The show—created by US *Saturday Night Live* writer Anne Beatts and based on her own experiences—was aimed at the hip and the young, who were probably more inclined to stay in their bedrooms listening to Devo. Channel 4 showed the series in the UK during the early '80s, but its overt references to American popular culture—including appearances by US new wave bands which were the height of cool stateside but ruefully naff in the average Brit-kid's eyes—were destined to ring few teenage bells here. It has not been seen in the UK since, which gives it ultimate cult status in my book. *Square Pegs* may have disappeared but the memory of Patty and Lauren running around the Weemawee High race track wearing ten tracksuits to lose weight is an enduring one.

Link: **www.ecto.org/braces/in/tv/square_pegs.html**
Square Pegs also wins the Cult TV Award for Oddest Web Link. Why not check out the link above —part of a website devoted to the mirthless documenting of TV characters who wore braces in their mouths.

Stepping Stones
ITV. A Yorkshire Television production. UK, 1977-81

Undistinguished lunchtime pre-school effort from Yorkshire. Presented, at least originally, by Paul Copley and Diana Davies. Made you switch back from home dinners to Yellow Fish and Savoury Mince at the school canteen. Insipid title tune stayed in your head all the way through double maths:"Stepping stones, stepping stones, one and two and three ..."Where was **Pipkins** when you needed it?

Stiletto
*See **Danger Mouse***

Crow henchman of the evil **Baron Silas Greenback**, Stiletto was a cod-mafioso, compete with Sicillian accent voiced by the show's writer Brian Trueman (see also **Chorlton & the Wheelies**).

Stingray

ITV. An AP Films/ATV/ITC production. Created by Gerry and Sylvia Anderson. Produced by Gerry Anderson. Directed by Alan Patillo, Desmond Saunders, David Elliot and John Kelly. Written by Gerry and Sylvia Anderson, Dennis Spooner and Alan Fenell. Music by Barry Gray. UK, 1964–5

"I name this child . . . Phones". It was the 21st century* and the World Aquanaut Security Patrol (WASP), was kept busy patrolling the oceans (see **Marine Boy**) abating trouble with Titan (voiced by Ray Barrett). The latter was a bit of a maniac (see **Zoltar**) and—not content with lording it over Titanica (a made-up under-water world)—he fancied ruling all the oceans and land and sent armies of Aquaphibians in **Titan Terror Fish** (a kind of armoured shoobunkin) to squash the humans and start a rein of evil. His idiot spy was Agent X20 (voiced by Robert Easton) who mingled unobtrusively into the crowds with his furtive, creeping manner and enormous, bulbous eyes.

But WASP was not to be had over. Even though the boss, Commander Shore (voiced by Ray Barrett), had lost the use of his legs and floated about in a hovercraft, there were still a few resources. For example, Captain **Troy Tempest**—a plastic beefcake (voiced by Don Mason)—was on hand to pilot Stingray, the WASP submarine, which was launched from an underwater tunnel at Marineville. Tempest's Texan co-pilot was the fag-puffing Phones, also known as George Sheridan. **Lady Penelope** (see **Thunderbirds**) and the beautiful, brooding **Marina** completed the crew, although their exact jobs were a bit vague. Marina was mainly there, it seems, to keep Tempest's testosterone bubbling in the manly fight against Titan and the protection of Pacifica, Marina's underwater home. Marina—a beguiling cross between Botticelli's Venus and a gudgeon—was the mute, green-haired mermaid, whom Troy had previously plucked from the oily grasp of Titan. Her lack of vocal chords stopped her from ever being able to tell Troy how she felt. But that did not prevent her from looking daggers at Atlanta Shore—the commander's able-bodied young daughter (voiced by Lois "Moneypenny" Maxwell)—whose Tempest tempting made Marina's mermaid scales stand on end. Rumours of a naked catfight episode have never been substantiated.

The third of Anderson's Supermarionation shows (it followed 1961's *Supercar* and 1963's *Fireball XL5*), *Stingray* had the distinction of being the first British television series to be filmed in colour. The Beeb showed it in black and white. A whopping 39 scaly skirmishes were filmed, at a cost of an equally whopping (then) £1m. It is inappropriate to lampoon the show, as it was fairly tongue-in-cheek to begin with and quite capable of lampooning itself. Just savour the delicious irony in that crooning closing song as we hear: "Marina, Aqua Marina, why can't you say the words that my heart is longing to hear? ..." Verdict: deep.

* It still is of course, but it wasn't then—back then it was the future, whereas now the future is the present and that future is all in the past.

Stone Rollers
*See **Bailey's Comets***

Rock-related competitor of Barnaby Bailey's teenage roller skate derby team in the De Patie-Freleng competitior of Hanna-Barbera's **Wacky Races**. This team is not to be confused with the **Boulder Mobile**.

Storybook International
ITV. No one is admitting to making it. UK tx 1981-87

"I am the storyteller, and my story must be told." Admit it, you taunted suspected liars with that song in the playground, rubbing your chin furiously as you danced the dance of disbelief. If not, you missed out on the only feasible use for *Storybook International*, a painfully long series of gawdy sub-Cinderella token gift stories and folk fables from around the world, worringly akin to **The Singing Ringing Tree**. Remember the story teller from the opening titles, with pointy shoes and whimsical feathered cap, wrapping himself around a tree? Full of woodcutters in shiny tunics, barely worn from a lifetime of no actual woodcutting, evil matriarchs, high-busted Estonian girls and evil, moustachioed man (see also **Dick Dastardly** and **Danger on the Danube Delta**), this **Jackanory** wannabee with a dangerously imbalanced lute-to-plot ratio was at very best a sobering lesson in how not to lip-sync. From the episode "Simpleton Peter", to "Morwen of The Woodlands" ("A Prince grows bored with his once young and beautiful wife ...") the series traipsed through every moral lesson known to man and is even now being flogged—perhaps unsurprisingly—to American schools as a curriculum-based learning programme. As its title suggests, the series was dubbed into about as many languages as rights could be sold for, including English, proving the widely held belief that everyone in medieval times spoke like Pam Ayres (see also **Pogle's Wood**). Well, didn't they? In Germany he was Johann, in England he was John. He was an idiot, but luckily, he's gone (I might have made that last line up).

Superted

A Siriol Animation production. Produced by Mike Young. Directed by Dave Edwards. Written by Robin Lyons. UK, 1982

An unconvincing polkadot alien called, er, Spotty imbued a toy bear with special powers. The bear became Superted—pronounced syooperted—and went off on a stream of tawdry animated adventures the production of which was sponsored by something called Sianel Pedwar Cymru.

Swap Shop
*See **Multi-Coloured Swap Shop, The**. BBC TV. A BBC production. UK, 1981-82*

The cunning new name for the **Multi-Coloured Swap Shop** relaunch. It sank after a year.

Sylvester Sneekley
*See **Penelope Pitstop***

By day he was Penelope's doting guardian. By night he was the evil **Hooded Claw** whose aim it was do do away with Penelope and claim the riches bequeathed to her. He had a nasty-looking nose and a camp voice supplied by Daws "**Snagglepuss**" Butler.

Take Hart

BBC TV. A BBC Bristol production. Produced by Patrick Dowling. UK, 1977

"Oh, hallo Morph." **Vision On** presenter Tony Hart steward-ed this popular, art-based spin-off show in a series of open-necked shirts, matched only by those of the producer, **Why Don't You** mastermind Patrick Dowling (see also **Vision On** and **Adventure Game, The**). Mocked-up at the BBC's Whiteladies Road outpost in Bristol, the light-filled artist's garret shared a studio with **Animal Magic,** *Why Don't You, Wildtrack* and the rest of the BBC Bristol portfolio.

Effortless demonstrations of art and craft techniques were ably given by the reassuring and emphatically non-patronis-ing Mr Hart. "Then just spill a bit of wax here ... like that, and ... just brush away the glitter ... there ... we ... are ... and ... there's our Mona Lisa." Children were empowered through Tony to visualise, imagine, experiment and ultimately balls up their own projects at home without the fear of "getting it wrong" or being laughed at by peers.

However, there was the opportunity to be publicly humili-ated via the *Take Hart* Gallery. Children were encouraged to send in their own string-and-Quality-Street-wrapper *chefs d'oeuvre*, along with their all-important age, to be displayed to the tune of John Williams playing "Cavatina" on the Spanish guitar. "This use of felt pen really gives a feeling of movement," Tony would comment, often rather generously. "Katie's really had fun with different textures in this piece," he might say of someone's Tippex and sandpaper effort. But send your treasured *meisterwerk* to Tony and that would be the last you ever saw of it. The old *Vision On* disclaimer was still going strong: "I'm sorry we can't return your pictures, but there is a prize for each one we show." This was later modified to "small prize".

The art demos were broken up by charming stop-frame animations, often involving mutable sand, à la **Sesame Street**, or aerial films of Tony in the carpark with a roller, painting a huge motif that only came together with the last

bit of white paint. But most memorable were the animated interludes involving **Morph**. Morph was a bit of brown plasticine, animated and created by Peter Lord and David Sproxton. Morph lived in a wooden box and was most often the shape of a miniaturised man, but could roll himself into a ball and knock over Tony's ink pot at the drop of a hat. In later series he acquired a slightly pugnacious companion called Chaz who enjoyed lousing things up for both Tony and Morph.

But for every silver lining there has to be a cloud. In the case of *Take Hart* that cloud came in the superfluous shape of Mr Bennett (aka **Play School**'s Ben Thomas) the caretaker, an imbecilic menial whose efforts at slapstick were laughable only because they were embarrassing (see also **Rentaghost**). That the embarrassment was clearly visible on Tony's face should have been pause for directorial thought, but sadly the Bennett quotient was gradually increased, like a dose of deadly poison, causing the show to wither into a shadow of its former glory. That shadow was called *Hartbeat*—a kind of post hip-hop *Take Hart* relaunch which had the added value of Margo, a comely assistant. With Margo, Morph, Chas and Bennett all competing for camera time, Tony—inevitably—became marginalised. The mix was unneccessarily diluted in an attempt to hold a viewing public, whose attention was increasingly being demanded by cooler "street" shows, pop music and tweeny magazines. That *Hartbeat*, by 1996, its dying year, concerned itself with "images of thin people" and "boy bands" showed a programme, and possibly a nation, in poor health. In its time, *Take Hart* was inspirational and charming stuff. Even if you never could be bothered to get your crayons out once it was over.

Tarzan, Lord of the Jungle
A Filmation production. USA

The boy Greystoke in animated jungle fun with Cheeta the chimp, and a lot of wailing into the trees to call the elephants. You know the story. Small aristocratic boy lost in jungle, was brought up by monkeys and ended up thinking he was one.

He talked to the animals (see also **Dr Snuggles**) in their own "language" and protected them from the marauding threat of humans (see also **Marine Boy**). This scenario—had it been real—might have offered two valuable lessons in anthropology and philosophy. Firstly, it might have proven once and for all that the compulsion to cover ones genitals up was, in fact, congenital. After all, the loincloth is hardly a monkey garment. Secondly, you might have been tempted to prophesy that there would always be a vine along when you most needed one. Sadly it wasn't real, so those arguments may not hold up. The butch baboon boy of Africa met his Amazonian avatar in Hanna-Barbera's "me-too" production, **Jana of the Jungle**.

Think of a Number

BBC TV. A BBC Bristol production. Series producer: Cynthia Felgate. Produced by Albert Barber. Written and created by Johnny Ball. UK

Many people paid money to be teachers could have learned a great deal from actor Johnny Ball. He devised, scripted and presented this educational show, which spawned a host of spin-offs. Ball—a veteran of **Play School**, and **Play Away** and adept at playing the fool to get children's attention—used bad puns, visual gags and clear, concise language to engage a generation of children in learning science and maths. Problems became unproblematic. Using only a buffoonish expression, manic delivery and a set of enormous cupboards—out of which props and video footage would appear—the progenitor of Fatboy Slim girl Zoe would take you on a journey through time, from which you would emerge knowing things you didn't know you wanted to know. Physics, astronomy … you name it, it came alive under Ball's stewardship. Pure Genius. The show was produced at the BBC's Bristol outpost, whence came the equally good **Vision On**, **Take Hart**, **Animal Magic** and **Why Don't You**. Ball was also responsible for spin-offs *Think Backwards* and *Think Again*.

Three Musketeers, The

A Hanna-Barbera production. USA, 1968

Undistinguished swashbuckle from Hanna-Barbera, based on Dumas' novel. It was shown as part of the **Banana Splits** and should not be confused with the highly entertaining **Dogtanian and the Muskehounds**.

Tiswas

ITV. An ATV production. UK, 1974-82

"Ooooooooooooooooooooo—kaaaaaaaaaaaaaaaaaaaaaaaayyyyyyy!"

Saturday morning, 10 o'clock. Get out your bread and con-densed milk sandwiches and turn off **Multi-Coloured Swap Shop**—there's a party going on over on ITV. It was time for *Tiswas*. And, twitching with tartrazine as you tucked into your eighth bowl of Golden Nuggets, that familiar stomping rock theme introduced the perfect anarchic antidote to the conservatism of *Swap Shop*. A young Birmingham DJ, Chris Tarrant, led a motley band of TV buccaneers in this controver-sial two and a half-hour matinee-style show for kids. *Tiswas*, at root, was roughly the same recipe as the BBC's more polite offering: a bunch of old cartoons, pop music and special guests, made whole by a studio compere of sorts (see also **Banana Splits, The**). The difference was, well, blindingly obvious.

Swap Shop might have been showing a schoolmarmish Delia Smith cookery segment. But on Tiswas, the **Phantom Flan Flinger** was stalking studio 3 with a plentiful supply of shaving-foam-on-paper-plate flans. They were launched ran-domly, the "flan" lodging in the hair of guests, presenters and crew. Children were pulled up by the ears from under the desk, wide-eyed as pies flew through the air, buckets were emptied, Wunda-gloo was activated and mayhem broke out on all sides—all generated by people who were supposed to be grown up. Adults were only allowed on the show inside a cage, where they were watered at regular intervals, at the bidding of

Mr Tarrant and by a band of only-too-willing bucketeers. Regular visits from guests such as Michael Palin, Terry Jones and Spike Milligan kept the madness levels high.

Cut to **Algernon Winston Spencer Castleray Razzmatazz** (aka unknown comedian Lenny Henry), a cod-rasta in an enormous hat, waxing lyrical about the benefits of DCM (De Condensed Milk) and spilling it all over himself. Cut to Bob Carolgees as **Houdi Elbow** in his jimjams, or later with Charlie the peanut-catching monkey or **Spit the Dog**, his phlegmatic puppet, and a host of terrible shaggy dog stories with pun punchlines (people who live in grass house shouldn't stow thrones, etc). Cut to **Batman**. Back to the studio where Trevor "Lenny Henry" McDoughnut is reading the news in enormous glasses, "Sylvester" McCoy (see **Vision On**) is getting a drubbing in **Compost Corner**, administered by Lenny Henry again as David Bellamy and John Gorman (formerly of the "Lily The Pink"-singing group Scaffold) is dressed as Albert the cleaner and giving everyone a ticking off for getting so much flan and water over his precious studio. Cut to *Return To The Planet Of The Apes*.

The Independent Broadcasting Authority (IBA) was suspicious of *Tiswas*—perhaps because it showed kids having actual fun, irresponsible adults, the odd wet t-shirt in the cage and boasted a minimal educational content. Live television is always a gamble and rock stars lighting up alleged joints on screen cannot have helped *Tiswas* greatly. Sally James, in her now legendary pop interview, did not help by asking Kevin Rowland what the name Dexy's Midnight Runners meant, only to be shushed embarrassedly by the mop haired singer of "Come On Eileen" as a hormonal 10 year-old looked fixedly down her leather-clad front: "Er, I'll tell you later Sally". It was just one in a whole boatload of bloopers the various crew members and presenters committed, upping the adult viewing figures, but vexing the regulating authority. By all accounts *Tiswas* got a stern talking-to from the IBA and was forced to introduce some educational content.

But where had it come from, all of a sudden? The answer is that it had been developing for some time. If you lived in the Midlands in 1974 you would have seen the first 11-episode season, aired by ATV with John Asher at the helm along with Mr Tarrant. The show returned and had survived over 100 episodes before the other ITV regions gradually came on board. One such was London's LWT, which had been broadcasting its own *Saturday Scene*. *Tiswas* acquired its presenter, the racily be-gartered Sally James in time for the start of its 1977 season.

By 1980 *Tiswas* was a national show. Sadly, the rot set in. The IBA sought to clamp down on the violent flan flinging and dodgy gags. Tarrant ran. He took Carolgees and Gorman with him and started one of the worst shows (apart from **Crackerjack**) ever aired: *OTT*, an adult version of *Tiswas*. The morning show limped on, but was clearly lacking its mainstay. Gordon Astley was recruited to take Tarrant's place, but what could he do when Sally James announced her imminent departure? When she jumped in 1982, the show aired its last. It was replaced with an unremitting void and vague sense of betrayal (actually a show called **Fun Factory**, but the net result was the same).

Thunderbirds

ITV. An AP Films production for ATV/ITC. Created by Gerry and Sylvia Anderson. produced by Gerry Anderson and Reg Hill. Written by Gerry and Sylvia Anderson, Allan Fennell, and others. Directed by Alan Patillo and others. Music by Barry Gray. UK, 1965

The scene: **Tracy Island**, a small island in the Pacific, owned by millionaire Jeff Tracy (voiced by Peter Dyneley). A bored ex-astronaut, Tracy needed something to do with his time, so he set up International Rescue, a secret organisation dedicated to good Samaritan work all over the globe. When trouble called, the swimming pool would slide open and spaceships would fly out. It was all very covert, but Tracy had good reason: he did not want his island hideaway to be dicovered by rogue mesmerist The Hood, an arch villain. But perhaps the paranoia was all part of his mid-life crisis. He was helped by his sons (he had a few): Scott (Shane Rimmer), Virgil (David Holiday), Alan (Matt

Zimmerman), Gordon (David Graham), and John (Ray Barrett). Just enough sons to man the Thunderbirds, Tracy's motley fleet of hi-tech rescue craft.

Thunderbird 1 was controlled by eldest sibling Scott. It was a slim rocket and usually the first craft to be dispatched. Thunderbird 2 (this encyclopaedia's favourite) was Virgil's domain. It was a giant olive-green cargo ship. Thunderbird 3 was an orange spaceship, piloted by the short-fused Alan. Alan drove a race car in his spare time and was sleeping with Tin Tin, the daughter of Tracy's Malaysian butler. Gordon, the clown, slipped into Thunderbird 4, the yellow submarine, which lived inside Thunderbird 2. But what of John? Poor John was the sole inhabitant of Thunderbird 5, the satellite space station which beamed messages of distress back to Tracy Island. It could surely have done that without John. Perhaps he was the black sheep. The thunderbirds were kitted out by the bespectacled Brains (not to be confused with **Brain**), who lived in his white lab coat.

Swinging in from time to time was the highly civilised **Lady Penelope**, an aristocratic limey, permanently smoking. She was IR's London agent. She was known to do a bit of work for WASP too (see **Stingray**). Driving her about in her pink Rolls was **Parker**, her deferential proletarian driver. Even in 2063 the one with the regional accent drives the toff. Classy stuff.

Sometimes people would get stuck under ground, or trapped in space, or stuck under water with limited oxygen or . . . it never really mattered. There was plenty to keep viewers interested. From Tracy Island's smooth transformation from '70s Caribbean superpad to high-tech public service operation, to the Thunderbirds themselves, the detail was gripping. Then there were the puppets themselves. More expensive and of a higher quality than the previous three Supermarionation shows, *Thunderbirds* allowed its cast several heads, so that moods could change. This resulted in long shots while Virgil retained the same expression of surprise, or moments of inappropriate seriousness. Each episode cost a staggering $60,000 to produce, with each puppet costing about $500. Now, in 2001, *Thunderbirds* is as popular as ever, with showings on

Channel 4 and vintage collectables fetching prices that verge on the Dark Side.

———

Tintin
*See **Hergé's Adventures of Tintin***

———

Titan Terror Fish
*See **Stingray***

Not really a fish but an armoured submarine which could spit projectiles out of its scaly fish mouth. There was a whole fleet of them, formulated and controlled by Titan and piloted by his army of newt-like aquaphibians, a kind of deep sea-dwelling paramilitary organisation whose sole mission was to blow up **Stingray** and its occupants and so control the oceans. Although the Titan Terror Fish was reasonably formidable, it is not to be confused with the genuinely terrifying giant goldfish out of **The Singing Ringing Tree**, which really was the stuff of nightmares.

———

Tog
*See **Pogles Wood***

A sort of pink and white striped squirrel with a speech impediment. Odd, but **Pippin** liked him.

———

Toadies
*See **Chorlton and the Wheelies***

Frankly, they were mushrooms. They spied on the Wheelies for **Fenella**. The Christmas carol they sang in "Chorlton & the

Iceworld" is one of the forgotten masterpieces of children's television. Probably. They were voiced by Joe Lynch.

Tomorrow People

ITV. A Thames Television production. Produced by Ruth Boswell, Vic Highes and Roger Price. Directed by various including Stan Woodward, Roger Price, Leon Thau and Vic Hughes. Created by Roger Price. Written by Roger Price, Jon Watkins and Brian Finch. Music by Dudley Simpson and Brian Hodson. UK, 1973-79

Wow, digital watches! Science Fiction fantasy involving something called homo superior: the next stage of human evolution. A group of these teenage superior homos known as The Tomorrow People, had developed a whole bunch of teles: telepathy, telekinesis and teleportation. These were, respectively, the ability to read other people's thoughts, to move objects without touching them and to transport theselves from one place to another without using the Tube. Actually, that last bit only partly true: their headquarters was in an old tunnel of the London Underground, which they called the Lab. But, for all their futuristic tendencies, they referred to teleporting as 'jaunting'—ie: "Let's jaunt!" Quaint. TIM was the talking computer whose "biotronic" capabilities allowed him to have a reassuringly human interface.

The Tomorrow People had also developed an inability to kill, which gave them a slight disadvantage over less than pacifistic enemies. Stun guns at the ready, then, this band of teenagers were dispatched by something called the Galactic Federation to protect planet earth (see also **Battle of the Planets**), which they did by "jaunting" about various sets made of card and sticky-backed plastic (see **Blue Peter**) and—in the case of a young Peter Davison—in a pair of silver underpants.

'Breaking out' as a superior homo was a difficult and traumatic process for adolescents, but the established Tomorrow People found those on the verge of recognising their true selves and took them under their wing. This device allowed the cast to fluctuate with alarming regularity. A gripping 68 30-minute episodes were made and aired over six seasons by Thames (see **Rainbow**). The show was created by Roger Price, who had intended to produce a show to rival **Dr Who**. But sometimes even the best laid plans . . . Let's jaunt. Next . . .

Tom's Midnight Garden

BBC TV. A BBC production. Produced by Paul Stone. Directed by Christine Secombe. UK, 1988

More of a classic than a cult piece, but no TV encyclopaedia—not even this one—would be complete without it. The credits above relate to an elegantly produced and respectful six-part adaptation of the famous children's novel of the same name by Philippa Pearce. Although the BBC made three adaptations of the novel—the first appearing in 1968 as part of the schools programme *Merry Go Round*, and the second 1974, as a stand-alone drama in three parts—the six-part series was to be the one most remembered.

Tom (Jeremy Rampling) was sent away to a handy Aunt Alan and Uncle Gwen (or was it the other way around?) to evade some form of pox (measles, his brother's—in those days it could kill you, probably). Sadly, the aunt and uncle lived in Norfolk which—as well you know—is where all sinister and dubious things happen. You need only think of Bernard Matthews.

It happened that aunty and uncle had a curious grandfather clock which was capable of striking the hour thirteen. Spooky. It just makes you want to go out into the garden in the middle of the night, doesn't it? Tom did, and discovered himself in a magical (read eerie) *jardin* (see also **The Singing Ringing Tree**). In this garden was little orphan Hattie, a girl. They became friends. No shenanigans, though, because she kept getting older, each time he went out there at night. What was going on? You kept thinking there must be some kind of clue in that grandfather clock, ticking and tocking and striking the wrong time . . . wrong time . . . wrong time . . . Well, it was beyond me.

On his last night the whole system collapsed and he stumbled out into the dustbins—no weird garden, no Hattie. But just who *was* that crazy old woman up in the top of the house? Read the book, it's much better than mine. The series was repeated in 1991 and released on video, but is now deleted for some bewildering reason. *Tom's Midnight Garden*—the TV adaptation—is not to be confused with *A Stitch in Time*, a tapestry-related tale of similar timewarp capers, dramatised with cunning use of haunting Irish jiggery which used to spook you up a treat on the way back from your Granny's.

Top Cat

ABC, syndicated. A Hanna-Barbera production. produced by Bernie Wolf. Directed by Ray Patterson. UK tx BBC 1. USA, 1961

Possibly the most perfectly realised of Hanna-Barbera's cartoon capers, *Top Cat* followed the money-making pursuits of the eponymous Top Cat ("whose intellectual close friends get to call him TC, providing it's with dignity")—a smooth-talking New York alley cat from the 13th precinct in a purple waistcoat and hat, through which his cat ears protruded in a beguiling fashion. He tipped waiters with a coin on a string, stole his morning newspaper and jumped onto the back of taxis.

A seasoned hustler, TC lived in a trash can and used **Officer Dibble**'s police phone as his own. Dibble, a second-rate neighbourhood beat cop, voiced by movie actor Allen Jenkins—was unhealthily obsessed with booking TC, although he never pinned anything on him. All he could ever do was command him to "clean up this alley". Meanwhile TC, with the aid of his loyal band of hoodlum toms—tried everything within his powers to make a nickel. Such scams involved passing off the rotund **Benny the Ball** as Catwalladur—the missing heir to a fortune—which brought him into unfortunate contact with a **Muttley**-esque snickering dog. In one episode Benny looked so bedraggled a passing millionaire philanthropist gave him a cheque for a million dollars, and the local tradesmen all flocked to TC's alley to offer him their finest wares. But of course TC tore the cheque up, thinking it was for a few cents and returned to his hustling ways, banging impatiently on his trash can lids to call his cohorts.

Fancy Fancy was the brown romeo in the white scarf, constantly putting his amorous pursuits on hold to bail out TC. **Spook** was the green one with the, like, kooky voice, man. **Choo Choo** could generally be relied upon, while **Brain** could not. And Benny, well Benny was just there, oblivious to all around him. Billed in the UK as *Boss Cat* to avoid a cat food brand-name lawsuit, *Top Cat* was really a send-up of the Phil Silvers show, with actor Larry Steng providing TC's Bilko croon and Private Doberman actor Maurice Gosfield providing the voice for Benny the Ball. There is little in animation history to surpass the interchanges between TC, Dibble and Benny the Ball: a masterpiece of comic scripting, voiced with perfect timing. Only **Danger Mouse** came close to this kind of team work.

Given his flagging fortunes and inability to make any gelt, it remains a surprise how TC stayed on Top, but he did. Perhaps it was sheer charisma. As the theme tune (second only in excellence to Hanna-Barbera's **Help! It's The Hair Bear Bunch**) testified: "He's the boss, he's a VIP, he's the championship. He's the most tip top ...Top Cat."

Touché Turtle and Dum Dum

A Hanna Barbera production. USA, 1962

"Touché awayyyyyy!" The drawn-out adventures of an ineffectual turtle musketeer wannabe and his hairy dog sidekick Dum Dum. Standard Hanna-Barbera fare of the period (see **also Lippy the Lion** and **Wally Gator**).

Toytown
*See **Larry the Lamb***

Pretend home of equally pretend lamb. Bah.

Tracy Island
*See **Thunderbirds***

Secret ocean hideaway of **International Rescue**. Not to be confused with **Danger Island**.

Treacle Tree
*See **Doctor Snuggles***

Anthropomorphised plant, with face, who dreamed of going away on adventures, just like the strangely-trousered inventor and part-time messiah **Doctor Snuggles**, whose antics he observed. Sadly he was wood and as such, rooted to the ground outside **Rickety Rick**, a shed made out of, er, wood. There is something decidely macabre about that whole scenario.

Troy Tempest
*See **Stingray***

Chunky, handsome submarine pilot and WASP captain. He patrolled the oceans with **Phones**, **Lady Penelope** and **Marina**. He was voiced by Don Mason.

Trumpton

BBC TV. A Gordon Murray Puppets production. Created, written and produced by Gordon Murray. Animated by Bob Bura and John Hardwick. Narrated and sung by Brian Cant. Music by Freddie Philips. UK, 1967

It was the nearest town to **Camberwick Green**. The town clock started each episode, "telling the time steadily, sensibly, never too quickly, never too slowly". Captain Flack and his firemen carried this stop-frame animation from Gordon Murray. You know the ones: **Pugh, Pugh, Barney McGrew, Cuthbert, Dibble, Grubb**. Picking up the telephone in his fire station, Flack would fulfill the same role as the army in Camberwick Green: solving minor problems. "Elevate," Flack would say, and the fire engine's ladder would go up so Grubb could rescue some errant kitty or perform some other non-dangerous function. The mayor, meanwhile, was more concerned with his chain of office than council matters. Every day at three o'clock, the fire brigade would play a fantastic waltz in the bandstand and that would be the end of the show. Verdict: excellent use of waltz, but not as good as **Chigley**.

Tucker's Luck

BBC 2. A BBC production. Produced by David Hargreaves. Created by Phil Redmond. UK, 1983-85

Cheeky cockerney chappie Tucker Jenkins (pronounced Jinekins) got too old for school and span off into his own show for teenagers who had grown older with him. The gritty adolescent action followed the trials of the later teenage years: trying to find a job; picking up your girlfriend from, er, school on your 50cc motorbike; being broke; putting aftershave mistakenly on your inexperienced Johnson; getting into fights and dabbling with beer, curry and chips. But most of all: wearing a black leather jacket and white t-shirt in a bid to look like the Fonz. Tucker (Todd Carty) was joined by an older, slimmer Alan Humpries (George Armstrong) and Trisha "shtewwpid" Yates

(Michelle Herbert). Todd went on to become Mark Fowler in *EastEnders*: the person Tucker would have become were he to have been diagnosed with clinical depression—something which could indeed have been brought on by snogging Trisha Yates for money. Don't knock it, it's done him all right, and at least he's not **Bungle**.

Turbo Terrific
*See **Wacky Races***

Super car, driven by the square-jawed, big-egoed **Peter Perfect**. He was not, of course, perfect: his Achilles heel was southern belle **Penelope Pitstop**.

Tyrone/Super Hero Tyrone
*See **Baggy Pants and the Nitwits***

Bumbling, mumbling, sexually frustrated retired super hero and star of *The Nitwits*, voiced by Arte Johnson. He was short, unsteady of foot and facially-haired. He was also married to the matronly and unapproachable Gladys—hence the sexual frustration. He looked a little like **Captain Caveman** in a dirty mac.

U

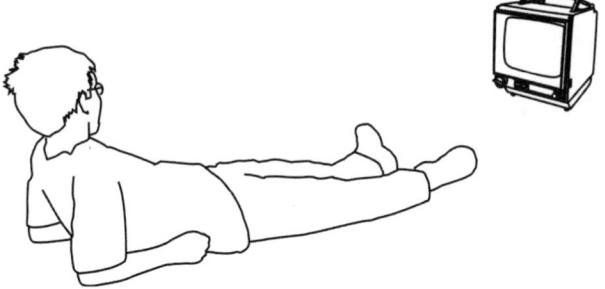

Uncle Bill
See Doctor Snuggles

Louche relative of Dr Snuggles, cropping up in exotic locations and living a life of mystery. He was based on a real life person: creator Jeffrey O'Kelly's own, er, Uncle Bill.

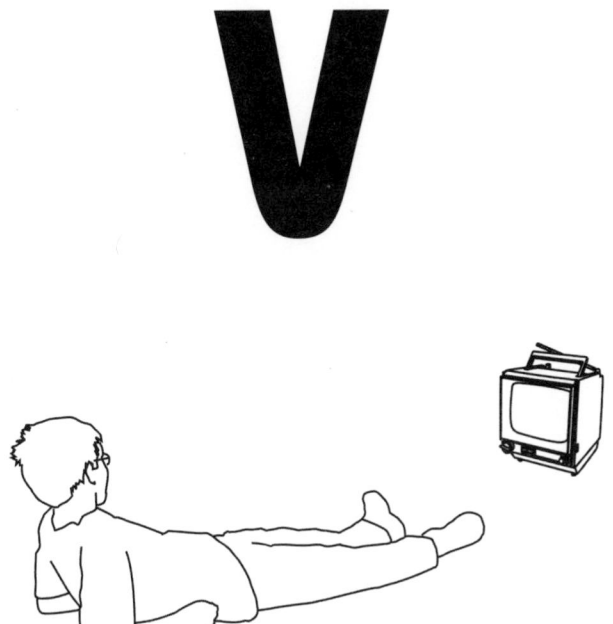

Valley of the Dinosaurs

CBS. A Hanna-Barbera production. USA, 1974

Hanna-Barbera's Amazon vortex extravaganza was shown in the UK on **the Multi-Coloured Swap Shop**. The latter show was the better for it, until *Valley* ... was replaced in that slot by **Hong Kong Phooey**. While rafting in the South American jungle, John Butler (voiced by Mike Road), his wife Kim (Shannon Farnon), their two children, Katie and Greg and Digger the Dog were sucked into a giant whirlpool. Plausibly, when they came out of the other side, they were in the Stone Age.

Equally plausibly, they made friends with a family of hirsute Neanderthals, Gorak, Gera, Tana and Lok, with their pet stegosaurus Glomb. A moving and poignant tale of two cultures ensued. Every so often an aeroplane would be sighted in the sky and the Butlers would wave frantically and jump up and down, as though in some cargo cult ritual, but the pilots never saw them and they were never found. Bleak, really. But since this was an American show, each family had lots to learn from the other.

Velma

*See **Scooby Doo***

She may have been dumpy, but she had brains. That was the formula anyway. In fact, the bespectacled Velma was one of those keeners who told on you at school when you hadn't done your work. She lost her glasses with comforting regularity, causing her to crawl around on all fours in a state of near-panic. Shame, though, that the four-eyed should be portrayed—as is so often the case—as a stereotypical charmless brainiac. Seeing is not everything (see **Vision On** *below*). Best quote: "Hmm, I think I'm beginning to figure out this kooky deep-freeze mystery."

Vision On

BBC TV. A BBC Bristol production. Devised and produced by Patrick Dowling. Directed by Peter Wiltshire and Clive Doig. UK

Radio was a bit dull if you were deaf. And television was only half useful. Montage sequences with a voiceover were lost on those who didn't hear (although a non-hearing capability was a distinct advantage with most **Hanna-Barbera cartoons** [see **Wally Gator**]). Here at last, though, was a children's television show designed to work just as well for deaf people as it it did for hearing people. Who can forget presenter Tony Hart delivering the famous *Vision On* gallery disclaimer, with Pat Keysell signing apologetically in the corner: "We are sorry we cannot return your pictures, but there is a prize for each one we show"? The show focused on stimulating visual awareness, with long mute sequences of art and crafts, keeping the hearing on board with plenty of music.

Dowling's visual feast included DIY danger with papier maché and solder supremo Wilf Lunn, the usual apeing about from Sylvester McCoy (see **Tiswas** and **Jigsaw**) and stop-motion mayhem from the white-coated Prof. He never moved his feet, but shot across fields in his lab coat. Meanwhile, Tony was out with his football pitch roller, marking up giant white murals in the car park, that could only be seen from above. Hart, of course, carried this show and soon had his own visual stimulus vehicle: **Take Hart**. Although *Vision On* was the brain-child of Patrick Dowling (see **Take Hart**, **Why Don't You**, **Adventure Game**), the contribution of director Clive Doig should not be underestimated if his own **Jigsaw** was anything to go by. *Vision On*: flawless teatime telly. Sadly missed by those who remember it.

Vision On: *by kind permission of Roc Renals*

Vortex
See Adventure Game, The

Nebulous conceptual purgatory, into which erring contestants were nominally flung if they stepped on the wrong space on a game board on this Patrick Dowling-produced, cheaply-made forerunner to the *Crystal Maze*. Fired the imaginations of children, for a while.

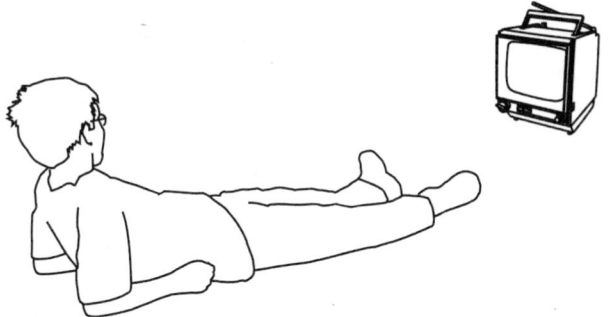

Wacky Races, The

CBS. A Hanna-Barbera production. Created by William Hanna and Joseph Barbera. Directed by Iawo Takamoto. USA, 1968

"Muttley! Get me out of this crrream puff, you dum-dum!"

Excellent Hanna-Barbera cartoon, not shown nearly often enough. Eleven idiosyncratic vehicles competed in an ever-lasting series of automobile races across country, hampered at every turn by the evil and ridiculously-hatted **Dick Dastardly** (voiced by Paul Winchell in sinister English accent with rolled 'r's). His dual-fanged mongrel sidekick **Muttley** (Don Messick) was always on hand to help, but the hound's loyalty was none too strong. Obsessed by winning by foul means or fouler, Dastardly used a host of unsporting devices such as saws on his wheels, oil spills, giant magnets and elaborately contrived plots.

Here's one: "This toy soldier, Muttley, has a line with a cork, on which is a lighted wick. The soldier will march and fall into that hole in the road. The cork will plug the hole, bringing the wick up to light the fuse which leads to the dynamite attached to the bottom of that tank which is filled with choc-o-late fudge. And when it explodes, the cars below will become gooey choc-o-late fudge, bu-wa-ha-ha-ha-ha-haaa."

Dastardly's plans, of course, always backfired—"Drat, and double drrat!"—causing Muttley to scorn him with his trade-mark wheezing snicker (see also **Spot** and **Hong Kong Phooey**). Typically, the moustachioed maniac would repay his mongrel's muttish mockery with a well-aimed glob of goo, causing the hound to growl his grumbling sound-effect: "Snckn-fstn-mckn-snckn-wawa-grr".

So just who were "those way-out, wacky racers"? Well ... The **Bouldermobile** was driven by the Slag Brothers: Rock Slag, voiced by Daws Butler and Gravel Slag, voiced by Don Messick. Guess what it was made of (hint: a boulder). In 1968 US parlance, the word "slag" was simply another word for "scree". The drivers were two forerunners to **Captain**

329

Caveman, complete with lumpy clubs. The **Compact Pussycat** was steered by the flighty, cosmetics-driven **Penelope Pitstop** (Janet Waldo). It had various in-built automations, such as extendable mirrors. As she would say: "Neatness counts". **Professor Pat Pending** (Don Messick), drove the **Convert-a-Car,** a Heath Robinson-esque, high-tech vehicle, capable of changing into a plane, tank, boat. In one episode he confounded opponents by changing into an exact copy of the Slag Brothers. Next up, the **Creepy Coupé** (pronounced coop) was the gothic-style motor of the **Gruesome Twosome**: **Big Gruesome** (Daws Butler) was an enormous Frankenstein character with a floppy fringe, while **Li'l Gruesome** (Don Messick) was a mini mauve dracula in a white suit. With candles for headlamps and its own "batty belfry" the creepy coup could switch to ghost, snake or dragon power via a host of ghoulish goons living in its tower.

The **Crimson Haybailer** was less a combined harvester and more of a German monoplane on pram wheels, manned by **Red Max** (Daws Butler), a kind of Von Richthoven take-off. Sometimes he did take off. The **Ant Hill Mob** (Mel Blanc) was a band of dwarf hoodlums in bespoke tailoring—visually a cross between the Munchkins and Showaddywaddy (see also **Cheggers Plays Pop**)—who drove the **Bullet-Proof Bomb** and spent too much time trying to protect **Penelope Pitstop**. Ever changing in number—sometimes six, sometimes seven, sometimes eight—they were led by **Clyde**: not Clyde Barrow of Bonnie Parker fame, but a gruff-voiced midget in a pork pie hat.

The **Arkansas Chuggabug** was a hillbilly themed vehicle, more like a motorized verandah than a car. It had a cast iron stove for an engine and was driven by the non-proactive **Lazy Luke** and his pet, Blubber Bear (both voiced by John Stephenson). The bear sat on the rocking chair and Luke sat on the bear.

The **Army Surplus Special**—one half steam roller, one half tank—was driven by a couple of miliary goons: the thick-necked **Sergeant Blast** and **Private Meekly**, a gawky nincompoop. The **Turbo Terrific** was the modestly named supercar, driven by the treacle-voiced **Peter Perfect** (Daws Butler). He was not, of course, perfect. His Achilles' heel was southern belle Penelope Pitstop, whose "Hey-elp, hey-elp" frailty drove him to acts of attempted heroism (see also **Snork Maiden** and **Moomintroll**), which rarely won him the race (see also **The Perils of Penelope Pitstop**). Dastardly and Muttley drove the **Mean Machine**, of course. It goes without saying that they never won. The races were narrated in rhyming couplets by Dave Wilcock, who switched at some point in every episode to the radar screen, on which the crazy cars would appear as white bean-shaped blobs, with one or two going backwards.

The cartoon owed a great deal to Blake Edwards' feature film *The Great Race*. This 1965 comedy (see also **Pink Panther**) featured colourful goodies and baddies competing in an international auto race in the '20s. The film starred Jack Lemmon, Tony Curtis and Nathalie Wood, who was often to be seen in her smalls covered in pie. The Dick Dastardly character—a little like the child catcher from *Chitty Chitty Bang Bang* (see also **Dreamy Boom Boom**) in top hat and waxed moustache—was played by Ross Martin and had a sidekick called Motley. The winning cartoon format was taken up in the early '70s by rival animators De Patie-Freleng in the equally good **Bailey's Comets**.

Wait Till Your Father Gets Home
A Hannah-Barbera production. USA, 1972

Superlative cartoon, based on the sitcom *All in The Family*. The action centred around a middle-class family, whose hard-working, old-fashioned father Harry Boyle (voiced by Tom Bosley) was having problems relating to the "free thinking" younger generation. Eldest son Chet (Lennie Weinrib) was, like, a loafing, 22 year-old unemployed hippy, forever on the cadge. Youngest son Jamie (Jackie Haley) was a nine-year old amoral capitalist, always with an eye to the fast buck. Alice, 16, (Kristina Holland) was a fat, greedy, "romantic radical", and the opposite of stay-at-home wifey, Irma (Joan Gerber). The latter experimented—briefly and apologetically—with financial independence.

Stressed from the strains of running his own business and handing out the hard-earned to his leeching children, Boyle had further troubles from Ralph, his fascist neighbour (voiced by comedian Jack Burns). Here was a card-carrying pinko hater, with a conspiracy theory to match every occasion. Along with Whitaker—a vicious granny—Ralph led a suburban vigilante squad, nominally tasked with eliminating The Reds, but which was extreme only in its incompetence. Harry tried in vain to talk him down from his wilder fantasies, but more often than not became embroiled in them.

Wait Till Your Father Gets Home, while typical of its time in its promotion of certain social values (ie hard work, nuclear family, suburban dwelling, conservatism), had the wit, irony and indeed drawings (reminiscent of the stylised graphic work of early **Pink Panther**) to offset this and provide one of Hannah-Barbera's best-realised efforts. The package was topped by a great theme tune. It aired in the US in 1972, winging its way to the UK, via syndication, very shortly thereafter. The UK programmers' mistake was to show it during prime kids' TV time, when much of the material was intended to be appreciated by adults, possibly returning from that hard-day-at-the-office. Its ability to laugh gently both at itself and the US family sitcom in general made this a serious forerunner to more anarchic rethinks of the format, such as *King of The Hill* or *The Simpsons*.

The show was first aired as a one-off segment on Paramount's *Love American Style* on ABC. NBC bought the pilot and 48 episodes—across two series—were subsequently syndicated by Rhodes Productions. Hardly seen since on terrestrial TV, the show was last seen heading towards Cartoon Network.

Wally Gator

A Hanna-Barbera Production. US, 1962

Wally Gator: a pun on the word Alligator. The humour stopped there. This 1962 Hanna-Barbera formula piece had Wally, an anthropomorphised crocodillian in a bad hat, living—like all captive animals—in zoo luxury (see also **Hair Bear Bunch, The**). He was tended by his zoo-keeper—the realistically named **Mr Twiddles**—who was always keeping a watchful eye on his errant reptile to make sure it didn't pop out and shock well to-do ladies. As far as Wally was concerned, he was a human, just like any other, so he thought nothing of nipping into town and tucking into a slap up dinner, or some other side-splitting caper. The show, hardly inspiring as a concept, was made to grate unremittingly on the ear and nerves by the cunning use of journeyman voice artists Daws Butler as Wally (see also **Snagglepuss** etc) and Don "Muttley" Messick as Twiddles (see **Scooby Doo, Wacky Races** etc). It was originally aired in the US on *The New Hanna Barbera Cartoon Show*, although syndication brought Wally spluttering and shrieking to our screens in his own right.

Weemawee High
See Square Pegs

Fictional high school setting of excellent US sitcom **Square Pegs**, in which two freshman girls, lacking in self-esteem, try without success to fit in. The name was surely chosen for its comic effect, as it was inserted into every other sentence.

Why Don't You?
BBC TV. A BBC Bristol production. Produced by Patrick Dowling, then Hilary Murphy. UK, 1973-95

Remember the Dorriss? *Why Don't You?* set out to provide fun things to do, see, make and cook for bored children on their school holidays. Anything from diabolos made out of empty bubble-bath bottles (cover up that brand name) to a film of someone's matchbox-collecting hobby and some ghastly child singing about riding his bike around Bristol was fair game in an average episode. One way-out, wacky feature was the use of tennis balls with slits in them for mouths and eyes drawn on. Two shaky hands (see also **Blue Peter**) would hold one and the balls would tell a joke: "Knock knock..."

Typically in my day you could see the show all the way through the Christmas holidays, sandwiched between **Lippy the Lion** and some old Harold Lloyd film. It was unique at the time in being presented by a team of (often precocious) actual children who lounged about on beanbags and crates and bounced around on orange spacehoppers. The original *Why Don't You?*, produced by Patrick Dowling and later by Hilary Murphy, was recorded in Bristol and cast from locals, although later incarnations were produced in Belfast, Liverpool, Cardiff and other locations.

The Dorris was a mysterious evil entity which lived under cushions in the studio and sometimes whooshed across the floor, or so they pretended. The Dorris' true identity (and point) was kept a mystery. But whoosh it went—especially when there was a weak link to the next segment. The Irish version of the show replaced the Dorris with an ill-advised comedy sheep.

Jane remembers her time as a presenter: "I was 14 when I did *Why Don't You?* I did it in the summer holidays. The thing about BBC Bristol was that it was so small. They only had this one big studio then, so you could only be in there for your allotted time. You just had to get it done. All the sets from other programmes would be there, stacked up behind yours. John Craven used to be there quite a lot. There were lots of people around like Tony Soper from **Wildtrack**, Terry Nutkins from **Animal Magic** and the man who was the voice of K9 off **Doctor Who** [see **Jigsaw**]. It was good fun ... very seventies. They filmed some of the outside broadcast parts of *Animal Magic* out the back by the BBC Club. So you'd be rehearsing and there was bloody Salty the Seal flapping about ... all these animals. We started knitting this really long scarf, and kept it up for the whole series. It was really long by the end."

The show's rhetorical question, from which sprung the title, was: "Why don't you switch off your TV set and go and do something less boring instead?" About one in five letters to the show observed, somewhat wittily: "If I switched off my TV set I wouldn't be able to watch *Why Don't You.*" In its early '70s heyday, the format was perfect. In the end of course, the message got through. Everyone switched off and it was axed in favour of shows with a higher gunge and hip hop quotient. Hilary Murphy also worked on **Multi-Coloured Swapshop** and later wrote questions for **Blockbusters**.

Wildtrack

BBC TV. A BBC Bristol production. UK, 1978–85

Sensible, science-led natural history show for kids, presented by Tony Soper and Su Ingle.

Willo the Wisp

BBC 1. Written and directed by Nick Spargo. UK, 1981

Willo the Wisp was animator Nick Spargo's forest-based series, featuring the various and fantastic voices of the late Kenneth Williams. The action was set in Doyle Woods and followed the capers of various hastily-drawn creatures, all surveyed by the Wisp, a swirly caricature of Williams himself. The romantically-named Mavis Cruet was the hapless, dumpy Fairy with buck

Willo the Wisp

teeth, having perpetual trouble with her spells. Arthur the Caterpiller—who bore a remarkable resemblance to Nero from **Danger Mouse**—was a bit of a smart-alec. Evil Edna was the wicked witch of Doyle Woods: a hideous television with dark intentions. Moog, a squat pink bovine/canine combination, was useless. Twit was the yellow bird and Carwash was the sleek gentleman cat. 26 5-minute films were made and shown on BBC1 in the **Wombles** slot, before the early evening news. Williams was without doubt a genius. Had it not been for his energetic characterisations, this averagely animated series would surely not have earned its place in the annals of cult history. It is revealing that the BBC once released it as a series of audio cassettes, although, sadly, these are no longer available.

Windy Miller
See Camberwick Green

In the old English tradition, journeyman Windy was named after his profession. He was a proper yokel in a smock and a **Fenella** Hat (see also **Ffestiniog**). On his birthday, the army brought him a cake in their armoured truck.

Willy Fogg
See Around the World with Willy Fogg

Willy The Terrible Fox
*See **Doctor Snuggles***

Species: fox. Type: sly, of course. There's a clue in the name.

Wingstead Hall
*See **Chigley***

Stately home of landed lazybones and confirmed bachelor **Lord Belborough**. In recent years Belborough had been forced to allow the public in, for money, and give them rides on his restored locomotive **Bessie**.

Winnie Vinegar Bottle
*See **Doctor Snuggles***

Mean-spirited, condiment-centric witch (though not in the same class as **Fenella**). She lived in the salt and pepper mountains.

Wombles, The
BBC TV. A FilmFair production. Created and written by Elizabeth Beresford. Directed by Ivor Wood. Music by Mike Batt. Narrated by Bernard Cribbins. UK, 1973

Cast your eye over the credits, above. A total of 60 5-minute episodes, repeated endlessly, made sure those mythical names lodged in the head for good. *The Wombles* was probably one of the most enduring children's animations of the '70s. Why? These obsequious hairy big-nosed midget goody-two-shoes conservationists waddled around Wimbledon Common, self-righteously picking up our litter and converting it into useful items for their burrow, teaching us all not to be so messy. Where did they get off? And—more importantly—why did they become such a universally recognised household name?

Was it the quality of Elizabeth Beresford's scripts, which were well plotted, amusing and educational? Was it the narration by actor Bernard Cribbins, whose vocal characterisations were so apposite? Was it the lurching charm of FilmFair's stop-motion animation? Was it the puppets themselves, all named after places your parents would force you to look up in the atlas? Tobermory, the handyman; Orinoco, the idiot; Wellington, the speccy brainiac; Bungo, the other idiot (see also **Bungle**); Tomsk, the bingeing food obsessive; sexy—but hairy—Madame Cholet, the, er, woman and cook (reassuring stereotype amid the subterranean troll mayhem . . .); or Great Uncle Bulgaria, the tottering patriarch in a tartan hat? Was it the excellent burrow set, complete with newspaper walls?

None of the above. It was that horrific song, shamelessly written by Mike Batt. "Underground, overground," it dug into the deepest, darkest recesses of your brain and festered. You sang it in school, you sang it in the bath, you sang it in bed. It is still there. You find yourself humming it absent mindedly during meetings. You've programmed it into your mobile phone, which goes off during a conference call with your biggest client in the States and, later, at home during sex.

Batt went on to annoy anyone who came home too late to see *The Wombles* with a series of Womble-related chart topping hits, the most naggingly annoying of which was *Remember You're A Womble*, in which Mr Batt and his besuited cohorts urged us to remember-member-member what a womba-womba-womble we were. Thanks for that, Mike. Member indeed.

A Womble feature film duly arrived, as rights were exploited seemingly without end: plastic Tomsk toothbrush holders that went manky and smelled, Madame Cholet pencil cases, "Orinoco Flow" by Enya (surely a mistake)—you name it. Finally, in 1991, there came a new half-hour adventure in which the hairy waddlers got on our backs about the Amazon rainforests, neatly forgetting that they had already accounted for sales of twenty Womble book titles. Paper has to come from somewhere, you know.

Despite it all, *The Wombles* remained a firm teatime favourite, shown after **Blue Peter**, just in time for your parent or guardian to come home from work, stand in front of it and talk loudly about the car's MOT while you ate Lego blithely on the carpet.

Wonderland Zoo
See Hair Bear Bunch, The

Home of **Hair**, **Square** and **Bubi**. Also home and workplace of their tormentor **Mr Peevly**, the zoo keeper, and his slow witted henchman **Botch**. The zoo was not all that bad: the food was free and Peevly was easy enough to outwit. Rather the zoo, with its rules and regulations, than the wild North Woods, into which Peevly threatened to send them back each episode.

Wonder Years, The
ABC. A New World Entertainment production. USA, 1988

This sweet—some might say syrupy—drama series followed the late childhood and growing pains of schoolboy **Kevin Arnold** (Fred Savage). Said growing pains were documented and narrated by Arnold himself, having grown up into a worldly wise man with a slightly grizzled voice (Daniel Stern). The story began in 1968 when Kevin was 12 and contrasted the usual rites-of-passage dilemmas and—since this was America—moral lessons with a sort of period documentary. The latter gave context and rooted the action in a slightly hazey, sentimentalised past, where everything seemed to happen in late summer, when the lawn sprinklers were on. It could often pour a little too much sugar in the Kool-aid for some people's taste.

Kevin—younger brother to the oafish, bullying Wayne and

flower power wanabee Karen, who was absent in mind if not in precocious body—had a tumultuous on-off relationship with his neighbour, the pristine Winnie Cooper (Danica McKellar), superior in her white alice-band. The script writers and actors were adept at portraying the hesitant awkwardness of pre-teen love and friendship with humour and slightly mawkish sensitivity. Kevin was an average sort of kid. He was sensitive, but not so much as to be marginalised. He was sporty, but not so much as to be on the right teams. He was well-intentioned, but prone to self-centred behaviour, from which he could always learn a valuable lesson while Mom cooked a meatloaf in her pinny and Pop watched Buzz Aldrin on the nine-inch Pye black & white.

Mom was a bit flowery and distant—stranded but making do in a marriage which had lost its bloom. Pop worked too hard and came home tired, stressed and grumpy. The only person with whom Kevin could talk it all through was his long-suffering best friend and geek, Paul Pfeiffer (Josh Saviano). **Pfeiffer** had growing pains of his own, of course, not that Kevin ever came far enough out of his own world to see that. Most of Pfeiffer's problems stemmed from the uncanny resemblance he bore to Morocco Mole (see **Secret Squirrel**): ie, no love-life dilemmas there. Kevin never noticed the looks in Pfeiffer's eyes as if to say, "you have it so easy, and you make such a fuss".

The show's enduring appeal—six seasons, and over 100 episodes—was due in large part to the quality of the child actors. They were cute, they were good. But children, like kittens, don't stay cute forever. Eventually they must pubesce and become croaking, greasy, big-nosed adolescents who are far less appealing to the average parent viewer. After some consideration about this show's target audience, it was decided that the show should be included as a children's show, as the storylines definitely aim to instruct and include a young audience. But *The Wonder Years'* nostalgic appeal—helped by a singalong soundtrack—to adults of the Baby Boom generation with kids of their own is probably more germane. It was shown in the UK on Channel 4.

Link: a truly frightening guide to *The Wonder Years* is available at **http://ourworld.compuserve.com/homepages/reynders/wy-frame.htm**

Woogie The Freckled Camel
See Doctor Snuggles

All you need to know is in the name. It lived in a rainbow and looked after the **Lavender Sheep**.

Wordsworth
See Jamie & the Magic Torch

Yokel-voiced dog of young be-jimjammed Jamie. Wore a Santa hat over his eyes.

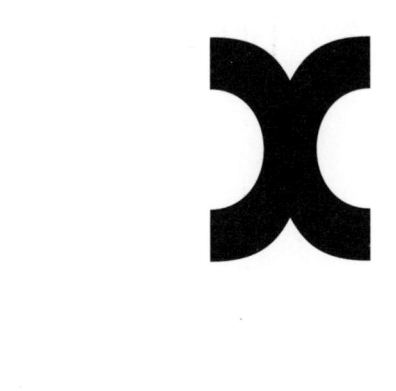

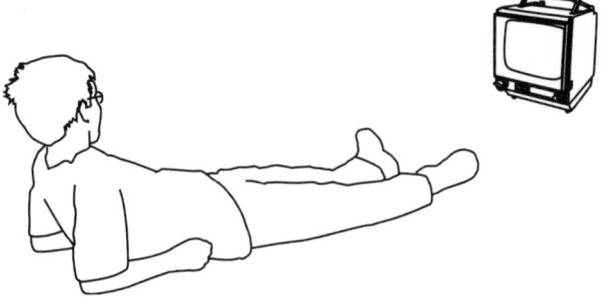

Xylophone hammering

Doodleoodleoodleoodleoodleoodle, Pee-oww! The sound-effect used by US animators **Hanna-Barbera** in almost all their cartoons. It happened in that anticipatory moment, just before a character made a running exit, when he, she or it was still hanging in the air, gathering momentum. Can also be done with high-tuned bongoes. The *piece-de-résistance* was **Hong Kong Phooey**, as his car actually made the sound as it drove along.

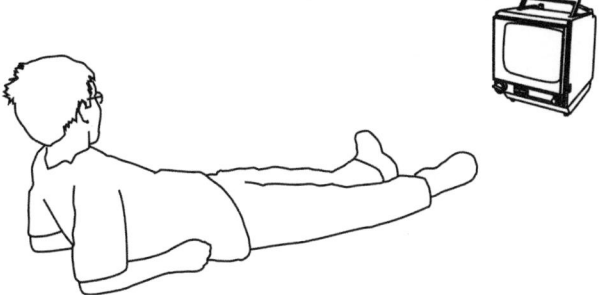

"Yo Ho Ho"s
*See **Bailey's Comets***

Pirate-centric team competing against Barnaby Bailey and his. There may have been the odd bottle of rum. Pointless pirate theme not to be confused with **Captain Pugwash**, or **Crackerjack**.

z

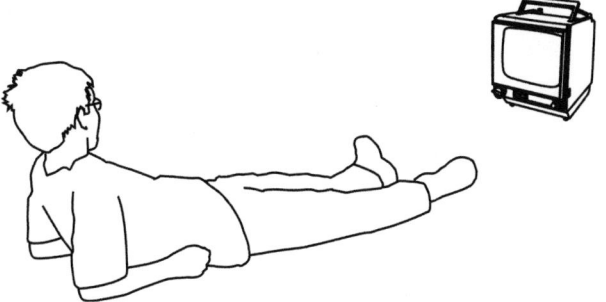

Zebedee
*See **The Magic Roundabout***

Red-faced, spring-arsed, bouncy fellow with a waxed moustache, who acted as Florence's conduit to the curious goings on in the garden. He had a habit of dropping in at the end of the show and telling you to go bed. Canny parents convinced their addled offspring that when Zebedee said it they had to go. Thanks for that, Zebedee.

Zippy
*See **Rainbow***

More a metaphor than a being. This orange creature, with a rugby ball-shaped head, epitomised all boorish, childish behaviour, and was obviously a boy. Suffering a serious attention deficit, he ate all the sausages, knocked down other peoples brick buildings, interrupted and talked over others. He was a problem child who came complete with his own solution: the zip on his mouth.

Zoltar
*See **Battle of the Planets***

Evil adversary of the crew of the Phoenix, and commander of **Spectra.** As with most space-based villains, his goal was to control the universe. Why? Sounds like a lot of work. But at least it supplied a lot of work for Jason, Mark and the rest. They always defeated him (and made it back for another game of pool in their flares), but still Zoltar came back for more. Inability to learn, delusions of grandeur, mask with pointy ears, suspected use of lipstick: borderline case. What can you do, though, age seven?

Zoomer

*See **Chorlton and the Wheelies***

He wore a flying-hat, he zoomed, he spoke like Dick Van Dyke
doing cockerney. He was voiced by Joe Lynch.